Diverse Families, Competent Families: Innovations in Research and Preventive Intervention Practice

Diverse Families, Competent Families: Innovations in Research and Preventive Intervention Practice has been co-published simultaneously as *Journal of Prevention & Intervention in the Community*, Volume 20, Numbers 1/2 2000.

The *Journal of Prevention & Intervention in the Community*™ Monographic (formerly the *Prevention in Human Services* series)* "Separates"

For information on previous issues of *Prevention in Human Services*, edited by Robert E. Hess, please contact: The Haworth Press, Inc., 10 Alice Street, Binghamton, NY 13904-1580 USA.

Below is a list of "separates," which in serials librarianship means a special issue simultaneously published as a special journal issue or double-issue *and* as a "separate" hardbound monograph. (This is a format which we also call a "DocuSerial.")

"Separates" are published because specialized libraries or professionals may wish to purchase a specific thematic issue by itself in a format which can be separately cataloged and shelved, as opposed to purchasing the journal on an on-going basis. Faculty members may also more easily consider a "separate" for classroom adoption.

"Separates" are carefully classified separately with the major book jobbers so that the journal tie-in can be noted on new book order slips to avoid duplicate purchasing.

You may wish to visit Haworth's website at . . .

http://www.haworthpressinc.com

. . . to search our online catalog for complete tables of contents of these separates and related publications.

You may also call 1-800-HAWORTH (outside US/Canada: 607-722-5857), or Fax 1-800-895-0582 (outside US/Canada: 607-771-0012), or e-mail at:

getinfo@haworthpressinc.com

Diverse Families, Competent Families: Innovations in Research and Preventive Intervention Practice, edited by Janet F. Gillespie, PhD, and Judy Primavera, PhD (Vol. 20, No. 1/2, 2000). *Provides a portrait of the real lives and practical challenges of our nation's families as they face a new millenium. You will discover family adaptation and competence in a variety of contexts and situations such as day-to-day issues of coping and survival, as well as major milestones such as sending children off to school, becoming a caregiver for a family member, and more.*

Employment in Community Psychology: The Diversity of Opportunity, edited by Joseph R. Ferrari, PhD, and Clifford R. O'Donnel, PhD (Vol. 19, No. 2, 2000). *"Fascinating and instructive reading, indeed a must read for all community psychology faculty, students, and potential employers. Sixteen community psychologists offer compelling, diverse and unique perspectives on their employment journeys." (Kenneth I. Maton, PhD, Professor of Psychology, University of Maryland)*

Contemporary Topics in HIV/AIDS Prevention, edited by Doreen D. Salina, PhD (Vol. 19, No. 1, 2000). *Helps researchers and psychologists explore specific methods of improving HIV/AIDS prevention research.*

Educating Students to Make-a-Difference: Community-Based Service Learning, edited by Joseph R. Ferrari, PhD, and Judith G. Chapman, PhD (Vol. 18, No. 1/2, 1999). *"There is something here for everyone interested in the social psychology of service-learning." (Frank Bernt, PhD, Associate Professor, St. Joseph's University)*

Program Implementation in Preventive Trials, edited by Joseph A. Durlak, PhD, and Joseph R. Ferrari, PhD (Vol. 17, No. 2, 1998). *"Fills an important gap in preventive research. . . . Highlights an array of important questions related to implementation and demonstrates just how good community-based intervention programs can be when issues related to implementation are taken seriously." (Judy Primavera, PhD, Associate Professor of Psychology, Fairfield University, Fairfield, Connecticut)*

Preventing Drunk Driving, edited by Elsie R. Shore, PhD, and Joseph R. Ferrari, PhD (Vol. 17, No. 1, 1998). *"A must read for anyone interested in reducing the needless injuries and death caused by the drunk driver." (Terrance D. Schiavone, President, National Commission Against Drunk Driving, Washington, DC)*

Manhood Development in Urban African-American Communities, edited by Roderick J. Watts, PhD, and Robert J. Jagers (Vol. 16, No. 1/2, 1998). *"Watts and Jagers provide the much-needed foundational and baseline information and research that begins to philosophically and empirically validate the importance of understanding culture, oppression, and gender when working with males in urban African-American communities." (Paul Hill, Jr., MSW, LISW, ACSW, East End Neighborhood House, Cleveland, Ohio)*

Diversity Within the Homeless Population: Implications for Intervention, edited by Elizabeth M. Smith, PhD, and Joseph R. Ferrari, PhD (Vol. 15, No. 2, 1997). *"Examines why homelessness is increasing, as well as treatment options, case management techniques, and community intervention programs that can be used to prevent homelessness." (American Public Welfare Association)*

Education in Community Psychology: Models for Graduate and Undergraduate Programs, edited by Clifford R. O'Donnell, PhD, and Joseph R. Ferrari, PhD (Vol. 15, No. 1, 1997). *"An invaluable resource for students seeking graduate training in community psychology . . . [and will] also serve faculty who want to improve undergraduate teaching and graduate programs." (Marybeth Shinn, PhD, Professor of Psychology and Coordinator, Community Doctoral Program, New York University, New York, New York)*

Adolescent Health Care: Program Designs and Services, edited by John S. Wodarski, PhD, Marvin D. Feit, PhD, and Joseph R. Ferrari, PhD (Vol. 14, No. 1/2, 1997). *Devoted to helping practitioners address the problems of our adolescents through the use of preventive interventions based on sound empirical data.*

Preventing Illness Among People with Coronary Heart Disease, edited by John D. Piette, PhD, Robert M. Kaplan, PhD, and Joseph R. Ferrari, PhD (Vol. 13, No. 1/2, 1996). *"A useful contribution to the interaction of physical health, mental health, and the behavioral interventions for patients with CHD." (Public Health: The Journal of the Society of Public Health)*

Sexual Assault and Abuse: Sociocultural Context of Prevention, edited by Carolyn F. Swift, PhD* (Vol. 12, No. 2, 1995). *"Delivers a cornucopia for all who are concerned with the primary prevention of these damaging and degrading acts." (George J. McCall, PhD, Professor of Sociology and Public Administration, University of Missouri)*

International Approaches to Prevention in Mental Health and Human Services, edited by Robert E. Hess, PhD, and Wolfgang Stark* (Vol. 12, No. 1, 1995). *Increases knowledge of prevention strategies from around the world.*

Self-Help and Mutual Aid Groups: International and Multicultural Perspectives, edited by Francine Lavoie, PhD, Thomasina Borkman, PhD, and Benjamin Gidron* (Vol. 11, No. 1/2, 1995). *"A helpful orientation and overview, as well as useful data and methodological suggestions." (International Journal of Group Psychotherapy)*

Prevention and School Transitions, edited by Leonard A. Jason, PhD, Karen E. Danner, and Karen S. Kurasaki, MA* (Vol. 10, No. 2, 1994). *"A collection of studies by leading ecological and systems-oriented theorists in the area of school transitions, describing the stressors, personal resources available, and coping strategies among different groups of children and adolescents undergoing school transitions." (Reference & Research Book News)*

Religion and Prevention in Mental Health: Research, Vision, and Action, edited by Kenneth I. Pargament, PhD, Kenneth I. Maton, PhD, and Robert E. Hess, PhD* (Vol. 9, No. 2 & Vol. 10, No. 1, 1992). *"The authors provide an admirable framework for considering the important, yet often overlooked, differences in theological perspectives." (Family Relations)*

Families as Nurturing Systems: Support Across the Life Span, edited by Donald G. Unger, PhD, and Douglas R. Powell, PhD* (Vol. 9, No. 1, 1991). *"A useful book for anyone thinking about alternative ways of delivering a mental health service." (British Journal of Psychiatry)*

Ethical Implications of Primary Prevention, edited by Gloria B. Levin, PhD, and Edison J. Trickett, PhD* (Vol. 8, No. 2, 1991). *"A thoughtful and thought-provoking summary of ethical issues related to intervention programs and community research." (Betty Tableman, MPA, Director, Division of Prevention Services and Demonstration Projects, Michigan Department of Mental Health, Lansing)*

Career Stress in Changing Times, edited by James Campbell Quick, PhD, MBA, Robert E. Hess, PhD, Jared Hermalin, PhD, and Jonathan D. Quick, MD* (Vol. 8, No. 1, 1990). *"A well-organized book. . . . It deals with planning a career and career changes and the stresses involved." (American Association of Psychiatric Administrators)*

Prevention in Community Mental Health Centers, edited by Robert E. Hess, PhD, and John Morgan, PhD* (Vol. 7, No. 2, 1990). *"A fascinating bird's-eye view of six significant programs of preventive care which have survived the rise and fall of preventive psychiatry in the U.S." (British Journal of Psychiatry)*

Protecting the Children: Strategies for Optimizing Emotional and Behavioral Development, edited by Raymond P. Lorion, PhD* (Vol. 7, No. 1, 1990). *"This is a masterfully conceptualized and edited volume presenting theory-driven, empirically based, developmentally oriented prevention." (Michael C. Roberts, PhD, Professor of Psychology, The University of Alabama)*

The National Mental Health Association: Eighty Years of Involvement in the Field of Prevention, edited by Robert E. Hess, PhD, and Jean DeLeon, PhD* (Vol. 6, No. 2, 1989). *"As a family life educator interested in both the history of the field, current efforts, and especially the evaluation of programs, I find this book quite interesting. I enjoyed reviewing it and believe that I will return to it many times. It is also a book I will recommend to students." (Family Relations)*

A Guide to Conducting Prevention Research in the Community: First Steps, by James G. Kelly, PhD, Nancy Dassoff, PhD, Ira Levin, PhD, Janice Schreckengost, MA, AB, Stephen P. Stelzner, PhD, and B. Eileen Altman, PhD* (Vol. 6, No. 1, 1989). *"An invaluable compendium for the prevention practitioner, as well as the researcher, laying out the essentials for developing effective prevention programs in the community. . . . This is a book which should be in the prevention practitioner's library, to read, re-read, and ponder." (The Community Psychologist)*

Prevention: Toward a Multidisciplinary Approach, edited by Leonard A. Jason, PhD, Robert D. Felner, PhD, John N. Moritsugu, PhD, and Robert E. Hess, PhD* (Vol. 5, No. 2, 1987). *"Will not only be of intellectual value to the professional but also to students in courses aimed at presenting a refreshingly comprehensive picture of the conceptual and practical relationships between community and prevention." (Seymour B. Sarason, Associate Professor of Psychology, Yale University)*

Prevention and Health: Directions for Policy and Practice, edited by Alfred H. Katz, PhD, Jared A. Hermalin, PhD, and Robert E. Hess, PhD* (Vol. 5, No. 1, 1987). *Read about the most current efforts being undertaken to promote better health.*

The Ecology of Prevention: Illustrating Mental Health Consultation, edited by James G. Kelly, PhD, and Robert E. Hess, PhD* (Vol. 4, No. 3/4, 1987). *"Will provide the consultant with a very useful framework and the student with an appreciation for the time and commitment necessary to bring about lasting changes of a preventive nature." (The Community Psychologist)*

Beyond the Individual: Environmental Approaches and Prevention, edited by Abraham Wandersman, PhD, and Robert E. Hess, PhD* (Vol. 4, No. 1/2, 1985). *"This excellent book has immediate appeal for those involved with environmental psychology . . . likely to be of great interest to those working in the areas of community psychology, planning, and design." (Australian Journal of Psychology)*

Prevention: The Michigan Experience, edited by Betty Tableman, MPA, and Robert E. Hess, PhD* (Vol. 3, No. 4, 1985). *An in-depth look at one state's outstanding prevention programs.*

Studies in Empowerment: Steps Toward Understanding and Action, edited by Julian Rappaport, Carolyn Swift, and Robert E. Hess, PhD* (Vol. 3, No. 2/3, 1984). *"Provides diverse applications of the empowerment model to the promotion of mental health and the prevention of mental illness." (Prevention Forum Newsline)*

Aging and Prevention: New Approaches for Preventing Health and Mental Health Problems in Older Adults, edited by Sharon P. Simson, Laura Wilson, Jared Hermalin, PhD, and Robert E. Hess, PhD* (Vol. 3, No. 1, 1983). *"Highly recommended for professionals and laymen interested in modern viewpoints and techniques for avoiding many physical and mental health problems of the elderly. Written by highly qualified contributors with extensive experience in their respective fields." (The Clinical Gerontologist)*

Strategies for Needs Assessment in Prevention, edited by Alex Zautra, Kenneth Bachrach, and Robert E. Hess, PhD* (Vol. 2, No. 4, 1983). *"An excellent survey on applied techniques for doing needs assessments . . . It should be on the shelf of anyone involved in prevention." (Journal of Pediatric Psychology)*

Innovations in Prevention, edited by Robert E. Hess, PhD, and Jared Hermalin, PhD* (Vol. 2, No. 3, 1983). *An exciting book that provides invaluable insights on effective prevention programs.*

Rx Television: Enhancing the Preventive Impact of TV, edited by Joyce Sprafkin, Carolyn Swift, PhD, and Robert E. Hess, PhD* (Vol. 2, No. 1/2, 1983). *"The successful interventions reported in this volume make interesting reading on two grounds. First, they show quite clearly how powerful television can be in molding children. Second, they illustrate how this power can be used for good ends." (Contemporary Psychology)*

Early Intervention Programs for Infants, edited by Howard A. Moss, MD, Robert E. Hess, PhD, and Carolyn Swift, PhD* (Vol. 1, No. 4, 1982). *"A useful resource book for those child psychiatrists, paediatricians, and psychologists interested in early intervention and prevention." (The Royal College of Psychiatrists)*

Helping People to Help Themselves: Self-Help and Prevention, edited by Leonard D. Borman, PhD, Leslie E. Borck, PhD, Robert E. Hess, PhD, and Frank L. Pasquale* (Vol. 1, No. 3, 1982). *"A timely volume . . . a mine of information for interested clinicians, and should stimulate those wishing to do systematic research in the self-help area." (The Journal of Nervous and Mental Disease)*

Evaluation and Prevention in Human Services, edited by Jared Hermalin, PhD, and Jonathan A. Morell, PhD* (Vol. 1, No. 1/2, 1982). *Features methods and problems related to the evaluation of prevention programs.*

Diverse Families, Competent Families: Innovations in Research and Preventive Intervention Practice has also been published as *Journal of Prevention & Intervention in the Community*, Volume 20, Numbers 1/2 2000.

Cover design by Thomas J. Mayshock Jr.

The Haworth Press, Inc., 10 Alice Street, Binghamton, NY 13904-1580 USA

Library of Congress Cataloging-in-Publication Data

Diverse families, competent families : innovations in research and preventive practice / Janet F. Gillespie, Judy Primavera, editors

p. cm.

"Has been co-published simultaneously as Journal of prevention & intervention in the community, Volume 20, Numbers 1/2, 2000."

Includes bibliographical references and index.

ISBN 0-7890-0797-5 (alk. paper)–ISBN 0-7890-0830-0 (alk. paper)

1. Family psychotherapy–United States. 2. Family–United States–Psychological aspects. I. Gillespie, Janet F. (Janet Frances), 1954- II. Primavera, Judy III. Journal of prevention & intervention in the community.

RC488.5 .D598 2000
616.89′156–dc21

00-040928
CIP

Diverse Families, Competent Families: Innovations in Research and Preventive Intervention Practice

Janet F. Gillespie
Judy Primavera
Editors

Diverse Families, Competent Families: Innovations in Research and Preventive Intervention Practice has been co-published simultaneously as *Journal of Prevention & Intervention in the Community*, Volume 20, Numbers 1/2 2000.

The Haworth Press, Inc.
New York • London • Oxford

ALL HAWORTH BOOKS AND JOURNALS
ARE PRINTED ON CERTIFIED
ACID-FREE PAPER

INDEXING & ABSTRACTING

Contributions to this publication are selectively indexed or abstracted in print, electronic, online, or CD-ROM version(s) of the reference tools and information services listed below. This list is current as of the copyright date of this publication. See the end of this section for additional notes.

- *Abstracts of Research in Pastoral Care & Counseling*
- *Behavioral Medicine Abstracts*
- *BUBL Information Service. An Internet-based Information Service for the UK higher education community <URL:http://bubl.ac.uk/>*
- *Child Development Abstracts & Bibliography*
- *CNPIEC Reference Guide: Chinese National Directory of Foreign Periodicals*
- *EMBASE/Excerpta Medica Secondary Publishing Division <URL: http://elsevier.n/>*
- *Family Studies Database (online and CD/ROM)*
- *FINDEX <www.publist.com>*
- *Gay & Lesbian Abstracts*
- *HealthPromis*
- *IBZ International Bibliography of Periodical Literature*
- *MANTIS (Manual, Alternative and Natural Therapy). MANTIS is available through three database vendors: Ovid, Dialog, & Datastar. In addition it is available for searching through www.healthindex.com*
- *Mental Health Abstracts (online through DIALOG)*
- *National Center for Chronic Disease Prevention & Health Promotion (NCCDPHP)*
- *National Clearinghouse on Child Abuse & Neglect Information*
- *NIAAA Alcohol and Alcohol Problems Science Database (ETOH)*
- *OT BibSys*
- *Psychological Abstracts (PsycINFO)*

(continued)

- *Referativnyi Zhurnal (Abstracts Journal of the All-Russian Institute of Scientific and Technical Information)*
- *Social Services Abstracts <www.csa.com>*
- *Social Work Abstracts*
- *Sociological Abstracts (SA) <www.csa.com>*
- *SOMED (social medicine) Database*
- *Violence and Abuse Abstracts: A Review of Current Literature on Interpersonal Violence (VAA)*

Special Bibliographic Notes related to special journal issues (separates) and indexing/abstracting:

- indexing/abstracting services in this list will also cover material in any "separate" that is co-published simultaneously with Haworth's special thematic journal issue or DocuSerial. Indexing/abstracting usually covers material at the article/chapter level.
- monographic co-editions are intended for either non-subscribers or libraries which intend to purchase a second copy for their circulating collections.
- monographic co-editions are reported to all jobbers/wholesalers/approval plans. The source journal is listed as the "series" to assist the prevention of duplicate purchasing in the same manner utilized for books-in-series.
- to facilitate user/access services all indexing/abstracting services are encouraged to utilize the co-indexing entry note indicated at the bottom of the first page of each article/chapter/contribution.
- this is intended to assist a library user of any reference tool (whether print, electronic, online, or CD-ROM) to locate the monographic version if the library has purchased this version but not a subscription to the source journal.
- individual articles/chapters in any Haworth publication are also available through the Haworth Document Delivery Service (HDDS).

ABOUT THE EDITORS

Janet F. Gillespie, PhD, is Associate Professor and Graduate Director in the Department of Psychology at SUNY College at Brockport, where she also serves on the College's Institutional Review Board. Dr. Gillespie received her PhD from Southern Illinois University at Carbondale with concentrations in clinical-child and community psychology. Dr. Gillespie's publications include articles on school-based preventive interventions, children's social problem solving, social skills training and group therapy with children, and research ethics. Her research interests also include quality-of-life issues and family competence. Dr. Gillespie is a member of the American Psychological Association and the Society for Community Research and Action.

Judy Primavera, PhD, is Associate Professor of Psychology at Fairfield University in Fairfield, CT. Dr. Primavera is also Director of the Adrienne Kirby Family Literacy Project, located at Action for Bridgeport Community Development in Bridgeport, CT. Dr. Primavera has authored numerous research articles and presented papers on family literacy, school transitions, childhood bereavement, parental divorce, domestic violence, and service learning/volunteerism. She received her PhD from Yale University, with a concentration in clinical-community psychology. Dr. Primavera is a member of the American Psychological Association and the Society for Community Research and Action.

Diverse Families, Competent Families: Innovations in Research and Preventive Intervention Practice

CONTENTS

Research on Family Resilience: Room for All and Strength from Each

Janet F. Gillespie
Judy Primavera

What qualities embody or define "strength" in a family? Indeed, what qualities define a family? How can the work of human services professionals enhance, strengthen and support families' lives? Researchers and practitioners alike grapple with such questions. The answers we provide, today and in the future, will shape and direct educational efforts, preventive interventions, and treatment approaches for children and their families into the 21st century. Politicians and media sources announce that "the family" is in jeopardy from multiple stressors at institutional and individual levels. Yet parents continue to nurture the children in their care, and want the best for them, as parents always have; and families continue to overcome odds, thrive, evolve, and inspire.

The articles in this volume, we hope, portray the real lives and practical challenges of our nation's families as they face a new millennium. The studies included investigate family adaptation and competence in a variety of contexts and situations. These situations include the day-to-day issues of coping and survival, as well as major milestones such as sending children to school and becoming a caregiver for a family member. This collection of papers also spans multiple levels of families' existence, examining home, school, and the larger community.

The first group of articles provides a framework for the special

---

[Haworth co-indexing entry note]: "Research on Family Resilience: Room for All and Strength from Each." Gillespie, Janet F., and Judy Primavera. Co-published simultaneously in *Journal of Prevention & Intervention in the Community* (The Haworth Press, Inc.) Vol. 20, No. 1/2, 2000, pp. 1-3; and: *Diverse Families, Competent Families: Innovations in Research and Preventive Intervention Practice* (ed: Janet F. Gillespie, and Judy Primavera) The Haworth Press, Inc., 2000, pp. 1-3. Single or multiple copies of this article are available for a fee from The Haworth Document Delivery Service [1-800-342-9678, 9:00 a.m. - 5:00 p.m. (EST). E-mail address: getinfo@haworthpressinc.com].

issue theme of family diversity. The paper by Jones and Unger points out the necessity of re-examining the ways that single parent families are viewed, by delineating multiple subtypes of that family structure and providing empirical evidence of the danger in overgeneralizing about single parents. Grant et al.'s findings speak to commonalities in families' coping efforts around a stressful life event such as sudden financial loss. Bouchard and Lee's paper looks at the lives of fathers of preschoolers and provides new insights on ways to maximize the quality of men's experience in their fathering role. Finally, Goyette-Ewing's paper proves that there is no one type of "latchkey child," but rather different types of families, confronting the same type of issue in finding afterschool supervision for their children.

The second section highlights issues of parent and child competencies in the context of school. Speer and Esposito point out the usefulness of looking at family adaptation over time, including the ways in which changes for better or worse in a family's functioning influence their children's academic skills. Primavera's paper gives unique qualitative insights into the wide-ranging benefits of involving parents in their children's development of literacy skills. Patrikakou and Weissberg's paper investigates relationships between parents' perceptions of teachers' behavior and their willingness to become involved at school, identifying parents' perceptions of teacher "outreach" as a key factor in promoting parent interest. Levine and Trickett also address the issue of parent involvement in their paper on Latino parents' strategies for addressing their children's school-related concerns.

The final section of the volume highlights child and parent competencies in the context of the family itself. In the first paper, Tebes and Irish describe results of an innovative intervention for "sandwiched" generation mothers who must simultaneously care for an older family member and attend to the needs of their own children. Their findings, with families who were predominantly middle-class, have implications for other caregivers as well, as the paper supports the notion that group and supportive therapy interventions serve families best when participants can learn from each other. The other papers in the section are studies of families of ethnic minority status. It is significant that many, if not most, submissions for this special issue studied ethnic minority families who were also families of low income status. These studies reiterate that chronic economic stress remains a disproportionately represented vulnerability factor in the United States (Danziger &

Gottschalk, 1991). However, many of the articles here provide hopeful findings that economic strain is not insurmountable, and of course, not incompatible with good parenting. The resilient, African American, single mothers profiled in Brodsky and DeVet's paper testify to the many ways that low-income mothers show excellent parenting skills and exemplify Gillespie's (1997) characterization as "the heroes they so often are." Furthermore, Canning and Fantuzzo's findings reveal that parents living in impoverished urban neighborhoods have much to "teach the teachers" who develop the parent counseling and parent education programs. Finally, the paper by Izzo, Weiss, Shanahan, and Rodriguez-Brown incorporates findings of research in cognitive and personality theory in presenting ways to help Mexican immigrant parents feel more efficacious in their parenting roles.

In the 1960's, a portion of a Breton, England fishermen's prayer became a favorite quote of President John F. Kennedy, and, later, the slogan of the Children's Defense Fund: "The sea is so great, and my boat is so small." The image of a child alone in the face of adversity suggested a need to re-shape the way this country tried to meet children's needs. The approach became one of strengthening and supporting families. Forty years later, in a new century, may we continue to work together to widen a welcoming space for families of all types, charting their safe course, and logging their success stories.

REFERENCES

Danziger, S., & Gottschalk, M. (1991). (Eds.) *Uneven tides.* New York: Russell Sage.

Gillespie, J. F. (1997). Community psychology and "this bridge": Traverse gently, with understanding. *American Journal of Community Psychology, 25,* 745-747.

Diverse Adaptations of Single Parent, Low-Income Families with Young Children: Implications for Community-Based Prevention and Intervention

C. Wayne Jones
University of Pennsylvania

Donald G. Unger
University of Delaware

SUMMARY. Distinct family caregiving structures among low-income single parent families were identified. The relationships between these structures and family needs, social resources and family functioning were described. Unmarried low-income, primarily African-American mothers whose children were enrolled in community-based early childhood programs were interviewed. While global measures of functioning or distress were unrelated to type of family caregiving structure, there were significant differences with respect to specific sources of stress or conflict, stability of the caregiving structure across time, and

Address correspondence to: C. Wayne Jones, Department of Child and Adolescent Psychiatry, Children's Hospital of Philadelphia, 111 North 49th Street, Philadelphia, PA 19139 (E-mail: cwjones@mail.med.upenn.edu).

This work was supported by Grant MCJ-420598 from the Maternal and Child Health Program (Title V, Social Security Act), Health Resources and Services Administration, Department of Health and Human Services.

[Haworth co-indexing entry note]: "Diverse Adaptations of Single Parent, Low-Income Families with Young Children: Implications for Community-Based Prevention and Intervention." Jones, C. Wayne, and Donald G. Unger. Co-published simultaneously in *Journal of Prevention & Intervention in the Community* (The Haworth Press, Inc.) Vol. 20, No. 1/2, 2000, pp. 5-23; and: *Diverse Families, Competent Families: Innovations in Research and Preventive Intervention Practice* (ed: Janet F. Gillespie, and Judy Primavera) The Haworth Press, Inc., 2000, pp. 5-23. Single or multiple copies of this article are available for a fee from The Haworth Document Delivery Service [1-800-342-9678, 9:00 a.m. - 5:00 p.m. (EST). E-mail address: getinfo@haworthpressinc.com].

perceived sources of primary support. Implications of these findings are discussed with respect to planning community-based services that build upon and strengthen family competencies. *[Article copies available for a fee from The Haworth Document Delivery Service: 1-800-342-9678. E-mail address: <getinfo@haworthpressinc.com> Website: <http://www.haworthpressinc.com>]*

KEYWORDS. Single parents, early intervention, prevention

Nearly one-third of all births in the United States are to single parents (U.S. Department of Health and Human Services, 1995b). This shift in family forms has sparked enormous interest by researchers, practitioners, and policy-makers, in part due to the relation between unmarried motherhood and poverty. The annual median income for families headed by mothers is among the lowest for any family form (U.S. Bureau of the Census, 1995). The well-documented link between poverty and negative developmental outcomes for children (Huston, 1991; McLoyd, Ceballo, & Mangelsdorf, 1997) earns unmarried mothers, their children and their families, as a group, the classification of "high risk."

Little is known, however, about differences in needs and resources among low-income single parent families. A major barrier has been that unmarried mothers continue to be negatively stereotyped as a group, often treated as a fundamentally flawed or deficit-based family structure (Hanson, Heims, Julian, & Sussman, 1995). This negative public perception was promoted during the highly charged political discussions related to "family values" and welfare reform during the Presidential and congressional elections of 1992. Some urban anthropologists (e.g., Francis-Okongwu, 1996) suggest that the unresolved issues of race, class, and gender have kept the unmarried single parent family and its "flaws" at the center of public policy and mass media discussions of poverty. After all, single parenthood and poverty rates are not evenly distributed across racial and ethnic groups. Seventy percent of all African-American births in 1994 were to unmarried mothers, compared to 25% for Caucasians (U.S. Bureau of the Census, 1995a). African-American and Hispanic children living in single-mother households are two to three times more likely to live in poverty than Caucasian children (Maternal & Child Health Bureau, 1994).

A "pathologizing view" of low-income unmarried mothers is also partly due to the substantial number of intra and extr: sors encountered by single parents as a group. Many o have serious negative consequences that undermine c!... and development. Family stressors include high rates of parental unemployment and low maternal educational attainment, unstable and unsafe living arrangements, poor medical care and nutrition, family and community violence, parental substance abuse, and child abuse and neglect (Belle, 1984; Halpern, 1990; Hanson & Lynch, 1992; Pelton, 1989). For teenage mothers, many of these stressors are compounded, given that teen mothers have the highest poverty rate of all at 87% (U.S. Bureau of the Census, 1995a). Moreover, numerous frustration-producing negative life events and chronic ongoing conditions of single parents are outside their personal control which can affect their emotional health and constrain their functioning as parents (McLoyd, 1990; McLoyd et al., 1997).

While these group effects are well-documented, variability within single parent families with regard to their unique characteristics, needs, functioning, and resources has not been adequately studied. In prior research, family configurations are rarely given a primary focus. Instead, single parents are referred to as a unidimensional family form without regard to the many different possible household and caregiving configurations that exist. Studies have also tended to focus on dysfunctional aspects rather than on strengths, and under-represent diversity in family process and functioning (Littlejohn-Blake & Darling, 1993; Stevenson, 1994; Taylor, Chatters, Tucker, & Lewis, 1990).

Single-parent families may differ on a variety of dimensions, such as how they become single-parent families, the degree to which the other parent is involved in family life, the composition of households, and how social network members help with parenting (Chilman, 1990; Lewis, 1989; Thompson and Ensminger, 1989). There is some evidence that a critical component of how low-income, African-American families adapt to stress involves the utilization of network members, particularly kin and "fictive kin," for support in meeting their daily material and social-emotional needs (Martin & Martin, 1978; Scott & Black, 1989; Taylor, 1986).

The implication of these findings to date is that there are a variety of patterns in which low-income nonmarried mothers organize their families in order to cope with the demands of raising their children. The variations in this population that are important to take into account for program planning and development are unknown, which has led to insufficiently differentiated policies and programs (Lerner, Castellino, Terry, Villarruel & McKinney, 1995). Recognition of the diversity among low-income single parent families is critical for effective outreach efforts to families most in need. Parent participation in early childhood community-based prevention and intervention programs often depends on the program's ability to accurately identify the unique characteristics, needs, functioning, and resources of each family and match these with appropriate, culturally sensitive services (Simeonsson, Bailey, Huntington, & Comfort, 1986; Unger & Wandersman, 1988).

Early childhood education and intervention programs are one of the most common settings for delivering community-based prevention and intervention services targeting high risk, low-income single parent families. These programs include large scale national efforts such as Head Start and Early Intervention Programs (EIPs) as well as numerous local level initiatives involving the development of "at-risk" community-based preschools often associated with churches, hospitals and neighborhood activity centers. Although the specific priorities and philosophical orientations of these early childhood programs differ, they each share a common mission of reducing risk for children and improving general developmental outcomes. Many programs also include a variety of family support services for parents. When made available, the family support components of early childhood programs are designed to strengthen personal coping and parenting skills, as well as to facilitate parents' access to material assistance as needed.

This study moves the direction of inquiry regarding single parent families toward the study of intra-group differences of single parent families who have children enrolled in urban early intervention and childhood programs. The guiding assumption was that there were common sources of stress or challenges affecting most single-parents with young children, but that there was considerable individual variation among families within this group with respect to the specific resources available to cope with or manage these stresses or challenges. The data were from a comprehensive five year project, Family Partnerships, examining the role that family-focused early childhood programs played in the lives of low-income, single-parent families.

Two hypotheses were addressed in this study. The first focused on identifying common family caregiving structures among a single parent population. It was predicted that caregiving structures could be identified that were relatively stable across time. The second hypothesis focused on the relation between family caregiving structures and social resources, family functioning, and stress resulting from financial and emotional needs. It was predicted that need-based stress, family functioning, and sources of primary support would vary by type of family caregiving structure.

METHOD

Participants

The sample included 218 low-income nonmarried mothers with a young child recently enrolled in one of 21 different early childhood programs located within the inner cities of Philadelphia, PA and Wilmington, DE. The sample was comprised primarily of African-American women (88%). The remainder of the sample were either Hispanic (6%) or Caucasian (6%). The majority of the caregivers (72%) were between 20 and 34 years of age. The median age for the total sample was 27 years old, with a range between 15 and 63 years of age. Teenage parents comprised 7% of the sample. The median age of children under 18 years of age in the household was 2.7 years old. Reported annual income for 76% of the families was less than $15,000. All of the participants in the study depended upon public assistance for some portion of family income. The majority (85%) were not employed outside the home; 6% were attending school or training programs.

The focus children in the study ranged in age from one to five years, with a median age of 2.4 years. Forty-one percent of the focus children were female and 59% were male. A total of 146 children and their families (67% of the total sample) were recruited from 14 Early Intervention Programs (EIP), 33 children and their families (15%) were recruited from four Head Start Centers, and 39 children and their families (18%) were recruited from three "At Risk" preschools. According to the Overall Delay Index created for this study, 29.8% of the children in the sample were severely impaired, 16.1% moderately impaired, 24.8% mildly impaired. A third of the children were described by their parents as having multiple health problems. Most of the children in the sample (80%) received their services in a center-based program. Of the children in the sample recruited from EIPs, 20% received a combination of home and center based services.

Measures

Family caregiving structure. A description of family caregiving structure was obtained from the demographic questionnaire constructed by the authors. The demographic questionnaire contained a wide range of descriptive information about the focus child, the early childhood program, and the parent/family. Two indicators of family caregiving structure used in this study included: (1) the primary caregiver of the focus child, who was identified via a question about who in the household generally diapered, fed, bathed, played with, comforted, and got up at night with the child; and (2) a listing of other adults in the household and their relationship to the child and caregiver.

Household income. Like family structure, a measure of household income was obtained from the demographic questionnaire. The categories used were based on increments of $400, beginning at $400 per month and rising to $1251 and over.

Need-based stress. An abbreviated version of the *Family Needs Scale* (Dunst, Trivette, & Deal, 1988) was utilized to measure the frustrating demands that often characterize the daily transactions of the family with the environment. This 23-item scale assessed five categories of needs, which included basic resources (e.g., food, clean water, adequate housing, clothing, transportation), discretionary time (e.g., time for leisure, attending self-improvement activities, time with family), financial or money needs (e.g., help with budgeting and payment of bills), equipment/medical resources (e.g., specialized care), and employment needs. Adequate measures of reliability and validity of the original scale have been established (Dunst, Trivette, & Deal). The alpha reliability coefficient in this study was .93.

Social network functioning. An adaptation of the *Network of Relationships Inventory* (NRI) (Furman & Buhrmester, 1985) was used to measure caregiver perceptions of individual relationships within their family and extended social network. Subscales assessed: emotional support, reciprocity (i.e., the giving of support to others), negative interactions (i.e., conflict/hassles) and instrumental/informational support. All original NRI items were used intact except for items from the Instrumental Support and Punishment/Hassles subscales. Instrumental support items were modified to focus on the securing of basic necessities (e.g., food, toys, furniture), childcare, loans, and information. The Punishment/Hassles subscale was renamed "Negative Interactions" and items were modified to focus directly on interpersonal conflict. The modified version of the NRI resulted in a 30-item five-point Likert-type scale with endpoint ratings of "none" or "never" and "a great deal" or "all the time." The four relationship dimensions were confirmed by a factor analysis. A sum score for each dimension was calculated for the different types of network members assessed by the NRI. Caregivers rated each of these relationship qualities with the following people: the child's grandmother, the focus child's father, the caregiver's romantic partner, the caregiver's extended relatives (up to 2), and friends. These individuals were selected on the basis of previous network studies in which single parents often spontaneously identified them as important. Furman and Buhrmester (1985) reported internal consistency of scale scores to be .80. Internal consistency values for the subscales ranged from .85-.95 in this study.

Family functioning. The 12 item General Functioning Index (GFI) of the *McMaster Family Assessment Device (FAD)* (Epstein, Baldwin, & Bishop, 1983; Miller, Bishop, Epstein, & Keitner, 1985) was one of two measures utilized to assess family functioning. The FAD was based on the McMaster Model of family functioning and focused on perceptions of how the family unit worked together on essential tasks rather than on static "attributes" of the family. The GFI, one of the seven FAD subscales, served as a measure of global functioning. Participants rated how strongly they agreed or disagreed to statements on a four point Likert scale. Alpha reliability coefficient for the GFI was .88.

Parent-child interaction. Parent/Caregiver Involvement Scale (PCIS), an observational measure (Farran, Kasari, Comfort, & Jay, 1986), was used to assess (a) the quality of parent-child involvement, which addressed the question of whether specific behaviors were demonstrated by the caregiver, and (b) the appropriateness of involvement, which addressed the question of how closely these behaviors were matched to the child's development, interest level, and motoric capabilities. Each of 11 scales were rated on these two dimensions. The scales included: (a) physical involvement, (b) verbal involvement, (c) responsiveness to child, (d) play interaction, (e) teaching behavior, (f) control over child's activities, (g) directives, (h) sequencing among activities,

(i) positive statements, (j) negative statements and discipline, and (k) goal setting. Videotapes were coded by two different coders, who were not involved in the interviewing of parents. Interrater reliability was .88. The alpha coefficient was .92 for quality and .91 for appropriateness.

Procedure

All newly enrolled eligible low-income, single parents within the 21 participating Early Intervention Programs, Head Start Centers and At Risk preschools received information about the Family Partnerships study from school staff. Based on individual program administrator estimates of the number of low-income single-parents served annually within their individual programs, 20% of the eligible EIP participants (approximate N = 725) and 28% of eligible Head Start and At Risk programs (approximate N = 250) volunteered and were accepted into this study. Parents were given three options for the location of the interview, including the home, the early childhood program, or the research office located at a local community based mental health facility. Forty-three percent of the parents were interviewed in their homes, 44% selected their child's early childhood program, and 13% selected the research office.

The interview was comprised primarily of standardized questions and covered a variety of topics related to the family's experiences of the services they were receiving from the early childhood programs as well as child, parent and family functioning. A face-to-face interview format was utilized in order to control for the diversity of reading levels among participating parents. Questions and possible responses were read aloud and participants who desired could read along on the provided set of cards listing response choices. The interviews were conducted by 12 different interviewers over the course of the project, five of whom were African-American, one of whom was Asian, and six of whom were Caucasian. All interviewers were trained to use a "family-centered" format, such as providing parents with a clear orientation to each section of the interview, providing videos for the parents' older children to watch, providing discretion around the number and timing of interview breaks, and providing choices about the number of sessions desired to complete the interview and the location of the interview. The interview took approximately 2 1/2 hours to complete. Families received $30 and public transportation tokens to cover their travel costs.

Caregivers and their children were also asked to participate in a caregiver-child interaction task. The administration of the interaction task involved providing the caregiver with a standard set of toys, selected for different developmental age levels, and requesting that the caregiver play with the child for 15 minutes as she normally would. Another five minutes was spent in clean up activities. The entire 20 minute play session was videotaped in the child's home or school.

Developmental assessments of all children were conducted at the child's home or school. The Bayley Scales of Infant Development (Bayley, 1993), the Stanford-Binet (4th Edition, Form L-M, 1960), and the Functional Status IIR (Stein & Jessop, 1982) were used to construct a categorical "Overall delay" index which took into account motor, language, cognitive, and other delays. The Index was comprised of five categories of functioning: severely impaired, moderately impaired, mildly impaired, average, and above average.

RESULTS

There was significant diversity and yet similarities among low-income, single-parent families with young children, particularly in regard to their family structures or households. In this sample of single-caregiver families, the biological mother was most often identified as the parent responsible for the children's care. For example, the biological mother was living in the same household as the focus child in 92% (n = 200) of the families and was identified as the primary caregiver in 98% (n = 197) of these households. Fathers were residing in 13% (n = 26) of these households and were identified as the primary caregivers in 2% (n = 5) of the total sample.

There were five patterns of family structures, although the incidence of these structures varied considerably in the sample. First, the *solo parent* household was comprised of one parent with no other adults in the household (35.8%, n = 78). Second, the *three generational* household included the mother of the focus child living with her family-of-origin (26.1%, n = 57). Some of these families had additional relatives living in the household, while others did not. Caregiving was often shared. Third, the *couple-headed* household consisted of the mother living with a male partner or the father of the child (16.5%, n = 36). Some of the fathers/boyfriends did not have stable residence in these households. Others had significant relationships with the mothers but were not married–legally or by common law. Fourth, there was a *kinship* household or "augmented" family (Randolph, 1995), where the single parent lived in the home of relatives and/or other adults (other than the baby's grandmother) within their social network (15.6%, n = 34). In these households, the primary responsibility of caregiving was sometimes assumed by someone other than the biological single parent. Lastly, there was the *relative/foster parent* household that involved an informal or legal separation between the natural parents and their children. In these households, *unmarried relatives or single foster parents* were taking responsibility for raising the children. Ongoing contact with one of the natural parents was reported for 38.5% of the children residing in this type of household. This was the least frequently occurring family form in the sample (6%, n = 13).

Stability and change of family caregiving structures. Change was an important dimension in describing family structure. Over an approximately 9 month period, there was both change and stability among the family structures. A considerable degree of stability was found in three generational households where the mother was living with maternal grandmother (90% stayed the same), in the solo parent household (88% stayed the same), and in the relative/foster parent households (100% stayed the same). Structures experiencing more change included the kinship household (73% stayed the same) and the couple-headed household, with mother living with her partner or the baby's father (59% stayed the same).

Caregiver age and family structure. Age was another dimension that distinguished family structures. The target child, on average, was younger in three generational households (25.8 months) as compared to couple-headed households (31.6 months old) (t (91) = 2.37, $p <$ .05). Primary caregivers in three-generational households were also younger (X = 25.6 years old, ranging in age from 15-45), compared with solo parent households (X = 27.8 years old, ranging in age from 19-46), (t (91) = 3.2, $p < .05$). There were no other significant differences in age of the target child or in caregiver age across the other caregiver household structures.

Household income and family structure. The primary caregiver's economic status showed variations by single-parent family structures. Single parents living alone had significantly lower incomes than all other family structures, except for couple-headed single-parent households (X^2 (18) = 46.28, $p < .05$). Single parents living alone (72%) had an income of less than $800.00 per month, compared with 64% of mothers living with male partners or fathers of the children. Foster/relative care and three generational households reported the highest household incomes (76.9% and 54.4%, respectively, indicating an income of more than $800.00 per month).

Need-based family stress and family structure. Of the five categories of daily needs measured by the Family Needs Scale (Dunst et al., 1988), caregivers in our sample all strongly endorsed money needs (61%). Personal discretionary needs (50%) and employment needs (42%) were also highly endorsed by all family structures. However, single parents living alone reported significantly higher personal discretionary needs ($F(4, 210) = 3.17, p < .05$), and significantly higher employment needs, ($F(4, 210) = 2.65, p < .05$) than other family structures as indicated by univariate ANOVAs. Basic needs (20%) and special equipment or medical needs (28%) were identified less frequently than other family needs across all family structures.

Family functioning and family structure. Based upon the FAD reported norms for the General Functioning Index (GFI) (Miller et al., 1985), 59% of the single caregivers scored in the "distressed" range of family functioning (i.e., caregivers met the established caseness criteria for the GFI). However, there were no significant differences for the GFI scores by type of single caregiver household.

Univariate ANOVA results from the PCIS indicated that there were significant differences in the quality ($F\ (4{,}204) = 2.85, p < .05$) and appropriateness ($F\ (4, 204) = 2.83, p < .05$) of parent-child interaction between the solo parent household and the three generational household. Caregivers living with the baby's grandmother were rated lower along the quality and appropriateness dimensions than parents living alone ($t(127) = 2.35, p < .05$; $t(127) = 2.64, p < .01$; respectively). There were no other significant differences between single caregiver household structures.

Social relations and family structure: Diversity within and across single caregiver families. A series of univariate ANOVAs were performed to assess differences across household types on emotional support, instrumental and informational support, reciprocity, and conflict/hassles. There were only two distinct differences in social relations that were related to family caregiving structure. First, conflict with maternal grandmother was highest for caregivers living in three generational homes. These caregivers reported significantly more conflict with their mothers than caregivers living in all other family structures ($p < .05$). Second, when the baby's father was present in the couple-headed households, the relationship between caregiver and baby's father involved greater reciprocity, and caregivers also perceived more emotional and instrumental/informational support from the baby's father than when the baby's father was not present ($p < .05$).

There were many similarities across the family structures in how support and conflict within social networks was perceived. Differences in social relations were more often related to the type of social network member that the caregiver was describing as opposed to the type of household structure. Across all family structures, univariate analyses indicated differences related to social network members within each of the social relationship dimensions assessed by the NRI: perceptions of emotional support (F (5,218) = 31.7, $p < .01$), instrumental and informational support (F (5,218) = 32.0, $p < .01$), conflict and hassles (F (5,218) = 42.7, $p < .01$), and reciprocity (F (5,218) = 32.0, $p < .01$).

T-test analyses of mean score differences in the social relationship dimensions for all family household structures indicated that the caregiver's mother and the mother's romantic partner provided significantly greater ($p < .05$) emotional support than other network members. To a lesser extent, friends and relatives were perceived to be consistent sources of emotional support for parents. Instrumental/informational support, which tended to be provided at lower levels than emotional support, was provided primarily by the caregiver's mother ($p < .05$) and romantic partners ($p < .05$). The caregiver was most involved in reciprocating support with the baby's grandmother and her romantic partner ($p < .05$). Mothers identified 21% of the babies' fathers as their current "romantic partners." Even if they were not romantically involved with the mother, fathers still, on the average, had contact with their children regardless of family structure. For example, 70% of caregivers reported that their children had regular contact with their fathers.

Caregivers reported significantly higher levels of conflict in their relationships with the maternal grandmother ($p < .05$). Caregivers also reported significantly higher levels of conflict with the focus child's father ($p < .05$) and the romantic partner ($p < .05$) (if not the child's father) than in their relationships with extended family members. (The foster/relative households were not included in the prior comparisons due to the small sample size).

DISCUSSION

Five distinct family caregiving structures among low-income single parent families were identified: (a) the solo parent household, (b) the three-generational household, (c) the couple-headed household, (d) the kinship or augmented household, and (e) the relative/foster parent household. While global measures of family functioning or distress were unrelated to type of family caregiving structure, there were significant differences among the various structures with respect to the stability of the household structures across time, specific sources of stress or conflict, and perceived sources of primary support.

There was considerable fluidity among the family caregiving structures within relatively short periods of time, particularly for unmarried couple-headed households and single parent kinship households. Three-generation households and solo parents reported the least change in caregiving structures. An important implication for community-based programs is that meaningful assessments of family needs and resources must be ongoing and repeated frequently across time.

As expected, need-based stress and family caregiving structure were closely linked. This pattern was particularly evident for the solo parent household, where caregivers had the lowest financial resources of all four types of family organization, greatest employment needs, and the least time to participate in personal discretionary activities, such as those involving self-improvement or family fun. Previous studies (e.g., McLoyd et al., 1997) have also suggested that both parents and children in this group have the highest exposure to discrete and chronic stressors. Research has shown that single parents living alone with their children are at risk for a number of negative social, material, and psychological outcomes (Belle, 1982; Furstenberg, Brooks-Gunn, & Morgan, 1987; U.S. Dept of Health and Human Services, 1995).

Maternal anxiety, depression and other health problems are intensified for single parents living alone with their children (Guttentag, Salasin, & Belle, 1980; Liem & Liem, 1978; Neff & Husaini, 1980), especially when there are several young children in the household (Pearlin & Johnson, 1977). It is this group of families which may be impacted the hardest by the recent changes in welfare policies that require participation in education, training, and employment activities in order to continue receiving support. In order to strengthen solo parent households, programs will need to be prepared to address a broad range of instrumental, material and emotional needs. These families are likely to require the most services in order to maintain competent functioning.

Despite the number and intensity of needs reported by solo parents, this group did not significantly differ in family distress ratings from those living in the other three family caregiving structures. This result may partly be due to the high levels of distressed family relationships reported by all families. Such high levels of distress are consistent with findings from previous studies with families living in poverty (e.g., McLoyd, 1990). Disappointments and conflicts among family members leading to family distress is likely to be common among low-income single parents, in part because family and network members have similar constraints, impoverished circumstances, and needs.

These results suggest that any one single parenting family structure does not provide a more "functional" or "dysfunctional" family environment than another single parent family structure. Nor does the number of caregiving supports alone predict the functioning of the family or network system. Programs are therefore cautioned against over-rating the functioning of single parent families who appear to have more caregiving supports in the household (e.g., grandmother, other kin, or partner) while over-pathologizing the solo parent who appears to have very little support.

While family and network relationships were strained, the mothers as a group reported feeling supported within their specific individual relationships. As previously indicated by Belle's (1982) research with poor African American women, relationships which were sources of support and strength were also major sources of distress. This finding was especially true for the mother-daughter relationships in the three generational families in this study. The multiple dimensions of this relationship may partly be explained by the high demands for support reciprocity from grandmothers, and struggles around independence and parenting competency within the mother-daughter relationship (Jones, 1991).

Consistent with a family systems model (e.g., Boyd-Franklin, 1989; Minuchin, 1974) and/or a transactional model (e.g., Sameroff & Fiese,

1990), this blurring between social resources and social stressors suggests that programs should avoid treating social resources and social stressors as discrete, unidirectional and stable assets or liabilities. Ongoing training and supervision in family systems approaches to intervention and prevention (e.g., Minuchin, 1974; Dunst, Trivette, & Deal, 1994) is important so that providers see and create opportunities for building stronger, more flexible family relationships.

Another finding which supports the relational and contextual focus of a family systems approach to intervention and prevention involved the three generational family caregiving structure. Single mothers living with their mothers in a three-generational home were rated lower in the quality and appropriateness of parent-child interactions, suggesting poorer functioning than single parents living in other types of households. However, when this finding is placed in the context of the mother's age, the picture becomes more complex. An important resource for these mothers living with their children's maternal grandmothers was their higher household incomes than single mothers living alone. Viewed from a "competency lens," these results suggest that the three generational household may be an adaptive family caregiving structure for the younger single parent who has considerable need for both instrumental and emotional support and is seeking out family resources to help cope with and parent a child who has special needs.

Programs should exercise considerable caution in interpreting discrete and overly global ratings of functioning or stress, which for poor unmarried mothers, may only shed light on their general plight, not on the adaptive processes of coping. Research with teen parents, for instance, suggests that the adaptiveness of shared parenting between mother and grandmother may be influenced by such factors as length of mother's residence in the home, age of the mother, race, and life course issues of the grandmother (Chase-Lansdale, Brooks-Gunn, & Zamsky, 1994; Furstenberg et al., 1987; Henly, 1997; Unger & Cooley, 1992).

Children's biological fathers and the mothers' romantic partners often had important roles in the family caregiving structure of single parent families. Almost 17% of the unmarried mothers in this sample were living either with a male partner or the father of the child. Nationally, in 25% of nonmarital births, parents live together, at least for a time (U.S. Department of Health and Human Services, 1995). It is important that the couple-headed single-parent household be given more focus in future studies and intervention, since it may hold a key to better understanding the forces promoting stability and change in family relationships. Even when mothers were not living with the babies' fathers, fathers were often involved in some capacity with their children. By failing to ask about the father's involvement with the family, potential sources of support and opportunities for father involvement may be overlooked.

In summary, the findings support the contention that single parenthood is best treated as a group of diverse family structures, rather than a single undifferentiated entity, in both practice and in applied research. A change in the lens through which single parents and their family caregiving structures are viewed is also needed. Viewing these structures as intentional family problem-solving strategies or attempted solutions is more congruent with a strengths and competency based family support model (e.g., Boyd-Franklin, 1989; Dunst et al., 1994; Minuchin, 1974). For most low-income unmarried mothers, the lack of money severely restricts choices related to such important aspects of daily living as neighborhood, housing, purchases, and schools for children. These restrictions are often significant sources of stress. An important resource that may be available to low-income unmarried mothers for managing their needs and those of their children, and which is not defined by money alone, is family, kin and friends. The persons with whom these mothers choose to live with, therefore, may often be made in the service of recruiting support in adapting to or coping with current needs. This approach is consistent with the proactive and adaptive aging or socio-emotional selectivity theory (Lang & Carstensen, 1994) that adults selectively optimize their social networks as their needs change.

This study highlights the importance of attending to distinctions and similarities between different types of family organization among low-income, unmarried mothers, both when planning and evaluating services. The majority of the unmarried mothers who participated in this study were very poor and had many needs, yet the particular nature of the barriers they encountered and the pattern of supportive resources available to them often varied in relation to the type of "family" they created for themselves. This perspective attributes positive intent and competence to these families and calls attention to the ever changing dynamics of their lives. It is by understanding the children and their unmarried mothers within the context of these family adaptations and their complex, dynamic individual relationships that will lead to the most meaningful prevention and/or intervention models that match the needs of specific families in the service of supporting competence.

REFERENCES

Bayley, N. (1993). *Manual for the Bayley Scales of Infant Development II.* San Antonio, TX: Psychological Corporation.

Belle, D. (1982). Social ties and social support. In D. Belle (Ed.), *Lives in distress: Women in depression* (pp. 133-144). Beverly Hills: Sage.

Belle, D. E. (1984). Inequality and mental health: Low income and minority women. In L. Walker (Ed.), *Women and mental health policy* (pp. 135-150). Beverly Hills, CA: Sage Publications.

Boyd-Franklin, N. (1989). *Black families in therapy.* NY: Guilford.

Chase-Lansdale, P. L., Brooks-Gunn, J., & Zamsky, E. S. (1994). Young African-American multigenerational families in poverty: Quality of mothering and grand-mothering. *Child Development, 65,* 373-393.

Chilman, C. (1990). Low income families and public welfare organizations. In D. G. Unger & M. B. Sussman (Eds.), *Families in community settings: Interdisciplinary perspectives.* NY: Haworth.

Dunst, C. J., Trivette, C. M., & Deal, A. G. (1988). *Enabling and empowering families: Principles and guidelines for practice.* Cambridge, MA: Brookline Books.

Dunst, C. J., Trivette, C. M., & Deal, A. G. (1994). *Supporting and strengthening families: Methods, strategies and practices.* Cambridge, MA: Brookline Books.

Epstein, N. B., Baldwin, L. M., & Bishop, D. S. (1983). The McMaster Family Assessment Device. *Journal of Marital and Family Therapy, 9,* 171-180.

Farran, D. C., Kasari, C., Comfort, M., & Jay, S. (1986). *The Parent/Caregiver Involvement Scale.* Greensboro, NC: The University of North Carolina at Greensboro, Child Development and Family Relations, School of Human Environmental Sciences.

Francis-Okongwu, A. (1996). Keeping the show on the road: Female-headed families surviving on $22,000 a year or less in New York city. *Urban Anthropology, 25,* 115-163.

Furman, W. & Buhrmester, D. (1985). Children's perceptions of the personal relationships in their social networks. *Developmental Psychology,* 21, 1016-1024.

Furstenberg, F. F., Brooks-Gunn, J., & Morgan, S. P. (1987). *Adolescent mothers in later life.* NY: Cambridge University Press.

Guttentag, M., Salasin, S., & Belle, D. (1980). *The mental health of women.* NY: Academic Press.

Halpern, R. (1990). Poverty and early childhood parenting: Toward a framework for intervention. *American Journal of Orthopsychiatry, 60,* 6-18.

Hanson, M. J. & Lynch, E. W. (1992). Family diversity: Implications for policy and practice. *Topics in Early Childhood Special Education, 12,* 283-305.

Hanson, S. M. H., Heims, M. L., Julian, D. J., & Sussman, M. B. (Eds.) (1995). *Single parent families: Diversity, myths and realities.* NY: Haworth Press.

Henly, J. R. (1997). The complexity of support: The impact of family structure and provisional support on African American and White adolescent mothers' well-being. *American Journal of Community Psychology, 25,* 629-655.

Huston, A. C. (1991). Children in poverty: Developmental and policy issues. In A. C. Huston (Ed.), *Children in poverty: Child development and public policy,* (pp. 1-22). Cambridge: Cambridge University Press.

Jones, C. W. (1991). Role adjustment among low-income single parents with a retarded child: Patterns of support. *Journal of Family Psychology, 4,* 497-511.

Lang, F. R., & Carstensen, L. L. (1994). Close emotional relationships in late life: Further support for proactive aging in the social domain. *Psychology and Aging, 9,* 315-324.

Lerner, R. M., Castellino, D. R., Terry, P.A., Villarruel, F. A., & McKinney, M. H. (1995). Developmental contextual perspective on parenting. In M. H. Bornstein (Ed.), *Handbook of parenting, vol. 2: Biology and ecology of parenting,* (pp. 285-309). Hillsdale, NJ: Lawrence Erlbaum.

Lewis, E. A. (1989). Role strain in black women: The efficacy of social support. *Journal of Black Studies,* 20, 155-169.

Liem, R. & Liem, J. (1978). Social class and mental illness reconsidered: The role of economic stress and social support. *Journal of Health and Social Behavior, 19,* 139-156.

Littlejohn-Blake, S. M. & Darling, C. A. (1993). Understanding the strengths of African-American families. *Journal of Black Studies, 23*(4), 460-471.

Martin, E. & Martin, J. (1978). *The black extended family.* Chicago: University of Chicago Press.

Maternal and Child Health Bureau. (1994). *Child Health USA 1993.* (DHHS Publication No. HRSA-MCH-94-1). Washington, DC: U.S. Government Printing Office.

McLoyd, V. C. (1990). The impact of economic hardship on black families and children: Psychological distress, parenting, and socioemotional development. *Child Development, 61,* 311-346.

McLoyd, V. C., Ceballo, R., & Mangelsdorf, S. C. (1997). The effects of poverty on children's socioemotional development. In J. D. Noshpitz & N. E. Alessi (Eds.), *Handbook of child and adolescent psychiatry: Varieties of development (Vol. 4),* (pp. 191-206). New York: Wiley.

Miller, I. W., Bishop, D. S., Epstein, N. B., & Keitner, G. I. (1985). The McMaster Family Assessment Device: Reliability and validity. *Journal of Marital and Family Therapy, 11,* 345-356.

Minuchin, S. (1974). *Families and family therapy.* Cambridge, MA: Harvard University Press.

Neff, J. & Husaini, B. (1980). Race, socioeconomic status, and psychiatric impairment: A research note. *Journal of Community Psychology, 8,* 16-19.

Pelton, L. H. (1989). *For reasons of poverty: A critical analysis of the public child welfare system in the United States.* New York: Praeger.

Pearlin, L. & Johnson, J. (1977). Marital status, life-strains and depression. *American Sociological Review, 42,* 704-715.

Randolph, S. M. (1995). African-American children in single-mother families. In B. J. Dickerson (Ed.), *African American single mothers* (pp. 117-145). Thousand Oaks: Sage.

Sameroff, A. J. & Fiese, B. H. (1990). Transactional regulation and early intervention. In S. Meisels & J. P. Shonkoff (Eds.), *Handbook of early intervention,* (pp. 119-149). New York: Cambridge University Press.

Scott, J. W. & Black, A. W. (1989). Deep structures of African-American family life: Female and male kin networks. *The Western Journal of Black Studies, 13,* 17-23.

Simeonsson, R. J., Bailey, D. B., Huntington, G. S., & Comfort, M. (1986). Testing the goodness of fit in early intervention programs. *Pediatrics, 69,* 635-641.

Stein, E. K., & Jessop, D. J. (1982). A noncategorical approach to chronic childhood illness. *Public Health Reports, 97,* 352-362.

Stevenson, H. C. (1994). Research on African-American family life: Learning to interpret the dance. *The Family Psychologist, 10,* 38-40.

Taylor, R. J. (1986). Receipt of support from family among black Americans: Demographic and familial differences. *Journal of Marriage and the Family, 48,* 66-77.

Taylor, R. J., Chatters, L. M., Tucker, M. B., & Lewis, E. (1990). Developments in research on black families: A decade review. *Journal of Marriage and the Family, 52,* 993-1014.

Thompson, M. S. & Ensminger, M. E. (1989). Psychological well-being among mothers with school age children: Evolving family structures. *Social Forces, 67,* 715-730.

Unger, D. G. & Cooley, M. C. (1992). Partner and grandmother contact in black and white teen parent families. *Journal of Adolescent Health, 13,* 546-552.

Unger, D. G. & Wandersman, L. P. (1988). A support program for adolescent mothers: Predictors of participation. In D. R. Powell (Ed.), *Parent education as early childhood intervention,* (pp. 105-130). Norwood, NJ: Ablex.

U.S. Bureau of the Census. (1995a). Fertility of American women: June, 1994. *Current Population Reports,* series P20-482. Washington, DC: U.S. Department of Commerce.

U.S. Bureau of the Census. (1995b). Income, poverty, and valuation of noncash benefits: 1993. *Current Population Reports,* series P60-188. Washington, DC: U.S. Department of Commerce.

U.S. Department of Health and Human Services. (1995). *Report to Congress on out-of wedlock childbearing.* (DHHS publication No. (PHS) 95-1257). Hyattsville, MD: U.S. Public Health Service.

Economic Stress and Psychological Distress Among Urban African American Adolescents: The Mediating Role of Parents

Kathryn Grant
LaShaunda Poindexter
Trina Davis
Mi Hyon Cho
Anthony McCormick
Kevin Smith
DePaul University

SUMMARY. The present study tested the hypothesis that maternal depression and negative parenting mediate the relationship between economic stress and psychological symptoms among urban African American youth. Two distinct economic stressors were examined: (1) acute economic loss and (2) chronic economic strain. Each of these economic stressors was expected to predict maternal depression, which, in turn, was expected to predict negative parenting, which, finally, was expected to predict adolescent symptoms. Results suggest that maternal depression and negative parenting partially mediate the relationship between economic stress and adolescent psychological symptoms among urban African American youth. Directions for future research and intervention implications are outlined. *[Article copies available for a*

Address correspondence to: Kathryn Grant, Department of Psychology, DePaul University, 2219 North Kenmore Avenue, Chicago, IL 60614-3504 (E-mail: kgrant@wppost.depaul.edu).

[Haworth co-indexing entry note]: "Economic Stress and Psychological Distress Among Urban African American Adolescents: The Mediating Role of Parents." Grant, Kathryn et al. Co-published simultaneously in *Journal of Prevention & Intervention in the Community* (The Haworth Press, Inc.) Vol. 20, No. 1/2, 2000, pp. 25-36; and: *Diverse Families, Competent Families: Innovations in Research and Preventive Intervention Practice* (ed: Janet F. Gillespie, and Judy Primavera) The Haworth Press, Inc., 2000, pp. 25-36. Single or multiple copies of this article are available for a fee from The Haworth Document Delivery Service [1-800-342-9678, 9:00 a.m. - 5:00 p.m. (EST). E-mail address: getinfo@haworthpressinc.com].

fee from The Haworth Document Delivery Service: 1-800-342-9678. E-mail address: <getinfo@haworthpressinc.com> Website: <http://www.haworthpressinc.com>]

KEYWORDS. Urban, poverty, stress, psychological symptoms, African American, adolescence, parenting, maternal depression

A central focus of research in developmental psychopathology is identification of sources of risk for psychological distress and disorder during childhood and adolescence. Psychosocial stress has been the focus of considerable investigation as one such source of risk. Extensive research has clearly established stressful life events as significant risk factors for psychological problems during childhood and adolescence in both cross-sectional (e.g., Banez & Compas, 1990; Hodges, Kline, Barbero, & Flanery, 1984) and longitudinal studies (e.g., DuBois, Felner, Brand, Adan, & Evans, 1992; Nolen-Hoeksema, Girgus, & Seligman, 1992). In particular, researchers have repeatedly demonstrated a relationship between the life stressors associated with poverty and poor mental health (e.g., Osofsky, 1995; Durant, Pendergrast, & Cadenhead, 1994).

Researchers are now turning their attention to the search for processes or mechanisms by which stressful life events contribute to psychological symptoms (Cicchetti & Cohen, 1995). Identification of the mechanisms through which stressful life events and chronic stressors exert their impact on adjustment is important for improving our understanding of the role of stress in the etiology of child and adolescent psychopathology and for the development of interventions to reduce negative outcomes associated with stress (Cicchetti & Cohen, 1995).

Few studies have employed the methodology necessary to address the "how" and "why" questions associated with process research. Conger and colleagues (e.g., Conger, Ge, Elder, Lorenz, Simons, 1994; Conger, Conger, Elder, Jr., Lorenz, Simons, & Whitbeck, 1993) are one of the few research groups to conduct research in this area. Results of their empirical work with rural families impacted by recent recession suggest that the relationship between acute economic loss and adolescent psychological problems is mediated by changes in parenting (Conger et al., 1992; Conger et al., 1993). As parents become distressed in response to economic problems, they become less nurturant and more hostile toward their children. These parenting changes lead, in turn, to adolescent psychological problems (Conger et al., 1995; Conger et al., 1994).

Conger's work has focused on white rural families faced with sudden income loss as a result of the farm crisis of the 1980's. Processes in the relationship between poverty and child and adolescent adjustment within chronically disadvantaged urban communities are less understood (Seidman, 1991; McLloyd, Jayaratne, Ceballo, Borquez, 1994). Understanding processes in the relationship between poverty and psychological problems among urban African American youth is particularly important as numerous studies indicate this population is at heightened risk by virtue of its disproportionate representation among the chronically poor (e.g., Duncan & Yeung, 1995; McLeod & Shanahan, 1993). According to the U.S. Bureau of Census (1992), 45.9% of African American children and adolescents live in poverty, roughly four times the rate of European American youth (Garrett, N'gandu, & Ferron, 1994). Further, although most poor are poor for only a short period of time, this is less true for African Americans (Gottschalk, McLanahan, & Sandefur, 1994). Disadvantaged African American youth are more likely to live in persistent poverty and to live in isolated urban neighborhoods (Huston, McLloyd, & Coll, 1995).

Little is known about the specific processes which may account for the relationship between poverty and psychological symptoms among urban African American youth. However, McLloyd (McLloyd et al., 1994) suggests these processes may be similar to those found in white rural youth. Specifically, McLloyd and colleagues (McLloyd et al., 1994) found an indirect link between maternal unemployment and adolescent symptoms, via maternal depression and maternal punishment, in their sample of African American families. This finding suggests that, similar to white rural youth, parent variables may mediate the relationship between poverty and symptoms among urban African American youth.

The present study builds on both McLloyd and Conger's work by testing the hypothesis that negative effects of economic stress on urban adolescents are mediated by the negative effects of economic stress on parenting. More specifically, this study will test a mediational model in which economic stress predicts maternal depression, which, in turn, predicts negative parenting, which, finally, predicts adolescent psychological symptoms.

METHOD

Participants

Fifty African American adolescents and their mothers participated in this study (parent participation was limited to mothers as over 90% of families living in extreme urban poverty are headed by single mothers; Garbarino, 1991). Adolescent mean age was 12.5 (range = 11-15) and 47.2% were female. Participating adolescents attended five public schools, in a large Midwestern city, at the time of their participation. Target schools were selected based on high percentages of low-income and African American students. Socioeconomic status of students attending target schools was based on eligibility for federally funded school lunch programs. According to these criteria, 86.5% of adolescents attending target schools were classified as low-income. Mothers' reports of gross family income ranged from \$307 to \$3500 per month (mean = \$1306), with most mothers (60%) reporting monthly income of \$1350 or below.

Measures

Economic Stress. Mothers completed two measures of economic stress. The Economic Loss Questionnaire, a modified subscale of Conger's (1992) Family Economic Pressure Index, assesses negative changes in finances over the past twelve months. Sample items include: "During the past twelve months did you change jobs for a worse one?", "During the past twelve months did you take a cut in wage or salary?" "During the past twelve months did you get laid off or fired?"

The Economic Strain Questionnaire, comprising modified versions of the remaining subscales of Conger's (1992) Family Economic Pressure Index, assesses chronic economic stress and strain. Sample items include "My family has enough money for the kind of home we would like to have" and "We have enough money to pay our bills." Participants are also asked to rate the extent to which financial matters are a source of conflict in their family. Conger and colleagues report adequate reliability and validity for each of the subscales of the Family Economic Pressure Index (Conger et al., 1995).

Maternal Depression. Maternal depression was assessed using the Beck Depression Inventory (BDI; Beck, Rush, Shaw & Emery, 1979). The BDI includes twenty-one items, each of which contains four statements. The respondent is asked to select the statements which are most true of him/her in the past week. Sample statements include: "I do not feel sad," "I feel sad," "I am sad all the time and I can't snap out of it," "I am so sad or unhappy that I can't stand it." Higher scores indicate higher levels of depression. Reliability and validity for the BDI are well-established (Beck et al., 1979).

Parenting. Parenting was assessed using the Parenting Practices Questionnaire (PPQ; Robinson, Mandleco, Olsen, & Hart, 1995). The PPQ is a 62 item questionnaire assessing a range of parenting strategies designed to capture Baumrind's authoritative parenting construct (Baumrind, 1966, 1971, 1978). Sample items include: "I give praise when my child is good," "I give comfort and understanding when my child is upset," "I explode in anger at my child." Reverse-scored positive parenting items (e.g., consistent discipline, nurturant parenting) and negative parenting items (e.g., inconsistent discipline, harsh/ explosive parenting) were summed to form the Negative Parenting score. The PPQ has demonstrated good reliability and validity (Robinson et al., 1995).

Psychological Symptoms. Adolescent psychological symptoms were assessed using the total problem score of the Child Behavior Checklist (CBCL; Achenbach, 1991; Achenbach & Edelbrock, 1986). The CBCL includes 113 behavior items which parents rate on a 3-point scale as "not true," "somewhat or sometimes true," or "very true or often true" of their child during the past six months. Both internalizing and externalizing symptoms are assessed. Sample items include "My child is nervous, highstrung, or tense," "My child is unhappy, sad, or depressed," and "My child gets in many fights." Normative data for the CBCL are based on a nationally representative sample of nonreferred children and adolescents, with separate norms for boys and girls. Reliability and validity for the CBCL are well established (Achenbach, 1991).

Procedures

Two African American clinical psychology doctoral candidates distributed flyers describing the project to sixth, seventh, and eighth graders attending target schools. Mothers interested in participating were instructed to provide a phone number or address and to return the flyer, via their child, to school. The two doctoral students collected the flyers, scheduled appointments, and administered questionnaires and videotaped interaction protocols in the homes of participating families. Questionnaires were administered in an interview format, with one of the doctoral students interviewing the mother, and the other interviewing the adolescent. Only maternal interview responses are reported in the present study. Participation took approximately one and one half hours. Families were paid $50 for their participation.

RESULTS

Results are presented in three stages: first, results of correlational analyses are summarized; second, mediational analyses are reviewed; finally, results of structural equation modeling are presented.

Correlational Analyses

Correlations among poverty, mediational, and symptom variables revealed several expected relationships. Economic loss was correlated with maternal depression (r = .39, $p < .01$) and adolescent symptoms (r = .35, $p < .05$), maternal depression was correlated with negative parenting (r = .45, $p < .01$) and adolescent symptoms (r = .39, $p < .01$), economic strain was correlated with maternal depression (r = .29, $p < .05$), and negative parenting was correlated with adolescent symptoms (r = .59, $p < .01$). Economic loss and economic strain were not significantly correlated, indicating these represent two distinct economic stressors.

Mediational Analyses

The following series of regressions are recommended to test for mediation effects: (1) regression of the mediator (e.g., negative parenting) on the independent variable (e.g., economic loss); (2) regression of the dependent variable (e.g., adolescent symptoms) on the independent variable (e.g., economic loss); (3) regression of the dependent variable (e.g., adolescent symptoms) on both the independent variable (e.g., economic loss) and the mediator (e.g., negative parenting) (Baron & Kenny, 1986; Holmbeck, 1997). The following conditions are necessary to provide support for the mediational hypothesis (Baron & Kenny, 1986; Holmbeck, 1997): (1) the independent variable is related to the mediator; (2) the mediator is related to the dependent variable once the independent variable is included in the equation; (3) the relation between the independent variable and the dependent variable decreases once the mediator is included in the equation.

Economic Strain and Psychological Symptoms. Implicit in these recommended analyses is a significant association between the independent variable and the dependent variable. By definition, a mediating variable explains or accounts for an existing relationship between two variables (Baron & Kenny, 1986; Holmbeck, 1997). A significant association between economic strain and adolescent symptoms was not found, thus precluding additional mediational analyses with these variables (Baron & Kenny, 1986; Holmbeck, 1997).

Economic Loss and Psychological Symptoms. Maternal depression and negative parenting were each examined as potential mediators of the relationship between economic loss and adolescent symptoms.

Results of mediational analyses conducted with maternal depression as the hypothesized mediator revealed the following predicted relationships. First, economic loss was significantly associated with maternal depression, $F\ (1, 48) = 6.53$, $p < .01$. Second, maternal depression was associated with adolescent symptoms, and this relationship remained significant once economic loss was included in the equation, $F\ (2, 47) = 3.82$, $p < .05$. Third, there was a significant decrease in the variance in adolescent symptoms accounted for by economic loss once maternal depression was included in the equation. In fact, economic loss no longer predicted a significant amount of variance in adolescent symptoms once maternal depression was included in the equation $F\ (2, 47) = 1.88$, $p < .11$. The results of these analyses support the hypothesis that maternal depression mediates the relationship between economic loss and adolescent psychological symptoms.

Results of mediational analyses conducted with negative parenting as the hypothesized mediator revealed the following predicted relationships. Economic loss was significantly associated with negative parenting, $F\ (1, 48) = 6.53$, $p < .01$, and negative parenting remained associated with adolescent symptoms once economic loss was included in the equation, $F\ (1, 48) = 5.28$, $p < .01$; however, the decrease in association between economic loss and adolescent symptoms was not substantial, and this relationship remained significant, $F\ (1, 48) = 2.93$, $p < .01$. These findings suggest that negative parenting partially mediates the relationship between economic loss and adolescent symptoms.

Structural Equation Modeling

Structural equation modeling is used both to test for mediating relationships (e.g., Dodge, Pettit, & Bates, 1994) and to examine indirect pathways between variables which are not directly related (e.g., McLloyd et al., 1994). For example, McLloyd and colleagues (1994) found no direct relationship between maternal unemployment and adolescent symptoms; however, they found that maternal unemployment predicted maternal depression, which, in turn, predicted increased punishment of the adolescent, which, finally, predicted adolescent psychological symptoms.

In the present study, we used structural equation modeling to examine the fit of two conceptual models. These models were based on the results of our mediational analyses. The first model focuses on the relationship between economic strain and adolescent symptoms. As we did not find a significant direct association between these variables, we tested whether or not maternal depression and negative parenting link economic strain and symptoms indirectly. More specifically, we hypothesized that economic strain would lead to maternal depression which, in turn, would predict negative parenting, which, finally, would lead to adolescent psychological symptoms.

The second model builds on the results of mediational analyses with economic loss and adolescent symptoms. Our mediational findings suggest that negative parenting and maternal depression mediate the relationship between economic loss and adolescent symptoms, with maternal depression more fully accounting for this relationship. Thus, we examined the hypothesis that both maternal depression and negative parenting, together, mediate the relationship between economic loss and adolescent symptoms, with significant variance in symptoms still predicted by economic loss. More specifically, we expected economic loss to lead to maternal depression, maternal depression to predict negative parenting, and, finally, negative parenting to lead to adolescent symptoms. Further, we expected economic loss to independently predict adolescent symptoms. The two models are depicted in Figure 1.

Economic Strain and Psychological Symptoms. Predictions for model 1 were set up as a path model with four observed variables (economic strain, maternal depression, negative parenting, adolescent symptoms) and tested using the LISREL 8.12a program (Joreskog &

FIGURE 1. Two conceptual models tested using structural equation modeling

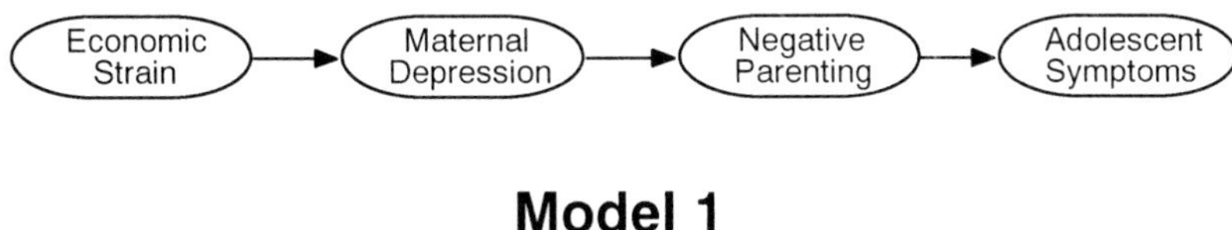

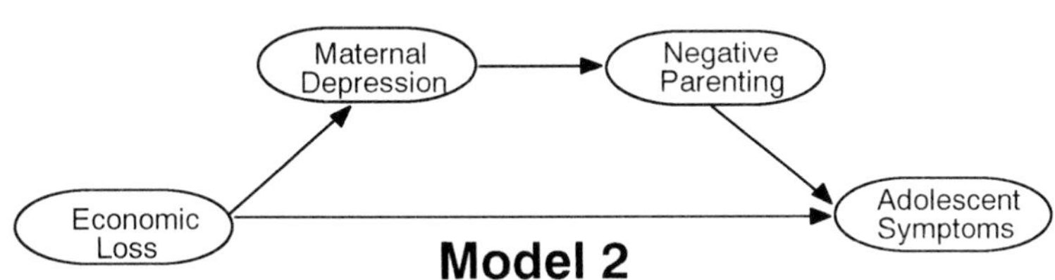

Sorbom, 1989). Evidence for the fit of the conceptual model was excellent and included a critical N greater than 200 (Critical N = 298.94) (Hoelter, 1983), a goodness-of-fit index greater than .90 (GFI = .98; AGFI = .94) (Joreskog & Sorbom, 1989) and a nonsignificant chi-square. In addition, all hypothesized pathways were statistically significant.

Economic Loss and Psychological Symptoms. Predictions for model 2 were set up as a path model with four observed variables (economic loss, maternal depression, negative parenting, adolescent symptoms) and tested using the LISREL 8.12a program (Joreskog & Sorbom, 1989). Evidence for the fit of this conceptual model was also excellent and included a critical N above 200 (Critical N = 299.69) (Hoelter, 1983), a goodness-of-fit index above .90 (GFI = .99; AGFI = .93) (Joreskog & Sorbom, 1989) and a nonsignificant chi-square. In addition, all hypothesized pathways were statistically significant.

DISCUSSION

The present study tested for mediating processes in the relationship between economic stress and psychological symptoms among urban

African American youth. Results suggest that the effects of economic stress on adolescent mental health are filtered, at least in part, through the effects of economic stress on parents.

These results build on McLloyd et al.'s (1994) finding that maternal depression and punishment indirectly link maternal unemployment with distress among African American youth. In fact, the present study provides stronger evidence for the mediating role of parenting in the relationship between economic stress and symptoms within this population. Whereas, McLloyd did not find a direct link between maternal unemployment and adolescent symptoms, the present study found a direct link between economic loss and psychological symptoms. In addition, an indirect link, similar to that found by McLloyd, was found between economic strain and symptoms via maternal depression and negative parenting. Both economic stressors examined in this study (economic loss and economic strain) were linked to adolescent symptoms via maternal depression and negative parenting.

Results of the present study, as well as McLloyd et al.'s (1994) results, are similar to the findings Conger and colleagues (e.g., Conger et al., 1993) have reported on economic stress, parenting, and symptoms among white rural youth. Taken together, these results suggest that processes accounting for the effects of economic stress upon adolescent mental health may be similar among adolescents of dissimilar backgrounds (e.g., African American vs. European American) living in dissimilar contexts (e.g., urban vs. rural).

However, it is important to bear in mind that parenting did not fully explain the relationship between economic stress and adolescent symptoms in the present study. It appears that additional factors, not examined in this study, also mediate this relationship. Such factors may range from cognitive attributions and coping styles to exposure to community violence, racism, and discrimination. Although results of the present study highlight similar processes in the relation between economic stress and symptoms across demographic groups, future research should examine the hypothesis that additional mediators (e.g., exposure to community violence/racism/discrimination) may be unique to urban African American youth.

In conclusion, social and public policy efforts to eradicate poverty are necessary if we are to truly protect youth from the negative effects of economic stress. In the meantime, intervention programs aimed at protecting youth from poverty's impact must include parents. Results of the present study suggest that we cannot protect children from the psychological costs of poverty without, first, protecting their parents.

REFERENCES

Achenbach, T. M. (1991c). *Manual for the Child Behavior Checklist and 1991 Profile.* Burlington, VT: University of Vermont Department of Psychiatry.

Banez, G. A. & Compas, B. E. (1990). Children's and parents' daily stressful events and psychological symptoms. *Journal of Abnormal Child Psychology, 18,* 591-605.

Baron, R., & Kenny, D. A. (1986). The moderator-mediator variable distinction in social psychological research: Conceptual, strategic, and statistical considerations. *Journal of Personality and Social Psychology, 51(6),* 1173-1182.

Baumrind, D. (1966). Effects of authoritative parental control on child behavior. *Child Development, 37,* 887-907.

Baumrind, D. (1971). Current patterns of parental authority. *Developmental Psychology Monographs, Part 2, 4,* 1-103.

Baumrind, D. (1978). Parental disciplinary patterns and social competence in children. *Youth and Society, 9,* 239-276.

Beck, A. T., Rush, A. J., Shaw, B. F., & Emery, G. (1979). *Cognitive Therapy of Depression.* New York: Guilford Press.

Cicchetti, D., & Cohen, D. J. (1995). *Developmental Psychopathology (Vols. 1 and 2).* New York: Wiley.

Conger, R. D., Conger, K. J., Elder, Jr., G. H., Lorenz, F. O., Simons, R. L., & Whitbeck, L. B. (1992). A family process model of economic hardship and adjustment of early adolescent boys. *Child Development, 63,* 526-541.

Conger, R. D., Ge, X., Elder, G. H., Jr., Lorenz, F. O., & Simons, R. L. (1994). Economic stress, coercive family process and developmental problems of adolescents Special issue: Children and poverty. *Child Development, 65,* 541-561.

Dodge, K. A., Petit, G. S., & Bates, J. E. (1994). Socialization mediators of the relation between socioeconomic status and child conduct problems. Special Issue: Children and poverty. *Child Development, 65,* 649-665.

Duncan, G. J., & Yeung, W. J. (1995). Extent and consequence of welfare dependence among America's children. *Children and Youth Services Review, 17,* 157-182.

DuBois, D. L., Felner, R. D., Brand, S., Adan, A. M., & Evans, E. G. (1992). A prospective study of life stress, social support, and adaptation in early adolescence. *Child Development, 63,* 542-557.

Durant, R., Pendergrast, R., & Cadenhead, C. (1994). Exposure to violence and victimization and fighting behavior by urban Black adolescents. *Journal of Public Health, 15(4),* 311-318.

Garbarino, J., Dubrow, N., Kostelny, K., & Pardo, C. (1992). *Children in danger: Coping with the consequences of community violence* (pp. 262). San Francisco: Jossey-Bass Inc.

Garrett, P., Ngandu, N., & Ferron, J. (1994). Poverty experiences of young children and the quality of their home environments. Special Issue: Children and poverty. *Child Development, 65(2),* 331-345.

Gottschalk, P., McLanahan, S., & Sandefur, G. D. (1994). *The dynamics and intergenerational transmission of poverty and welfare participation.* In S. H. Danziger, G. D. Sandefur & D. H. Weinberg (Eds.) Confronting Poverty (pp. 84-108). New York: Russell Sage Foundation.

Hodges, K., Kline, J. J., Barbero, G., & Flanery, R. (1984). Life events occurring in families of children with recurrent abdominal pain. *Journal of Psychosomatic Research, 28,* 185-188.

Hoelter, J. W. (1983). The analysis of covariance structures: Goodness-of-fit indices. *Sociological Methods of Research*, 11, 325-344.

Holmbeck, G. N. (1997). *Toward terminological, conceptual, and statistical clarity in the study of mediators and moderators*: Examples from the child-clinical and pediatric psychology literatures. *Journal of Consulting and Clinical Psychology, 65,* 599-610.

Huston, A., McLoyd, V. C. & Garcia-Coll, C. (1994). Children and poverty: Issues in contemporary research. *Child Development, 65,* 175-282.

Joreskog, K. G., & Sorbom, D. (1989). *LISREL VII: User's reference guide (1st ed.).* Mooresville, IN: Scientific Software.

McLeod, J., & Shanahan, M. (1993). Poverty, parenting, and children's mental health. *American Sociological Review, 58(3),* 351-366.

McLoyd, V. C. (1990). The impact of economic hardship on black families and children: Psychosocial distress, parenting, and socio-emotional development. *Child Development, 61,* 311-346.

McLoyd, V. C., Jayaratne, T. E., Beballo, R., & Borquez, J. (1994). Unemployment and work interruption among African American single mothers: Effects on parenting and adolescent social emotional functioning. Special Issue: Children and poverty. *Child Development, 65,* 562-589.

Nolen-Hoeksema, S., Girgus, J. S., & Seligman, M. E. P. (1992). Predictors and consequences of childhood depressive symptoms: A 5 year longitudinal study. *Journal of Abnormal Psychology, 101,* 405-422.

Osofsky, J., Wewers, S., Hann, D., & Fick, A. (1993). Chronic community violence: What is happening to our children? Special issue: Children and violence. *Psychiatry Interpersonal and Biological Processes, 56(1),* 36-45.

Robinson, C. C., Mandleco, B., Olsen, S. F., & Hart, C. H. (1995). Authoritative, authoritarian, and permissive parenting practices: Development of a new measure. *Psychological Reports, 77,* 819-830.

Seidman, E. (1991). Growing up the hard way: Pathways of urban adolescents. *American Journal of Community Psychology, 19,* 173-205.

The Marital Context for Father Involvement with Their Preschool Children: The Role of Partner Support

Geneviève Bouchard
Catherine M. Lee

School of Psychology
University of Ottawa

SUMMARY. Fathers from dual-earner families with preschool-aged children reported that they were frequently involved in disciplining their children, often helped them in their daily routines, and occasionally got up at night with them. Fathers' sense of competence in the paternal role was predicted by marital satisfaction and the perception that their partners view them as competent fathers. Fathers' satisfaction in the paternal role was predicted by marital satisfaction and adaptability within the couple relationship. These results highlight the marital relationship as an important context for the quality of men's experience in their fathering role. Implications for programs promoting father involvement are discussed. *[Article copies available for a fee from The Haworth Document Delivery Service: 1-800-342-9678. E-mail address: <getinfo@haworthpressinc.com> Website: <http://www.haworthpressinc.com>]*

Address correspondence to: Catherine M. Lee, PhD, Centre for Psychological Services, University of Ottawa, 120 University Private, Ottawa, Ontario, Canada K1N 6N5 (E-mail: cmlee@uottawa.ca).

This research was supported by a grant from the Social Sciences and Humanities Research Council of Canada to Catherine M. Lee.

[Haworth co-indexing entry note]: "The Marital Context for Father Involvement with Their Preschool Children: The Role of Partner Support." Bouchard, Geneviève, and Catherine M. Lee. Co-published simultaneously in *Journal of Prevention & Intervention in the Community* (The Haworth Press, Inc.) Vol. 20, No. 1/2, 2000, pp. 37-53; and: *Diverse Families, Competent Families: Innovations in Research and Preventive Intervention Practice* (ed: Janet F. Gillespie, and Judy Primavera) The Haworth Press, Inc., 2000, pp. 37-53. Single or multiple copies of this article are available for a fee from The Haworth Document Delivery Service [1-800-342-9678, 9:00 a.m. - 5:00 p.m. (EST). E-mail address: getinfo@haworthpress inc.com].

KEYWORDS. Fathers, father involvement, partner support, motivation

Paternal involvement with children has benefits for children, mothers, and fathers themselves (Lamb, 1997). However, despite men's equivalent competence in child care (Pruett & Litzenberger, 1992), women are still primarily responsible for childcare activities (Lee & Duxbury, 1998; Strazdins, Galligan, & Scannell, 1997). Various multidimensional models have been developed to examine the variables that facilitate or inhibit men's participation with their children (Pleck, 1997). The focus in this study is on fathers' perceptions of the ways their partners support them in their roles as fathers.

The link between marital quality and child adjustment is well-established (Cummings & O'Reilly, 1997). Happily married parents interact more positively with their infant (Levy-Schiff, 1994), preschool (Lindahl, Clements, & Markman, 1997) and school age children (Simons, Beaman, Conger, & Chao, 1993). Moreover, fathers reporting higher marital satisfaction and spousal support rate their preschool children more favorably (Goldberg, 1990). Studies of the link between the marital relationship and fathers' involvement with their children yield contradictory results with some researchers reporting a strong link (Levy-Schiff), others finding no relation (Deutsch, Lussier, & Servis, 1993), and others reporting associations only when the marital quality variable is dichotomized (McBride & Mills, 1993). Variables that influence the link between the marital relationship and fathers' involvement with their children are discussed below.

AGE OF CHILD

Many studies have been conducted during the transition to parenthood, examining the father's interaction with his newborn, infant, or toddler (Gable, Belsky, & Crnic, 1995). During this transition, individuals redefine their roles as they move from being a couple to being a family with very young children (Cowan & Cowan, 1995). However, differences between mothers and fathers may be accentuated during the transition to parenthood (Clark, Hyde, Essex, & Klein, 1997; Cowan & Cowan, 1995), making it inappropriate to generalize findings from this stage in the life cycle to later stages. Few studies have examined the preschool period, although it is a time when the child requires less physical caregiving than during infancy and toddlerhood, but continues to need considerable interaction with parents (Lewis, 1997).

MARITAL QUALITY AND SUPPORT

Researchers have examined diverse aspects of the marital relationship including closeness, satisfaction, sex role attitudes, and support of the father to determine how they are associated with fathers' involvement in childcare activities. Nevertheless, the precise role is not well understood. Some investigators hypothesize that the closer a couple feels, the more the father will be motivated to care for his children (Cox, Owen, Lewis, & Henderson, 1989; Volling & Belsky, 1991). Thus, father involvement is considered to be motivated by a desire to please one's partner, rather than for intrinsic reasons. Contrary to prediction, Crouter, Perry-Jenkins, Huston and McHale (1987) found a negative correlation between love for the wife and paternal involvement with children.

Another hypothesis suggests that less traditional views of gender roles are associated with less gendered division of tasks in the family and greater participation by men in child care, a traditionally feminine task. This hypothesis has received mixed support with some studies finding no significant effects (Crouter et al., 1987), others finding a significant relation between a man's attitudes and his involvement in child care (Deutsch et al., 1993), and some finding a positive relation with mothers' but not with fathers' sex role attitudes (Barnett & Baruch, 1987). A third hypothesis that has received some support proposes a spillover of effects from one dyad in the family (the couple) to another dyad (the father-child relationship), so that higher marital satisfaction is expected to be associated with fathers' greater involvement with their children (Levy-Schiff & Israelashvili, 1988).

It is necessary to move beyond general predictions of a correlation between marital quality and father involvement to examine mechanisms by which the marital relationship may affect a father's involvement with his children. De Luccie (1996) found that fathers' rating of frequency of maternal support were highly correlated with fathers' reports of the frequency of their involvement with their children. In an effort to determine what fathers found supportive in their partners' behavior, in this study we examined three different ways that the mother might support her partner in his role as a father.

Deci and Ryan (1991) proposed three dimensions of the interpersonal context that may facilitate or inhibit an individual's involvement in various activities including: (1) the extent to which a person encourages autonomy with respect to an activity; (2) the extent to which a person conveys confidence in another's competence in the activity; and (3) perceived availability to assist with the activity. These three concepts have been found to be critical in various activities such as school achievement and behavioral adjustment of children (Grolnick & Ryan, 1989; Grolnick, Ryan & Deci, 1991), behaviors of subordinates in the workplace (Deci, Connell & Ryan, 1989), and participation in health promoting treatments (William, Grow, Freedman, Ryan & Deci, 1996), but their applicability to father involvement has not been examined. They are, however, similar to the types of spousal support identified by Cutrona (1997) as promoting a harmonious couple relationship.

The current study was designed to examine the influence of the marital relationship on fathers' involvement with preschool children in dual-income families. Single income families were not included in the study, because the dynamics of father involvement may differ between single income and dual income families (Volling & Belsky, 1991). The father's role was examined in terms of what he does with his children, his sense of competence in child-related activities, and his satisfaction in the parental role. Couple variables include marital satisfaction, dimensions of the couple relationship (adaptability and cohesion), as well as partner support (esteem, autonomy, and availability) in the father role. Specifically, it was predicted that fathers' marital satisfaction, the level of couple adaptability and cohesion, and partner support of the father role would be positively related to fathers' involvement, fathers' perception of competence, and fathers' satisfaction with the father role. Furthermore, it was predicted that partner support variables would be more strongly associated with father involvement than would more global measures of marital functioning (satisfaction, adaptability, or cohesion).

METHOD

Participants

The sample consisted of 104 fathers in dual-income families with at least one preschool child. Fathers ranged in age from 25 to 48, with an average age of 35.7 (*SD* = 4.3). The sample was well-educated with 56% holding a university degree. Participants worked outside the home between 26 and 80 hours per week, earning between $40,000 - $60,000 in Canadian dollars. Fathers had been married (68%) or living with their partner (32%) for an average of 9.7 years and had at least one preschooler (mean age of 3.4 yrs) living at home with them. Fifty one percent of the preschoolers were boys and 49 percent were girls. Most of the fathers (55%) had two children living with them at home, 26% had one child, 17% had three children and 1% had four children. Their partners ranged in age from 26 to 44 years (*SD* = 4.2), with an average age of 34.6. These women worked an average of 36.7 hours per week (ranging from 25 to 60 hours), earning between $20,000 - $39,000 in Canadian dollars.

Measures

Father involvement scale. A 16-item scale developed for the study assessed father involvement. Fathers were asked to estimate their level of involvement in activities requiring direct interaction with their pre-school child (e.g., helping child with the morning routine), using a seven-point Likert-type scale, ranging from 1 = *almost never* to 7 = *almost always*, with a mid-point of 4 = *moderate*). Activities were drawn from existing scales (Ahmeduzzaman & Roopnarine, 1992; McBride & Mills, 1993; Russell, 1989) with additional items added to address emotional-care. Cronbach's alpha coefficient for this scale was .88.

Perceived competence in childcare activities scale. Fathers were asked to rate their sense of competence for each activity listed on the father involvement scale (e.g., putting child to bed) using a seven-point Likert-type scale ranging from 1 (*not competent*) to 7 (*very competent*). This scale, developed specifically for the current study, had a Cronbach's alpha coefficient of .90.

Parental satisfaction. A six item measure developed by Picard-Lessard (1995) assessed the father's satisfaction in his parenting role (e.g., "I'm satisfied with the way I'm raising my children," "I'm satisfied with the extent of responsibility I assume in taking care of my children"). In the current study, the alpha value for this scale was .86.

Marital satisfaction. Marital satisfaction was assessed by the Satisfaction subscale (10-items) of the Dyadic Adjustment Scale (DAS, Spanier, 1976). Baillargeon, Dubois and Marineau (1986) reported adequate psychometric properties for their French version of the scale. The Satisfaction subscale has been shown to reproduce the correlation values obtained with the full-scale DAS and other marital measures with little loss of information (Hunsley, Pinsent, Lefebvre, James-Tanner & Vito, 1995). Cronbach's alpha coefficient in this study was .87.

Adaptability and cohesion. The Marital Adaptability and Cohesion Scales III (MACES III; Olson, 1993) is a 20-item measure with two subscales measuring adaptability and cohesion, using a five-point Likert scale (1 = *almost never* and 5 = *almost always*). Adaptability refers to the capacity to be flexible in meeting demands. Cohesion refers to closeness in the marital relationship. Olson reported good internal consistencies for each subscale (.78 for adaptability and .82 for cohesion) with test-retest reliabilities of .83 and .80. Alpha values for the translated version were comparable to the original scale (.75 for the adaptability subscale and .88 for the cohesion subscale).

Partner support for father involvement. A 12-item scale was developed for this study, based on existing scales evaluating the interpersonal style of marital partners (Blais, 1989). The scale assesses three different kinds of support for the paternal role: support for autonomy (e.g., "my partner respects my opinion when we take a decision concerning our child," "my partner encourages me to be myself, as a father"), esteem support (e.g., "my partner has confidence in my abilities as a parent," "my partner shows me that she likes the way I parent my child"), and availability (e.g., "my partner is there when I need her as a parent," "my partner does what she can to make things easier in my role as a parent"). Fathers were asked to rate the frequency of each response on a seven-point Likert-type scale (1 = *almost never*, 7 = *almost always*). An exploratory factor analysis with this sample, using maximum likelihood extraction with oblimin rotation, supported the presence of three dimensions representing the three different types of support, explaining 74.6% of the total variance. Internal consistency for each factor was high (Cronbach's alpha coefficients = .86 support for autonomy, .89 esteem support, and .87 for availability).

Procedure

To be eligible, participants had to be: (a) living with at least one preschool child (2-5 years), (b) working at least 25 hours per week outside the home, and (c) married or in cohabitation with a partner who also worked at least 25 hours per week outside the home. Participants were recruited through 25 daycare centers. Questionnaires (N = 330) were distributed to daycare center directors who were asked to solicit potential participants. One hundred and seventeen completed questionnaires were returned via prepaid envelopes. Ten questionnaires were excluded from the sample because the fathers did not meet eligibility requirements.

RESULTS

Six questionnaires were excluded from the analysis because more than 20% of the items were missing for these participants on a measure. Analyses were conducted on data from 101 participants. Means, standard deviations and alpha levels for each of the variables are presented in Table 1.

Descriptive Data

Responses to the Father Involvement Scale indicate that fathers reported that they were often involved in the child's daily life (e.g., helped their children with the morning routine, read stories to their

TABLE 1. Means, Standard Deviations and Cronbach's Alpha Levels for the Variables

Measures (scale range)	M	SD	Low	Medium	High	alpha
Father Involvement (1 to 7)	5.02	0.84	2%	40%	48%	.88
Perception of Competence (1 to 7)	5.36	0.74	0%	28%	72%	.90
Parental Satisfaction (6 to 42)	34.57	5.49	2%	17%	81%	.86
Satisfaction with life scales (5 to 35)	18.72	3.31	16%	84%	0%	.86
Marital satisfaction (0 to 50)	35.84	5.45	1%	34%	65%	.87
Adaptability (10 to 70)	32.09	5.90	38%	62%	0%	.90
Cohesion (10 to 70)	38.81	6.82	14%	86%	0%	.88
Esteem Support (1 to 7)	5.24	1.18	5%	60%	35%	.89
Support for autonomy (1 to 7)	5.53	1.19	3%	21%	76%	.86
Availability (1 to 7)	5.83	0.98	1%	13%	86%	.87

children, put their children to bed at night, helped their children with their personal problems), and were very frequently involved in disciplining their children. Fathers reported they occasionally got up at night to care for their children and occasionally stayed home to care for their children when they were sick. Notably, the only activity in which fathers rarely took part was in selecting what their child would wear.

Responses to the Perceived Competence Scale show that fathers reported feeling moderately competent in the various child-related activities. At the item level, fathers reported feeling very competent in outdoor activities with their child and in comforting their child, and feeling only somewhat competent at selecting what their child would wear. On the Parental Satisfaction Scale, fathers reported feeling most satisfaction with their ease in the parental role, and only moderate satisfaction with the amount of time that they devote to their children. The mean DAS score for fathers in our sample was similar to the mean value reported by Hunsley et al. (1995). The means obtained on the adaptability and cohesion subscales of the MACES were also comparable to the means reported by Noller and Shum (1990). Thus, the sample was comparable to normative samples in terms of satisfaction in marital and parental roles. Responses to the Partner Support for Father Involvement scale indicated that participants perceived moderate to high levels of support from their partners.

Correlations Between Marital and Paternal Variables

Table 2 presents the correlation coefficients between the six different indices of the quality of the couple's relationship and the measures of father involvement in child care, perceived competence in child care, and parental satisfaction. The results support the hypothesis that the more a father felt satisfied in his marital relationship, perceived his couple relationship as being cohesive and flexible, and felt supported by his partner in his role as a father, the more he participated in various child activities, the more competent he felt in his role, and the more he enjoyed fathering.

Marital Variables Predicting Parental Variables

Hierarchical multiple regressions were conducted to determine the percentage of variance in father involvement, perception of compe-

TABLE 2. Correlations Between Father Involvement, Parental Competence, Parental Satisfaction and Various Marital Measures

Measures	Marital Satisfaction	Adaptability	Cohesion	Support for Autonomy	Esteem Support	Availability
Father Involvement	.22*	.38**	.32**	.25*	.44**	.24*
Parental Competence	.28**	.32**	.31**	.29**	.46**	.28
Parental Satisfaction	.34**	.41**	.41**	.35**	.42**	.29**

Note.* $p < .05$; ** $p < .01$.

tence, and parental satisfaction accounted for by the set of marital variables, and to determine whether the addition of specific dimensions of partner support toward the fathering role improved prediction of the three parenting variables beyond that afforded by more global measures of couple quality. Analyses were conducted separately for father involvement, perception of competence, and parental satisfaction. For all analyses, the order of entry moved from global to specific. Thus, the most global marital variable, marital satisfaction (measured by the DAS) was entered at Step 1; more precise dimensions of the marital relationship (adaptability and cohesion) were entered as a block at Step 2; finally, the three types of partner support specifically focused on the parental role (support for autonomy, esteem support, and availability) were entered as a block at Step 3. The results of these analyses are presented in Table 3.

Father involvement. At step 1, marital satisfaction is a significant predictor of father involvement but accounts for little variance. The addition of adaptability and cohesion to the equation at Step 2 yielded a significant increment, due exclusively to the adaptability variable. At Step 3, the addition of the three partner support variables to the equation also added significantly to the prediction of father involvement, exclusively due to the esteem support variable.

Parental competence. Marital satisfaction, entered at the first step of the equation, was a significant predictor of fathers' sense of competence, but explained little variance. The block of adaptability and cohesion entered at the second step did not significantly augment the

TABLE 3. Marital Variables Predicting Parental Variables (N = 104)

Predictor variable	B	β	R^2 change
Father Involvement			
Step 1			
Marital satisfaction	0.03	0.22*	
			0.05*
Step 2			
Adaptability	0.04	0.30*	
Cohesion	0.02	0.15	
			0.10*
Step 3			
Support autonomy	−0.09	−0.13	
Esteem support	0.38	0.53**	
Availability	−0.15	−0.18	
			0.11*
Parental Competence			
Step 1			
Marital satisfaction	0.04	0.28*	
			0.08*
Step 2			
Adaptability	0.02	0.20	
Cohesion	0.08	0.08	
			0.04
Step 3			
Support autonomy	−0.06	−0.10	
Esteem support	0.31	0.50**	
Availability	−0.08	−0.10	
			0.11*
Parental Satisfaction			
Step 1			
Marital satisfaction	0.34	0.34**	
			0.11**
Step 2			
Adaptability	0.22	0.24*	
Cohesion	0.15	0.19	
			0.09*
Step 3			
Support autonomy	0.22	0.05	
Esteem support	1.22	0.26	
Emotional support	−0.89	−0.16	0.04

Note. *$p < .05$; **$p < .001$

prediction of sense of competence. The addition of the three partner support variables at the third step significantly augmented the prediction of sense of competence, exclusively due to esteem support.

Parental satisfaction. At Step 1 marital satisfaction was a significant predictor of parental satisfaction. At Step 2 the addition of adaptability and cohesion added significantly to the prediction, due to the adaptability variable. The addition of the block of partner support variables at Step 3 did not contribute to the prediction of parental satisfaction. Thus, with respect to a father's satisfaction in his role as a father, the hypothesis was not supported.

In summary, marital adaptability predicted fathers' level of involvement and satisfaction with their parental role. Esteem support from the partner predicted a father's level of involvement and his feelings of competence as a parent.

DISCUSSION

Fathers in this study reported being involved in the day-to-day care of their preschool children, feeling competent as fathers, and deriving considerable satisfaction in their parental role. All of the marital variables were significantly correlated with the parental variables.

Marital satisfaction was related to all three aspects of the father's role–his involvement, his sense of competence, and his satisfaction, but accounted for only a modest amount of the variance. Thus, in contrast to some of the powerful effects found during the transition to parenthood (Levy-Schiff, 1994) the link between marital satisfaction and father involvement with preschoolers seems more modest. The inclusion of adaptability in the marital relationship predicted father involvement and satisfaction, but not sense of competence. The fact that cohesion in the marital relationship did not contribute to this increment may reflect overlap between cohesion and marital satisfaction. The significance of adaptability may lie in the flexibility with which partners deal with the stresses of their multiple roles. Adaptability may, of course also be related to a couple's nontraditional attitudes regarding gender roles.

Finally, the inclusion of supportive partner behaviors specific to the parental role added significantly to the prediction of father involvement and sense of competence, but not to his satisfaction in the parental role. Of the three types of partner support studied, one consistently contributed–esteem support, the extent to which a father perceived his partner to value his competence as a father. Interestingly, the perceived availability of the partner to assist the father in his parental role was not related to father involvement. One reason may be that the frequent provision of support may inadvertently undermine a person's sense of competence in that role or activity (Beach, Fincham, Katz, & Bradbury, 1997). Thus a mother who wishes to enhance her partner's involvement with their children might be best advised to refrain from well-intentioned advice that places her in an expert role and might undermine a father's sense of competence. Instead, she should focus on developing an appreciation of the man's contribution in his role as a father, communicating her confidence in his abilities, and recognizing the value of different ways to parent.

A number of limitations to these findings should be borne in mind. First, the sample was a relatively affluent one. Fathers reported a high level of involvement with their children, although they acknowledged areas in which they were less involved. It is possible that the high level of involvement may be related to SES or to self-selection into the study. The generalizability of findings to less involved fathers is unknown. Second, some of the key variables were measured with scales developed specifically for this study, although their psychometric properties were encouraging, they are not yet well-established. Third, as the study is correlational, no causal inferences can be made. Although direction of influence from marital to parental variables makes intuitive sense, it is possible that parental variables also influence marital functioning. Finally, data were gathered from fathers only, not from their partners, and patterns of interrelationships between marital and parental variables might differ if data were also obtained from mothers.

IMPLICATIONS

The current study has important implications for parent education and other supportive programs designed to optimize fathers' involvement with their children. The two variables that were most strongly associated with father involvement were a sense that his partner viewed him as a competent father and a perception of the parent-parent relationship as flexible. Although this sample included only married or cohabiting fathers, it seems likely that these variables could apply equally to separated or divorced families. Advocates maintain that the best interests of the child are served by the child maintaining a relationship with both parents. The development of a healthy co-parenting relationship is fundamental to children's adjustment to their parents' divorce (Emery, 1994). The abilities to recognize the competence of the child's other parent and to interact flexibly with them are considered an essential focus in evaluations of child custody (Ackerman, 1995). Mental health professionals have an important role to play in helping separated and divorced families to reach parenting arrangements that facilitate the child's access to both parents.

Promoting Couple Communication

It has been argued that there is a need to provide programs to facilitate the development of harmonious couple relationships (Cowan & Cowan, 1995; Cutrona, 1997). With the arrival of their first child, couples may experience a shift from egalitarian to a gendered division of labor. This shift is associated with distress in mothers. It is clear that couples need to learn to communicate about the challenges they are facing and ways that they can meet their multiple role demands. Prior to the arrival of children, early couple interventions should focus on the establishment of supportive behaviors between partners (Cutrona, 1997). Results from this study suggest that some types of interactions that may be intended as helpful may not in fact be useful in promoting father-involvement (Picard, Lee, & Hunsley, 1997). For example, correction of a father's behavior may inhibit his involvement rather than encourage it. Here once again, it is essential that couples learn to make clear requests for the kinds of interactions they find supportive.

Promoting Adaptability

Lee and Duxbury (1998) found that about one in five dual-income couples reported that one of the ways that they balanced their work and family responsibilities was by flexibility in roles. Thus, family roles were not rigidly defined and tasks were accomplished according to what worked best for the family at that particular time. Adaptability requires a willingness by both parents to experiment with new ways of interacting together and new, more fluid definitions of family roles. Interventions to strengthen families should focus on challenging rigid definitions of family functioning to promote openness to greater diversity in the ways families interact.

Facilitating Fathers' Development of Competence

Fathers require opportunities to develop their competence in parenting. Examination of the parenting sections of major bookstores reveals an array of books about child care. The majority, however, focus on mothers and children. Books packed with practical suggestions are written by and for mothers. Although men may find useful information embedded in books on mothering, they may also benefit from parenting books written by and for men. Parent resource centers provide opportunities for parents to learn about parenting through workshops, libraries, courses, and drop-in centers. There is growing awareness that these centers must offer services that target fathers as well as mothers in their advertising, activities, and hours of operation.

Developmental research has identified that mothers and fathers have more similarities than differences in their interactions with their children (Lamb, 1997); however, some significant differences also have been identified. The promotion of father involvement requires that women relinquish the rights to define unilaterally what is appropriate, desirable or acceptable parental behavior.

FUTURE RESEARCH

In examining fathers' roles in the new millennium, it is important to examine different ways of co-parenting to determine the optimal co-parent relationship to promote the child's well-being. Unfortunately, the term co-parenting is more frequently used to refer to divorced parents than it is in reference to married parents. Couples manage the tasks of their diverse roles in numerous ways. For example, the Canadian National Child Care Survey (Lero, Goelman Pence, Brockman, & Nuttall, 1992) found that in 61.5% of dual earner families with children under 13, the parents off-shifted–that is they worked different hours in order to maximize the time that their children could be cared for by one of them. Off-shifting makes economic sense by reducing the need for alternate child care; it allows children to maximize their time with parents, however, the toll it takes on parental relationship is not well understood. Greater attention to these nontraditional family arrangements is needed.

CONCLUSIONS

Findings from this study underline the complex interplay between marital and parental relationships by highlighting the importance of partner support in a father's involvement with his children and his satisfaction in that role. It is clear that interventions to enhance fathers' involvement with their children must focus not only on fathers, but also on their partners as active participants who affect the father's definition of his role within the family. Father involvement and satisfaction is best promoted when partners adopt an affirming, rather than a coaching or didactic role.

REFERENCES

Ackerman, M. J. (1995). *Clinician's guide to child custody evaluations.* New York: Wiley.

Ahmeduzzaman, M., & Roopnarine, J. (1992). Sociodemographic factors, functioning style, and social support, and fathers' involvement with preschoolers in African-American families. *Journal of Marriage and the Family, 54,* 699-707.

Baillargeon, J., Dubois, G., & Marineau, R. (1986). Traduction française de l'Échelle d'ajustement dyadique. *Revue canadienne des sciences du comportement, 18,* 25-34.

Barnett, R. C. & Baruch, G. K. (1987). Determinants of fathers' participation in family work. *Journal of Marriage and the Family, 49,* 29-40.

Beach, S. R. H., Fincham, F. D., Katz, J., & Bradbury, T. N. (1997). Social support in marriage: A cognitive perspective. In G. R. Pierce, B. R. Sarason, & I. G. Sarason, (Eds.), *Handbook of social support and the family* (pp. 43-65). New York: Plenum.

Blais, M. (1989). *Inventaire des styles interpersonnels du (de la) conjoint(e).* Unpublished manuscript. Université du Québec à Montréal, Montreal.

Clark, R., Hyde, J. S., Essex, M. J., & Klein, M. H. (1997). Length of maternity leave and quality of mother-infant interactions. *Child Development, 68,* 364-383.

Cowan, C. P., & Cowan, P. A. (1995). Interventions to ease the transition to parenthood: Why they are needed and what they can do. *Family Relations, 44,* 412-423.

Cox, M. J., Owen, M. T., Lewis, J. M., & Henderson, V. K. (1989). Marriage, adult adjustment, and early parenting. *Child Development, 60,* 1015-1024.

Crouter, A. C., Perry-Jenkins, M., Huston, T. L., & McHale, S. M. (1987). Processes underlying father involvement in dual-earner and single-earner families. *Developmental Psychology, 23,* 431-440.

Cummings, E. M., & O'Reilly, A.W. (1997). Fathers in family context: Effects of marital quality on child adjustment. In M. E. Lamb (Ed.), *The role of the father in child development* (3rd ed., pp. 49-65). New York: Wiley.

Cutrona, C. E. (1997). Social support as a determinant of marital quality: The interplay of negative and supportive behaviors. In G. R. Pierce, B. R. Sarason, & I. G. Sarason (Eds.), *Handbook of social support and the family* (pp. 173-194). New York: Plenum.

De Luccie, M. F. (1996). Mothers: Influential agents in father-child relations. *Genetic, Social and General Psychology Monographs, 122,* 287-307.

Deci, E. L., Connell, J. P. & Ryan, R. M. (1989). Self-determination in a work organization. *Journal of Applied Psychology, 74,* 580-590.

Deci, E. L., & Ryan, R. M. (1991). A motivational approach to self: Integration in personality. In R. Dienstbier (Ed.), *Nebraska symposium on motivation: Vol. 38, Perspectives on motivation* (pp. 237-288). Lincoln, NE: University of Nebraska Press.

Deutsch, F. M., Lussier, J. B., & Servis, L. J. (1993). Husbands at home: Predictors of paternal participation in childcare and housework. *Journal of Personality and Social Psychology, 65,* 1154-1166.

Emery, R. E. (1994). *Renegotiating family relationships: Divorce, child custody, and mediation.* New York: Guilford.

Gable, S., Belsky, J., & Crnic, K. (1995). Coparenting during the child's 2nd year: A descriptive account. *Journal of Marriage and the Family, 57,* 609-616.

Goldberg, W. A. (1990). Marital quality, parental personality, and spousal agreement about perceptions and expectations for children. *Merrill Palmer Quarterly, 36,* 531-556.

Grolnick, W. S., & Ryan, R. M. (1989). Parent styles associated with children's self-regulation and competence in school. *Journal of Educational Psychology, 81,* 143-154.

Grolnick, W. S., Ryan, R. M. & Deci, E. L. (1991). Inner resources for school achievement: Motivational mediators of children's, perceptions of their parents. *Journal of Educational Psychology, 83,* 508-517.

Hunsley, J., Pinsent, C., Lefebvre, M., James-Tanner, S., & Vito, D. (1995). Construct validity of the short forms of the Dyadic Adjustment Scale. *Family Relations, 44,* 231-237.

Lamb, M. E. (1997). Fathers and child development: An introductory overview and guide. In M. E. Lamb (Ed.), *The role of the father in child development* (3rd ed., pp. 1-18). New York: Wiley.

Lee, C. M., & Duxbury, L. (1998). Supports of employed parents from partners, employers, and friends. *Journal of Social Psychology, 138,* 303-322.

Lero, D. S., Goelman, H., Pence, A. R., Brockman, L. M., & Nuttall, S. (1992). *Canadian National Child Care Study: Parental work patterns and child care needs.* Catalogue No. 89-529E. Ottawa: Statistics Canada and Health and Welfare Canada.

Levy-Schiff, R. (1994). Individual and contextual correlates of marital change across the transition to parenthood. *Developmental Psychology, 30,* 591-601.

Levy-Schiff, R., & Israelashvili, R. (1988). Antecedents of fathering: Some further exploration. *Developmental Psychology, 24,* 434-440.

Lewis, M. E. (1997). Fathers and preschoolers. In M. E. Lamb (Ed.), *The role of the father in child development* (3rd ed., pp. 121-143). New York: Wiley.

Lindahl, K. M., Clements, M., & Markman, H. (1997). Predicting marital and parent functioning in dyads and triads: A longitudinal investigation of marital processes. *Journal of Family Psychology, 11,* 139-151.

McBride, B. A., & Mills, G. (1993). A comparison of mother and father involvement with their preschool age children. *Early Childhood Research Quarterly, 8,* 457-477.

Noller, P., & Shumm, D. (1990). The couple version of FACES III: Validity and reliability. *Journal of Family Psychology, 3,* 440-451.

Olson, D. H. (1993). Circumplex Model of marital and family systems: Assessing family functioning. In F. Walsh (Ed.), *Normal family processes* (2nd ed., pp. 104-137). New York: Guilford.

Picard, M., Lee, C. M., & Hunsley, J. (1997). Social supports received and desired: The experiences of recently divorced parents with their parents and parents-in-law. *Journal of Divorce and Remarriage, 27,* 57-69.

Picard-Lessard, M. (1995). *The role of on-site daycare in helping parents balance work and family responsibilities.* Unpublished dissertation. University of Ottawa, Ottawa.

Pleck, J. H. (1997). Paternal involvement: Levels, sources, and consequences. In M. E. Lamb (Ed.), *The role of the father in child development* (3rd ed., pp. 66-103). New York: Wiley.

Pruett, K. D., & Litzenberger, B. (1992). Latency development in children of primary nurturing fathers. *Psychoanalytic study of the child, 47,* 85-101.

Russell, G. (1989). Work/family patterns and couple relationships in shared caregiving families. *Social Behaviour, 4,* 265-283.

Simons, R. L., Beaman, J., Conger, R. D., & Chao, W. (1993). Childhood experience, conceptions of parenting, and attitudes of spouse as determinants of parental behavior. *Journal of Marriage and the Family, 55,* 91-106.

Spanier, G. B. (1976). Measuring dyadic adjustment: New scales for assessing the quality of marriage and similar dyads. *Journal of Marriage and the Family, 38,* 15-28.

Strazdins, L. M., Galligan, R. F., & Scannell, E. D. (1997). Gender and depressive symptoms: Parents' sharing of instrumental and expressive tasks when their children are young. *Journal of Family Psychology, 11,* 222-233.

Volling, B. L., & Belsky, J. (1991). Multiple determinants of father involvement during infancy in dual-earner and single-earner families. *Journal of Marriage and the Family, 53,* 461- 474.

Williams, G. C., Grow, V. M., Freedman, Z. R., Ryan, R. M., & Deci, E. L. (1996). Motivational predictors of weight loss and weight loss maintenance. *Journal of Personality and Social Psychology, 70,* 115-126.

Children's After School Arrangements: A Study of Self-Care and Developmental Outcomes

Michele Goyette-Ewing
Yale University

SUMMARY. Developmental correlates of children's after school arrangements were examined with suburban seventh graders and their mothers. Self-care children identified as unsupervised and "hanging out" had more difficulties than supervised children or unsupervised self-care children "at home" in terms of school achievement, susceptibility to peer pressure, self-reported behavior problems, and experimentation with alcohol. The study failed to identify any benefits of leaving children unsupervised after school in terms of adaptive behavior or competence. The findings have implications for providing more supportive services to working families as a means of increasing family competence. *[Article copies available for a fee from The Haworth Document Delivery Service: 1-800-342-9678. E-mail address: <getinfo@haworthpressinc.com> Website: <http://www.haworthpressinc.com>]*

KEYWORDS. Self-care, school age child care

The after school supervision of school-aged children is an issue of increasing social importance. Social and economic changes, such as

---

Address correspondence to: Michele Goyette-Ewing, PhD, Associate Research Scientist, Yale Child Study Center, Box 207900, Yale University, New Haven, CT 06525.

[Haworth co-indexing entry note]: "Children's After School Arrangements: A Study of Self-Care and Developmental Outcomes." Goyette-Ewing, Michele. Co-published simultaneously in *Journal of Prevention & Intervention in the Community* (The Haworth Press, Inc.) Vol. 20, No. 1/2, 2000, pp. 55-67; and: *Diverse Families, Competent Families: Innovations in Research and Preventive Intervention Practice* (ed: Janet F. Gillespie, and Judy Primavera) The Haworth Press, Inc., 2000, pp. 55-67. Single or multiple copies of this article are available for a fee from The Haworth Document Delivery Service [1-800-342-9678, 9:00 a.m. - 5:00 p.m. (EST). E-mail address: getinfo@haworthpressinc.com].

the entry of large numbers of women into the out-of-home work force and rising numbers of single-parent families, have influenced the trend toward leaving school-aged children unsupervised on a regular basis (Zigler & Hall, 1988). The inflexibility of parents' work schedules, and crises in the availability and affordability of day care contribute to the stresses on families who must juggle the multiple responsibilities of providing for their families and meeting their children's needs.

The number of unsupervised children in the United States is estimated to be 5 million (Fact Sheet on School-Age Children, 1996). Despite its relevance for so many children and families, empirical research on the supervision of school-aged children after school has increased slowly over the past twenty years.

Early work in the field mainly contrasted supervised and unsupervised children and found few differences between children who were supervised after school and those who were not. No significant differences between supervised and unsupervised children were found in their school adjustment and academic achievement (Gold & Andres, 1978a, 1978b; Galambos & Garbarino, 1985). Differences were not found between self-care and supervised children on measures of classroom orientation, and fear level (Galambos & Garbarino, 1985), classroom sociometric nominations, conduct grades, self-reports of self-competence, and parent and teacher ratings (Vandell & Corasaniti, 1988) or children's social and psychological functioning, for example, self-esteem, locus of control, and social and interpersonal competence (Rodman, Pratto, & Nelson, 1985).

Richardson and colleagues (1989) found eighth graders' substance use to be related to the number of hours children spend in self-care each week, however, this study looked only at hours in self-care and did not address characteristics of the self-care arrangements (i.e., at home, "hanging out").

Researchers have begun examining characteristics of after school arrangements and have been able to document a relationship between the *type* of self-care arrangement and children's behavior. Steinberg (1986) examined the after school experiences and susceptibility to peer pressure of fifth, sixth, eighth, and ninth graders. No differences were found between the self-care children and supervised children, however, when the type of self-care arrangement was examined differences were found. Children most removed from adult supervision (e.g., allowed to "hang out" after school) were the most susceptible to peer pressure, while children who went to a friend's house after school were less susceptible to peer pressure. Children who went to their own homes after school were least susceptible to peer pressure.

Galambos and Maggs (1991) sought to determine if sixth grade unsupervised "hanging out" children were engaging in more problem behaviors. They examined 4 types of latchkey arrangements representing a continuum of care, e.g., adult care, self-care at home, self-care at a friend's, and self-care "hanging out." Overall, no differences in adjustment were found between supervised children and children in self-care at home. However, when gender was considered, it was found that girls who were further from adult supervision (e.g., at a friend's house or "hanging out") reported more problem behavior and contact with more deviant peers than those in self-care at home or in adult care.

Some experts believe that there may be benefits gained from the responsibility of caring for oneself and urge that more research be done before conclusions are drawn about how children in self-care are faring (Cole & Rodman, 1987). It has been argued that, particularly for the older child, the responsibility of being on one's own after school is a positive rather than a negative influence (Garbarino, 1981). Proponents of self-care suggest that early responsibilities make children more independent and self-reliant than their constantly supervised peers (Stroman & Duff, 1982). These qualities are hypothesized to affect competence and the development adaptive behavior skills.

Taken together, these findings suggest that there are few documented differences when self-care at home and supervised children are directly compared, however, when children were in arrangements characterized as unsupervised "hanging out," they were more likely to self-report higher susceptibility to negative peer pressure and more problem behavior. School achievement and substance use have been previously assessed by some studies, however, not using the characteristics of the self-care environment (e.g., unsupervised at home versus unsupervised "hanging out"); the present study uses this methodology.

The purpose of the current study was threefold: (1) to replicate and extend findings regarding the relationship between characteristics of children's after school arrangements and their academic and behavioral adjustment, specifically, parent-reported and self-reported problem behavior, school achievement, susceptibility to negative peer pressure, and substance use; (2) to obtain mothers' reports about child care arrangements and child behavior; and (3) to assess the potential benefits of self-care related to children's adaptive behavior skills and competence.

METHOD

Participants

The sample consisted of 110 (54 males, 56 females) seventh graders and their mothers. Seventh graders were chosen because 12- to 13-year olds represent the oldest children considered to be in self-care, while still allowing for some variability in how many months children had been unsupervised after school. The children were all enrolled in a public middle school in a suburban community in the Northeast of approximately 27,000. Letters describing the study and requesting consent to participate were sent to the households of all 228 seventh graders. Forty-eight percent of the entire seventh grade participated.

The mean age of all children in the sample was 12.9 years with a range of 12.0 to 14.1 years. The child sample was 89.1% White, 0.9% Black, 2.7% Hispanic, 0.9% Asian, 3.6% other and 2.7% did not indicate ethnicity. The sample was drawn from a range of socioeconomic levels; the mean SES of families (Hollingshead, 1975) was 45 (range 17 to 64) and fell in the second highest of five categories (e.g., medium business owners, minor professionals, and technical workers). Most mothers in the sample were employed: 36.3% identified themselves as working full-time (35 hours a week or more), 49% were working part-time (less than 35 hours a week), and 13% were not employed. Mothers employed full time worked an average of 41.5 hours each week with a range from 35 to 75 hours. Mothers employed part-time worked an average of 19.9 hours per week with a range from 5 to 34 hours.

Measures and Procedures

Parent report questionnaires, child questionnaires, and school records were the data sources. Data were collected from children at school in groups of 6 to 12. Parent data were collected through the questionnaires sent and returned by mail.

Demographic questionnaires. Items on the demographic questionnaire assessed marital status, parental employment status, ethnicity, parental education and occupation, income level, and hours per week each parent worked outside of the home.

After school arrangements. Two independent raters classified the children into three groups (supervised, self-care at home, and self-care "hanging out") by examining mothers' reports of where the child was after school on most days during the preceding week and how many after school hours per week the child spent without an adult present. For example, if a parent endorsed "home with a parent, other adult, or older sibling," the child was placed in the supervised group. If the parent reported the child was "unsupervised, 'hanging out' in the mall, library, neighborhood, etc." the child was placed in the "self-care, hanging out" group. In addition, if the child reported that they spent most of their time "hanging out with friends" in places other than at home, raters placed an unsupervised child in the "self-care hanging out" group. Interrater reliability for placement into three groups was good (Kappa = .86). Consensus was reached on the 10 disagreements.

The duration in self-care variable was determined by the mother's report of the child's history of after school care since first grade, and the estimate of the total number of months spent in unsupervised after school arrangements.

Mothers' feelings about self-care. A 6-item survey was developed to describe parents' feelings about their employment situation. The 7-point Likert scale items measured how well mothers liked their jobs, whether they felt their child was negatively affected by their work status, whether they felt their children had negative feelings about their working, whether they wanted a change in their work situations, and whether they felt their jobs interfered with being able to spend time with their child. The answer to each question was analyzed separately and interpreted as qualitative data regarding mothers' employment situations.

Parent-rated child behavior problems and competencies. The Child Behavior Checklist (CBCL) (Achenbach & Edelbrock, 1981) is a well-established, norm-referenced measure of behavior problems for children aged 4 to 16. The CBCL provides subscales measuring externalizing and internalizing difficulties and social competence. For the present study, only the internalizing scale and the social competence score were used. The CBCL has been shown to have excellent reliability and validity.

Parent-rated child adaptive behavior. The Adaptive Behavior Inventory (ABI-Short Form) is a 50 item measure, with a 4-point Likert rating scale ranging from 0 indicating a complete lack of a skill to 3 indicating skill mastery (Brown & Leigh, 1986). The scale yields a standard score which is correlated with other measures of independent living skills, e.g., the Vineland Adaptive Behavior Scales (Sparrow, Balla, & Cicchetti, 1984). Internal consistency (Cronbach's alpha = .96) is excellent (Brown & Leigh, 1986).

Child-reported behavior problems. This 25-item measure by Galambos and Maggs (1991) assesses a wide range of problem behaviors, including minor acts typical for a seventh grader (e.g., did something that parents said not to do) and more serious actions (e.g., took things worth between $2 and $50). Children reported how many times in the preceding month they had engaged in each activity on a 5-point scale (1 = never, 5 = almost every day). Responses were summed for a total Self-Reported Behavior Problem Score (Cronbach's alpha = .82).

Child-reported substance use. Open-ended questions regarding lifetime substance use were asked to indicate how many times children had used cigarettes, alcohol, and marijuana in their lifetime (Richardson et al., 1989).

Child-reported susceptibility to peer pressure. Steinberg (1986) presented children with a series of 10 antisocial hypothetical dilemmas (ie. vandalism, cheating, and stealing). Participants were then asked to choose between two courses of action, one suggested by his or her "best friends," the other the child's own prosocial resistance to the suggestion. The child then indicated how certain he or she was of the decision on a 3-point scale (1 = I guess so, 3 = absolutely certain). Cronbach's alpha was .85.

School achievement. The Metropolitan Achievement Test (MAT6) is a nationally standardized, group-administered school achievement test, yielding a Total Battery Composite Score expressed as a z score with a mean of 50. It has adequate internal consistency (KR-20 = .95) (Prescott, Balow, Hogan & Farr, 1988).

RESULTS

Data were analyzed in the following manner: first, descriptive analyses of the after school arrangements were conducted, including the relationships between arrangement type and parental work status and parents' feelings about work and child care. A second set of analyses examined relationships between after school care arrangement and adjustment measures.

Demographics and Description of Groups

Three groups were compared in the current study, children supervised after school (n = 59), in self-care at home (n = 45), and those in self-care "hanging out" (n = 6). Chi-square analyses revealed no significant differences between the groups in terms of demographic variables, i.e., parental marital status, mothers' or fathers' level of education, family income, ethnicity, or socioeconomic status.

The groups differed in terms of child sex (χ^2 (2, N = 110) = 10.80, p < .005). Self-care girls were more likely to be at home (89% of self-care girls); self-care boys were more likely to be "hanging out" (57% of self-care boys). The extremely low number of girls in the self-care "hanging out" group precluded reliable results with a model that included child sex.

Parents' Work Status

While fathers' work status was not significantly related to children's after school arrangements, after school arrangements were related to mothers' work status. Mothers of self-care "hanging out" children (M = 37.03, SD = 11.78) and mothers of self-care at home children (M = 33.66, SD = 13.29) tended to work significantly more hours each week (F (1,105) = 28.50, p < .0001) than mothers of supervised children (M = 16.30, SD = 13.24).

To examine whether the mothers' work hours were associated with aspects of their care arrangements or developmental outcomes, Pearson correlations were computed. Working more hours each week was associated with having children who spent longer durations in self-care (r = .34, p < .0001), more hours per week in self-care during the seventh grade (r = .61, p < .0001), and who experienced greater numbers of changes in their care arrangements since first grade (r = .26, p < .005). Mothers who worked more hours each week were also less satisfied with their after school arrangement (r = −.18, p < .05).

Long maternal hours were not significantly associated with the developmental outcomes assessed: parent-reported internalizing problems, self-reported problem behavior, susceptibility to peer pressure, school achievement, adaptive behavior, or competence.

Mothers' Feelings About Work and Childcare

In further exploring the relationship between after school arrangement and mothers' work, chi-square results showed no significant differences in terms of how well mothers liked their jobs or whether they felt their child had negative feelings about their work status, $p > .05$. Employed mothers of self-care children were more likely to feel that their children had negative feelings about their working than mothers of supervised children who held a job (χ^2 (8, N = 91) = 16.82, $p < .03$). In addition, these employed mothers of self-care children were more likely to want a change in their work situations (e.g., working fewer hours) than employed mothers of supervised children (χ^2 (6, N = 90) = 13.08, $p < .05$). They were also more likely to feel that their job interfered with their being able to spend time with their child (χ^2 (4, N = 91) = 20.66, $p < .0005$) than employed mothers of supervised children.

Multivariate Analysis of Group Differences on Outcome Variables

Examination of differences between three groups. The three after school care groups were compared via multivariate ANOVAs on the nine developmental outcome variables: achievement, parent-reported internalizing difficulties, self-reported problem behaviors, susceptibility to negative peer pressure, cigarette use, marijuana use, alcohol use, competence, and adaptive behavior (see Table 1). The MANOVA led to a significant main effect for Group, $F(18,162) = 1.88$, $p < .05$. A series of univariate ANOVAs were performed for each of the nine developmental outcome variables; where significant Student-Newman-Keuls multiple comparisons were conducted. The ANOVA for academic achievement across groups was significant, $F(2,88) = 4.76$, $p < .01$. Student-Newman-Keuls multiple comparison procedure (SNK) showed that self-care "hanging out" children had lower school achievement than supervised children or self-care "at home" children, $p < .05$.

Child-reported problem behavior differed across groups, $F(2,88) =$

TABLE 1. Comparison of Mean Scores on Developmental Outcome Measures for Three Types of After School Arrangements

Variable	Type of After School Care			Univariate F
	Supervised	Unsupervised at Home	Unsupervised Hanging Out	
				F (2, 88)
Achievement	67.35[a] *SD* = 16.73	69.40[a] *SD* = 18.71	45.63[b] *SD* = 17.42	4.76**
Parent-Reported Internalizing Difficulties	50.15 *SD* = 8.15	53.79 *SD* = 8.98	54.67 *SD* = 11.27	2.14
Self-Reported Problem Behavior	28.83[a] *SD* = 4.94	31.49[a] *SD* = 6.90	43.00[b] *SD* = 17.20	11.02****
Susceptibility to Peer Pressure	24.70[a] *SD* = 8.01	28.13[a,b] *SD* = 9.49	33.83[b] *SD* = 7.94	3.80*
Cigarette Use	15.51 *SD* = 88.33	5.84 *SD* = 18.91	5.17 *SD* = 8.26	.26
Marijuana Use	.04 *SD* = .29	.11 *SD*. 39	.17 *SD* = .41	.57
Alcohol Use	1.55[a] *SD* = 3.54	4.96[a] *SD* = 9.65	11.67[b] *SD* = 23.94	4.20*
Competence	37.23 *SD* = 23.30	35.18 *SD* = 22.67	27.17 *SD* = 22.72	.52
Adaptive Behavior	117.49 *SD* = 13.45	116.34 *SD* = 13.01	107.83 *SD* = 13.08	1.46

Note. $^{*}p < .05$. $^{**}p < .01$. $^{****}p < .0001$

11.02, $p < .0001$. In particular, an SNK showed a higher number of problem behaviors for self-care "hanging out" children than for supervised children or self-care "at home" children, $p < .05$.

Susceptibility to peer pressure differed across groups, $F(2,88) = 3.80$, $p < .05$. An SNK indicated self-care "hanging out" children had the greatest susceptibility to negative peer pressure, and supervised children reported the least susceptibility to negative peer pressure, $p < .05$. The use of alcohol differed between groups $F(2,88) = 4.20$, $p <$

.05. Children in self-care "hanging out" had used alcohol significantly more than the self-care at home or the supervised children. No significant differences were found in the number of cigarettes smoked during the child's lifetime or experimentation with marijuana.

Neither of the hypothesized benefits of self-care were found as univariate ANOVAs for competence and adaptive behavior were not significant.

DISCUSSION

The present study sought to investigate the relationship between specific developmental outcomes and the presence or absence of supervision provided by children's after school arrangements. Findings supported prior research which indicated that self-care "hanging out" children had more self-reported behavior problems (Galambos & Maggs, 1991) than supervised children. It also provided further validation to Steinberg's (1986) finding that children "hanging out" after school were more susceptible to peer pressure than their peers in other care plans. Self-care children were more likely to have used alcohol, in concert with the findings of Richardson et al. (1989). Finally, prior studies (Galambos & Garbarino, 1985; Vandell & Corasaniti, 1988) which examined school achievement did not differentiate between children who were unsupervised at home and those who were "hanging out."

Until the type of unsupervised arrangement was considered, no differences between unsupervised and supervised children had been found in terms of academic achievement. The present study found that self-care children who "hang out" after school have lower school achievement than their peers in other care plans. This is important as academic performance has been found to make an independent contribution to delinquency even after the effects of socioeconomic status or prior conduct problems are controlled (Maguin & Loeber, 1996).

It is not merely the situation of being unsupervised that puts children at risk for behavioral difficulties, but that the structure of the unsupervised after school arrangement is associated with negative outcomes. Children who are at home unsupervised may feel that they are psychologically closer to their parents. The expectation that the child will remain at home and, perhaps, follow a routine, complete homework, and be available to adult monitoring by phone may provide many children with the structure and support they need. In addition, remaining at home after school may limit children's opportunities to engage in problem behaviors, experiment with alcohol, and associate with negative peers. It is crucial to work towards preventing these behavioral patterns developed in childhood and adolescence because they lead to some of our country's most severe and costly health and social problems (Kolbe, Collins, & Cortese, in press).

Contrary to arguments that self-care could be a stimulus to growth for children, the present study did not identify any benefits to children's adaptive behavior or competence. Taken together, these findings argue for the importance of families and communities providing adequate supervision and structure for school-aged children during the after school hours.

Future work should focus on refining our understanding of which children are adversely affected by their after school plans. A longitudinal study which assesses children's functioning prior to entering self-care may shed light on how children with differing experiences, skills, and abilities are affected by their after school arrangement. Cross sectional studies such as this one cannot address questions regarding which children are likely to begin self-care at an early age or what characteristics of children and families (e.g., previous problem behaviors and family functioning) contribute to their adjustment or risk. For example, are there predisposing characteristics of children and/or families which make them more likely to use less structured after school arrangements, and therefore, to have poorer developmental outcomes? Are there factors that contribute to families' abilities to make better plans for their children? Qualitative data from children regarding their feelings about their parents' work schedules, their own burgeoning autonomy, and the opportunities provided by their after school environments would provide yet another perspective on the problem of school-aged child care.

Families of supervised and self-care children did not differ in many respects. They did, however, differ in terms of the mothers' work status. Mothers of self-care children were much more likely to work full time. These mothers also were more likely to report that they felt that their child had negative feelings about their work and that their job interfered with spending time with their children. Employed mothers who were able to secure a supervised arrangement for their child or who had the flexibility in their work schedule to be at home in the hours after school were less likely to feel that their child had negative feelings about their work and were not as interested in changing their work situations. The number of hours that mothers worked was associated with characteristics of their care arrangement (e.g., duration, stability, and hours per week of self-care), however, long work hours were not correlated with developmental outcomes.

The findings of the present study suggest that family competence can be enhanced and the development of potentially serious behavior problems can be prevented by developing age appropriate ways of helping families to provide supervision and structure for their children's after school hours. This goal is an important one if we hope to reduce social problems such as delinquency and teen substance use. Increasing the availability of affordable, high quality after school programs for school-aged children is one way of supporting the well being of working families.

Given the continuing rise in single parent and dual-worker families, it is important that public awareness of the school-aged child care problems which face families increase. Parents, educators, clinicians, and all who are concerned with children's development need to be made aware of the potential problems associated with leaving school-aged children unsupervised and unstructured and the alternatives and services that may be helpful to them. In this way, parents can develop the best possible plans for the structure and supervision of their child's after school arrangement and advocates for children and families can work toward available, affordable, and developmentally appropriate services for all school-aged youngsters.

REFERENCES

Achenbach, T. & Edelbrock, C. (1981). Behavioral problems and competencies reported by parents of normal and disturbed children aged 4 through 16. *Monographs of Social Research in Child Development, 46,* #188.

Brown, L. & Leigh, J. E. (1986). *ABI: Adaptive Behavior Inventory.* Austin, TX: Pro-Ed.

Cole, C. & Rodman, H. (1987). When school-age children care for themselves: Issues for family life educators and parents. *Family Relations, 36*(1), 92-96.

Factsheet on School-Age Children (1996, September). Wellesley, MA: Center for Research on Women, Wellesley College.

Galambos, N. L. & Maggs, J. L. (1991). Out-of-school care of young adolescents and self-reported behavior. *Developmental Psychology, 27,* 644-655.

Galambos, N. L. & Garbarino, J. (1985). Adjustment of unsupervised children in a rural setting. *Journal of Genetic Psychology, 146*(2), 227-231.

Gold, D. & Andres, D. (1978a). Comparisons of Adolescent Children with Employed and Nonemployed Mothers. *Merrill-Palmer Quarterly, 24,* 243-253.

Gold, D. & Andres, D. (1978b). Developmental comparisons between ten-year-old children with employed and non-employed mothers. *Child Development, 49,* 75-84.

Hollingshead, A. D. (1975). Four Factor Index of Social Status. Unpublished working paper, Department of Sociology, Yale University, New Haven, CT.

Kolbe, L. J., Collins, J., & Cortese, P. (in press). Building the capacity of schools to improve the health of the nation: A call for assistance from psychologists. *American Psychologist.*

Maguin, E., & Loeber, R. (1996). Academic performance and delinquency. *Crime and justice: A review of research, 20,* 145-264.

Prescott, G. A., Balow, I. H., Hogan, T. P., & Farr, R. C. (1988). *Metropolitan Achievement Test (MAT6) Survey Battery Technical Manual.* San Antonio, TX: The Psychological Corporation.

Richardson, J. L., Dwyer, D., McGuigan, K., Hansen, W. B., Dent, C., Johnson, C., Sussman, S.Y., Brannon, B., & Flay, B. (1989). Substance use among eighth-grade students who take care of themselves after school. *Pediatrics, 84,* 556-566.

Rodman, H., Pratto, D. J., & Nelson, R. S. (1985). Child care arrangements and children's functioning: A comparison of self-care and adult-care children. *Developmental Psychology, 21,* 413-418.

Sparrow, S. S., Balla, D. A., & Cicchetti, D. V. (1984). *Vineland Adaptive Behavior Scales.* Circle Pines, MN: American Guidance Service.

Steinberg, L. (1986). Latchkey children and susceptibility to peer pressure: An ecological analysis. *Developmental Psychology, 22*(4), 433-439.

Stroman, S. H. & Duff, R. E. (1982). The latchkey child: Whose responsibility? *Childhood Education, 58*(2), 76-79.

Vandell, D. L. & Corasaniti, M. A. (1988). The relation between third graders' after-school care & social, academic, & emotional functioning. *Child Development, 59*(4), 868-875.

Zigler, E. & Hall, N. (1988). Daycare and its effects on children: An overview for pediatric health professionals. *Journal of Developmental and Behavioral Pediatrics, 9*(1), 38-46.

Family Problems and Children's Competencies Over the Early Elementary School Years

Paul W. Speer
Cynthia Esposito

Rutgers University

SUMMARY. Problems experienced by families from a sample of at-risk, urban children were observed and recorded by social workers over a two year period. Four groups of families were distinguished through social worker case notes based on family problems and needs; families were grouped into stable high needs, stable low needs, change for better and change for worse categories. Children were then followed for three years, from the beginning of kindergarten to the end of second grade, and assessed on classroom competence and academic achievement outcomes. Classroom competence included the teacher's rating of both the child's social skills in the classroom, and the academic competence of the child. Academic achievement included a standardized assessment of both math and reading skills. Results indicated that children from families with stable low needs consistently perform with more competence in the classroom than children from families with stable high needs or those whose need status increased. Children from families with stable high needs score comparably to children from families with

Address correspondence to: Paul W. Speer, Center for Social and Community Development, School of Social Work, Rutgers University, 100 Joyce Kilmer Avenue, Piscataway, NJ 08854-8045.

The authors wish to thank Theresa Fox for her many helpful contributions to this article.

[Haworth co-indexing entry note]: "Family Problems and Children's Competencies Over the Early Elementary School Years." Speer, Paul W., and Cynthia Esposito. Co-published simultaneously in *Journal of Prevention & Intervention in the Community* (The Haworth Press, Inc.) Vol. 20, No. 1/2, 2000, pp. 69-83; and: *Diverse Families, Competent Families: Innovations in Research and Preventive Intervention Practice* (ed: Janet F. Gillespie, and Judy Primavera) The Haworth Press, Inc., 2000, pp. 69-83. Single or multiple copies of this article are available for a fee from The Haworth Document Delivery Service [1-800-342-9678, 9:00 a.m. - 5:00 p.m. (EST). E-mail address: getinfo@haworthpressinc.com].

stable low needs on math, and no difference between groups were found in reading. Implications of these findings for strengthening family competence is discussed. *[Article copies available for a fee from The Haworth Document Delivery Service: 1-800-342-9678. E-mail address: <getinfo@haworthpressinc.com> Website: <http://www.haworthpressinc.com>]*

KEYWORDS. At-risk families, child development, social work interventions

Among children in the United States, those growing up with chronic poverty in urban settings are shown to fare worse in both school achievement and the development of social skills than their economically advantaged peers. These children are labeled 'at risk,' for they are exposed daily to the stress of living in poor neighborhoods. Poor neighborhoods are associated with unresponsive and under-resourced social institutions, high crime rates and frequent violence. Importantly, these neighborhood conditions affect children's families. For children growing up in families beset by problems associated with poverty, problems which are exacerbated by neighborhoods defined by numerous stresses, there is a dramatic impact on their academic and social development.

Many studies have examined the influence of family problems on outcomes for at-risk children. Family problems are variously labeled risk factors, stressors or negative life events (Barber, 1992; Forehand, Biggar, & Kotchick, 1998; Forehand, Wierson, Thomas, Armistead, Kempton, & Neighbors, 1991; McLoyd, 1990). Common problems for families facing chronic poverty include unemployment, early parenthood, a single parent family structure, lack of social support, parental drug and alcohol abuse, non-authoritative parenting styles and poor family role modeling (Baumrind, 1991; Chase-Lansdale, Brooks-Gunn, & Zamsky, 1994; Garbarino & Sherman, 1980, Hashima & Amato, 1994; Hawkins, Lishner, & Catalano, 1985; Jackson, 1994; Johnson & Abramovich, 1988; Pearlin & Johnson, 1977; Stevens, 1988). Current theory and a growing body of literature support the basic concept that as family problems increase, the risk for a series of negative outcomes substantially increases for children (Brooks-Gunn, Klebanov, Liaw, & Duncan, 1995; Sameroff, Seifer, Barocas, Zax, & Greenspan, 1987; Huston, 1991; McLoyd, 1990, 1998). Negative outcomes for these children can range from behavior problems and poor academic achievement to drug use, psychiatric disorders and suicide (Myers, Taylor, Arrington, & Richardson, 1992).

Regardless of the source of negative child outcomes, there is a body of research supporting the concept of resilience in children. Resilience represents the ability of children to exhibit competencies and successes despite the presence of stressful life events or circumstances (Werner, 1995). Furthermore, research has supported the notion that resilience can be enhanced by promoting positive family functioning, supporting family strengths, and identifying and intervening in family problems (Baruch & Stutman, 1994; Floyd, 1996; Lester, McGrath, Garcia-Coll, Brem, Sullivan, & Mattis, 1995; Schorr, 1988; Werner & Smith, 1992).

A successful transition into school which supports early school achievement is a very important condition of further success for children. Children who enter school and perform poorly from the beginning, academically or socially, tend to continue having negative experiences in school (Hawkins & Lishner, 1987; Dumas, 1997). However, when young children can achieve in the early grades of school, they set themselves on a path of further positive experiences and outcomes (Entwisle, 1995; Schorr, 1988). Although the mechanisms by which early school competence contributes to positive developmental outcomes are still being investigated, it seems that whatever the mechanism, early school performance tends to predict later success (Durlak, 1997).

The current study sought to build on the existing child competence literature by examining the effects of changes in family functioning, as reflected in the level of family problems and needs, on school outcomes for young elementary school children. Do families from impoverished communities who have few problems and needs–competent families–produce children who are more competent in school? Are children from families with many problems less competent in the school setting than their peers? Studies that address how changes in levels of family needs impact child outcomes would greatly benefit the existing literature on family competence.

The current study has three unique qualities. First, the family problems and needs were derived inductively, from the case notes of social workers working with families as part of a longitudinal transition-to-school intervention. Second, social worker notes about family needs were gathered in the kindergarten year and again in the first grade year to assess changes over this critical transition period, thus representing an important ecological unit (a chronosystem) for investigation. Lastly, the data on child outcomes (both social and academic competencies) are gathered longitudinally, allowing examination of the effects of the family context on child outcomes over time.

METHOD

Participants

Participants were part of a larger intervention study which involved extensive documentation about problems faced by families gathered by social workers who implemented the family support intervention. The family support intervention provided an array of support services, including basic needs provision, crisis intervention, special needs counseling, and referrals for issues such as drug abuse, domestic violence and child neglect. Participants were former Head Start attendees, and the families of those attendees, living in a mid-sized, northeastern city. For the present study, only participants from the experimental group of the larger intervention study were included, as this group had extensive documentation about the family problems gathered by a social worker, the family service worker (FSW), who implemented a family support intervention. Of the children in the families studied (N = 96), 71% were African-American, 17% Hispanic, 4% Caucasian, and 8% of mixed race. Gender composition of the children was 52% male; 48% female. A large percentage of parents (41.5%) had no high school diploma (average number of years in school was 11.4), and only 2.5% reported having a college degree. Twenty-five percent of mothers in the sample were teenagers at the time of the target child's birth. Mean per capita income, as self-reported by families in the study, was $2,451. Eighty-three percent of families reported receiving at least one form of public assistance (i.e., AFDC, WIC, food stamps).

Family Groupings

Families were grouped by needs status based on qualitative analysis from the notes of the FSW's providing support and intervention to the families. These notes extensively documented events affecting the family, and family functioning. For every participant family, categories were created for each event, issue, or circumstance documented by the FSW. The procedure used to derive the number of family problems was anchored in an inductive or grounded theory framework (Glaser & Strauss, 1967). Grounded theory provides a mechanism by which qualitative information is investigated, and themes in data are revealed and categorized, usually for the purpose of hypotheses creation. In this case, extensive FSW notes, taken over years, were used as data to determine the type and number of needs presented by the family and their level of functioning. Notes were read by one of the authors who created exhaustive categories for each family issue described until categories were saturated. Categories of stressors totaled 46.

Each family was then coded as either having or not having each of the 46 stressors. Next, sum totals were calculated for each family by year, for both the kindergarten and first grade years. The sum of problems for any one family ranged from 0 to 11 (M = 3.41) in the kindergarten year and 0 to 13 (M = 3.65) in the first grade year. Based on the differences between family problem type, four groups were created: stable low needs; stable high needs; change for worse and change for better. This grouping represents the independent variable in this study.

A sum of three problems was used as the cutoff between high and low need since most categories of problems were serious (e.g., drug abuse, domestic violence) and because the distribution of problems was positively skewed (i.e., the majority of families did not have most identified problems). Problem categories include drug abuse, death in the family, homelessness, need for medical services, divorce, hunger, incarceration and the like. Examples of categorized problems are presented by group in Table 1.

The grouping of families in the study was, therefore, based on the following method:

1. Stable Low Need–a sum score less than three for both years;
2. Change for Better–first grade sum is lower than kindergarten sum by two or more. Scores reduced by two but still falling within the very high needs or very low needs range are not counted;
3. Change for Worse–the first grade sum is more than kindergarten sum by two or more. Scores increased by two but still falling

within the very high needs or very low needs range are not counted;
4. Stable High Needs–a sum score of greater than or equal to three for both years.

A sample description from each of the four family group categories is as follows:

1. Stable Low Need–The summer before entering kindergarten, this child's mother got married and began looking for a new job. The mother accepted assistance from the FSW on her job search, and to find better housing. The mother found a job and the new stepfather attended school meetings. The child, a boy, brought lunch to school daily, sharing with other children, and was noted as nicely dressed and well-behaved. During the first grade year this family continued to do well, with his teacher commenting that he worked well independently and got along with other children. At the end of the first grade year, the family moved to a better apartment.
2. Change for Better–In the kindergarten year this child had great difficulty separating from his mother, crying hysterically for long periods. This apparent sign of parent-child problem affected his school functioning as well. He was switched to another teacher mid-year, but the crying continued. The teacher asked the FSW to sit in on a meeting with the mother, in which the mother divulged that her son had witnessed the sexual abuse of a neighborhood friend while at a babysitter's home. She also shared that her son's father was addicted to heroin, and that her son had called 911 during a parental fight. As a result of the meeting with teacher and FSW, the mother began counseling; shortly thereafter, her son's behavioral and academic progress improved. During the first grade year, this child separated from his mother easily, and was able to play with the other children. His mother regularly helped her son with his homework, and the child's father began on methadone, and attended a literacy program at the local library.
3. Change for Worse–During this child's kindergarten year, he lived with his mother, who attended classes at a local community college, and visited his father during the summers. Increasingly, the child had problem behaviors in school and at home and was

described as retreating from others and becoming angry at peers who joined him in play. At home he "put on his pajamas and watched TV alone." By the middle of his first grade year, however, this family was requesting rental assistance, food stamps and clothing. The child's teacher suspected drug abuse in the family. The child was increasingly unfocused, having a lot of trouble concentrating. In February, the house the family lived in was damaged by fire and the family became homeless.

4. Stable High Needs–This child's mother and two siblings lived in a small house with the maternal grandmother. The kindergarten year was marked by many problems, such as the child's lead poisoning, poor housing and concerns by the mother about going off welfare (she hadn't worked in 15 years). The child at age five was still sleeping in a crib; all three children had speech deficits. In April of the kindergarten year, the grandmother had a stroke. Early in the first grade year, while the mother sought work, the grandmother was placed in a nursing home and subsequently died. With nowhere else to go, the family was forced to move in with relatives in the South.

Due to the mobility of the families, the total number of families for which there is FSW data over both the kindergarten and first grade years is 88. Family groupings calculated from the inductive methods described reveal that 31% or 27 families were classified as stable low needs; 19% or 17 as changing for the better; 14% or 12 as changing for the worse; and 36% or 32 as stable high needs families.

Inter-rater reliabilities were computed for the coding of the categories between three trained raters. In order to compute the reliabilities, one rater completed the coding of the categories for all families in the kindergarten year. A second rater then coded half of the families and a third rater coded the other half. Inter-rater agreement using the kappa statistic reached .99, indicating excellent agreement between raters.

Measures

Three measures were used as dependent variables in the study. First was a measure of classroom competence which combined an assessment of social skills and academic competence from the Social Skills Rating Scale, Teacher Form (Gresham & Elliot, 1990). Social skill subscales include cooperation, self-control and assertiveness. A scale sum score was calculated (reliability alpha of .95 in kindergarten and .96 in first grade). Academic competence subscales include teacher ratings of children's performance in different content areas (reliability alpha of .95 in kindergarten and .97 in first grade). Due to the highly significant correlations between socials skills scores and academic competence scores for each school year (kindergarten r = .60, $p < .001$, 1st grade r = .73 $p < .001$, 2nd grade r = .67 $p < .001$), these subscales were standardized and averaged to create a Classroom Competence Index. This index captures the competence children display in the classroom setting, both academically and socially.

TABLE 1. Frequencies for Selected Problem Types by Family Grouping

	Stable Low Needs 31% (N = 27)	Change for Better 19% (N = 17)	Change for Worse 14% (N = 12)	Stable High Needs 36% (N = 32)
Avoidance of Family Social Worker				
K	4% (1)	29% (5)	25% (3)	28% (9)
1st	4% (1)	0% (0)	33% (4)	22% (7)
Family/School Relationship Problems				
K	0% (0)	29% (5)	8% (1)	13% (4)
1st	4% (1)	0% (0)	17% (2)	28% (9)
Material Needs (clothing, food, housing, house repairs, homelessness)				
K	11% (3)	18% (3)	17% (2)	97% (31)
1st	0% (0)	0% (0)	58% (7)	91% (29)
Psychosocial Needs (separation, divorce, violence, child abuse, sexual abuse, custody issues, child separation from family)				
K	0% (0)	29% (5)	0% (0)	59% (19)
1st	0% (0)	0% (0)	8% (1)	63% (20)
Physical and Mental Health (illness, hospitalization, death, depression, pregnancy, suicide)				
K	0% (0)	47% (8)	17% (2)	84% (27)
1st	7% (2)	24% (4)	75% (9)	88% (28)
Care of Child (child poorly rested, poorly groomed, neglected, frequently absent or tardy)				
K.	7% (2)	24% (4)	8% (1)	44% (14)
1st	4% (1)	12% (2)	67% (8)	56% (18)
Drug or Alcohol Use Affecting the Family (social worker reports alcohol or drug problems)				
K	26% (7)	59% (10)	25% (3)	78% (25)
1st	22% (6)	59% (10)	42% (5)	81% (26)

Additionally, two achievement tests, one each for math and reading, were used as dependent variables. The Woodcock-Johnson Psycho-Educational Battery-Revised (Woodcock & Johnson, 1989, 1990) is an individually administered assessment of achievement and cognitive abilities. Two subscales assessing mathematics skills (calculation and applied problems) and two subscales assessing reading (word letter identification and passage comprehension) were used. Age-normed scores are converted from the total number of correct items.

RESULTS

The sampling of family problems listed in Table 1 shows several important patterns. First, the stable high needs group had problems in a much greater proportion than the other three groups. Compared to the average rates across the other three family types, families with stable high needs had 2 times the proportion of family/school problems, 3 times the proportion of physical and mental health problems, 5 times the proportion of material needs and 10 times the proportion of psychosocial needs. Second, drug or alcohol use by family members was the problem experienced at the greatest or nearly the greatest proportion within each of the four family groupings. Third, a distinguishing pattern for the change for better group was that they improved family-school relations, stopped avoiding the social worker and reduced the level of psychosocial needs. In contrast, families that changed for the worse had an increase in a different constellation of problems, namely material needs, health needs, and problems in care for their child(ren).

Despite the low attrition rate in this study, teacher ratings of children's academic competence was highly sporadic over the three-year period. The sporadic nature of the teacher data gathered may be due to the fact that school conditions were stressful for teachers as well as students, thus limiting their ability or willingness to participate in the study. Due to the elevated rates of missing data from teachers, classroom competence analyses include only those children who had at least two data points over the three years. Based on this analytic approach, 15 children who had more than one data point missing were removed from the analyses. Means and standard deviations of social and academic performance are reported in Table 2 for the three-year period, as well as selected demographic characteristics of families.

Finally, children's social and academic outcomes were examined

TABLE 2. Means and Standard Deviations for Family Groupings on Classroom Competence, Math, Reading, and Demographics

Dependent Variable	Stable low need	Change for better	Change for worse	Stable high need
	Mean (SD)	Mean (SD)	Mean (SD)	Mean (SD)
Competence K	.580 (.713)	.281 (.997)	−.125 (1.06)	−.186 (.665)
Competence 1st	.441 (.665)	.087 (1.01)	−.734 (.762)	−.102 (1.03)
Competence 2nd	.693 (.844)	.116 (.702)	−.149 (.641)	−.171 (.865)
Math K	108.2 (14.0)	99.75 (16.5)	87.56 (17.8)	101.35 (18.9)
Math 1st	110.1 (13.2)	103.7 (19.4)	103.2 (6.55)	109.2 (14.5)
Math 2nd	104.3 (10.9)	94.08 (19.3)	98.56 (7.06)	106.5 (11.3)
Reading K	95.64 (8.09)	91.25 (10.2)	90.11 (10.5)	92.65 (12.6)
Reading 1st	103.9 (13.0)	99.77 (17.4)	93.44 (13.4)	101.4 (13.2)
Reading 2nd	103.7 (14.8)	97.75 (19.6)	94.22 (15.0)	101.6 (14.1)
Per capita income K	4406 (6824)	2189 (1965)	2223 (2291)	1256 (787)
Children in house K	2.47 (1.39)	2.89 (1.05)	3.55 (2.11)	3.33 (1.30)
Adults in household K	2.00 (1.00)	1.67 (.50)	1.82 (1.08)	1.89 (.85)
Years at current address K	4.26 (1.52)	3.33 (1.94)	3.0 (1.41)	4.15 (1.94)
Parent years of education K	11.8 (.76)	11.9 (.93)	11.55 (1.69)	10.78 (2.36)

for differences across families with differing levels of problems over time. To analyze the influence of family problems on child outcomes, one way ANOVA's were applied to children's classroom competence scores and math and reading scores. Results indicate that for classroom competence, differences in family group were significant for all three years; in kindergarten, F (3,57) = 3.6, $p < .05$; in first grade, F (3,55) = 2.9, $p < .05$; in second grade, F (3,56) = 4.4, $p < .01$. In kindergarten and second grade, children from stable low needs families were rated significantly higher in classroom competence than children from stable high needs and change for worse families. In first grade, children from stable low needs families were rated significantly higher in classroom competence than children from change for worse families, and the difference between stable low needs and stable high needs families approaches significance. In sum, teachers consistently rate children from families with stable low needs as more competent in their classrooms than their peers from other families.

Academic achievement outcomes differentiated family groups only for math and only in kindergarten and second grade, but not for first grade (kindergarten, F (3,68) = 3.2, $p < .05$; second grade, F (3,67) =

3.1, $p < .05$). Post hoc analyses indicate that in the kindergarten year, children from families that changed for the worse performed significantly worse than children from families with stable low needs or stable high needs. During the second grade year, children from families that changed for better performed significantly worse than children from families with either stable low needs or stable high needs. No significant differences were found in reading scores, for any year. Importantly, results of the achievement data found that children from families with stable levels of need (either high or low) performed better than children from families with changes in levels of need.

DISCUSSION

This study contributes to the literature on family competencies and child development by combining several unique research characteristics. First, the study is based on qualitative data gleaned from Head Start family social worker field notes. Descriptions derived from these data provide for a richer and more contextually sensitive representation of families. The richness of this data contributes to a better understanding of the problems faced by chronically poor families, and how those problems conglomerate and entrench themselves into families' lives. Understanding how family problems impact children can improve the practices of professionals who are in contact with these families. The qualitative method also informed the quantitative analyses, making possible a link between highly specified and contextual information about family functioning, and children's achievement and classroom performance outcomes.

Second, the study focused on the change in family setting over the first two years of the children's early elementary school experience. This is a very important time for children, because the transition into school marks the beginning of the need to adapt to increased social demands. Those who succeed early tend to stay successful, and those who fail at this point tend to remain unsuccessful. For such young children, and given the high stakes, a clearer understanding of the relationship between family functioning and children's abilities to succeed in school is of paramount importance. Additionally, the study gathered data longitudinally; data of this nature provide the best insights into relationships of interest, in this case family problems and children's academic and social outcomes.

Despite these valuable qualities to the study, several limitations should be noted. First, groups were derived from treatment families only (the only families for which detailed social worker notes existed). Second, some of the data gathered, particularly classroom competence data, was missing when examined longitudinally. Third, FSW notes were focused almost exclusively on family problems or needs. This "deficit orientation" overlooks the strengths that may counteract such deficits. Lastly, the families participating in this study represent some of the poorest in their community and, indeed, in the United States. This very narrow sample of research participants makes interpretation of the data, particularly generalizations from the findings, challenging. In contrast, studies of very poor, urban populations are increasingly important as poverty in the United States becomes concentrated.

Of the four family groups, only change for better families improved over the two years studied. Within this group, over 50% had less than four problems in the first year. In contrast, 78% of the stable high needs families, those who were not able to improve, had five or more problems in the first year. This can be contrasted further with families defined by stable low needs, for whom 56% had either no problems or only one problem during the first year. These findings address the intractability of the problems of chronically poor families, fully supporting the conception of risk as pervasive and entrenched (McLoyd, 1990, 1998). Moreover, after two years of social work services, 36% of families were defined as stable, high needs families, with 90% experiencing material needs, over 80% having physical or mental health needs and over 75% displaying problems with substance abuse. Despite the alarmingly high levels of need and the weak impact of the intervention for this group, an important story is told about family functioning and child outcomes from these data.

The overwhelming finding is that despite the tremendous poverty and risk all families in this study faced, children of the stable low needs families demonstrated significantly greater classroom competencies than their peers, in addition to significantly greater math achievement. It is important to note that stable low needs families did not differ statistically from other family groups in number of children in the household, number of adults in the household, length at current address or level of parent education. They did, however, differ on income, with stable low needs families reporting a per capita income 3.5 times greater than stable high needs families. Despite the magnitude of this difference, the most economically advantaged of the four groups is, by national standards, exceptionally impoverished. Although families in this study represent some of the most economically disadvantaged in the country, within these groups economic resources proved to be critical in distinguishing the level of problems faced by families. Second, while all four family groups represent the bottom rung of our economic strata, there are families who, despite facing risks and stresses, succeed in raising children who demonstrate social and academic competencies.

In contrast to 'at-risk' classifications, this study found that children from families with stable high needs performed well on academic tests; in fact, children in families with stable high needs outperformed children from stable low needs on math in the second grade year. While not statistically significant, the strong performance by children from families with stable high needs raises questions about strengths and competencies that may be easily overlooked. Relatedly, teachers rated this group of children very poorly on classroom competence despite standardized test results to the contrary. It is possible that these children performed well because the school environment was more stable and nurturing than the stressful home environments they faced. Importantly, our data show that although children from families with stable high needs face tremendous obstacles, they also possess academic capacities and competencies.

A cautionary note must be added to these findings. It is crucial that strengths and competencies be encouraged in families at risk, however, ignoring the structural inequalities in society that place them at risk may lead to "blaming the victim" (Ryan, 1971). These results speak most strongly to the following imperatives: that we support communities and chronically poor families with very young children and that we intervene earlier, so that children may enter elementary school from the stable context of a secure family environment. Finally, we must acknowledge that every child, no matter how at risk, has the potential for success; and we must continue to investigate the relationships between family and child functioning and changes in families' risk factors over both the short- and long-term.

REFERENCES

Barber, B. K. (1992). Family, personality, and adolescent problem behaviors. *Journal of Marriage and the Family, 54,* 69-79.

Baruch, R. & Stutman, S. (1994). *Strategies for fostering resilience.* Washington, DC: Institute for Mental Health Initiatives.

Baumrind, D., (1991). The influence of parenting style on adolescent competence and substance use. *Journal of Early Adolescence, 11*(1), 56-95.

Brooks-Gunn, J., Lebanov, P., Liaw, F. & Duncan, G. (1995). Toward an understanding of the effects of poverty upon children. In Fitzgerald, H., Letster, B. & Zuckerman, B. (Eds.), *Children Of Poverty: Research, Health, and Policy Issues* (pp. 3-36). New York: Garland Publishing Inc.

Chase-Lansdale, P., Brooks-Gunn, J. & Zamsky, E. (1994). Young African-American multigenerational families in poverty: Quality of mothering and grandmothering. *Child Development, 65,* 373-393.

Dumas, J. (1997). Home and school correlates of early at-risk status. In Kronick, R. (Ed.), *At-Risk Youth: Theory, Practice, Reform* (pp. 97-118). New York: Garland Publishing.

Durlak, J. A. (1997). *Successful prevention programs for children and adolescents.* New York: Plenum.

Entwisle, D. (1995). The role of schools in sustaining early childhood program benefits. *The Future of Children, 5,* 133-144.

Floyd, C. (1996). Achieving despite the odds: A study of resilience among a group of African American high school seniors. *Journal of Negro Education, 65*(2) 181-189.

Forehand, R., Biggar, H., & Kotchick, B. A. (1998). Cumulative risk across family stressors: Short- and long-term effects for adolescents. *Journal of Abnormal Child Psychology, 26,* 119-128.

Forehand, R., Wierson, M., Thomas, A. M., Armistead, L., Kempton, T., & Neighbors, B. (1991). The role of family stressors and parent relationships on adolescent functioning. *Journal of the American Academy of Child Psychiatry, 30,* 316-322.

Garbarino, J., & Sherman, D. (1980). High-risk neighborhoods and high-risk families: The human ecology of child maltreatment. *Child Development, 51,* 188-198.

Gresham, F., & Elliot, S., (1990). *Social skills rating system.* Circle Pines, MN: American Guidance Service, Inc.

Glaser, B., & Strauss, A. (1967). *The discovery of grounded theory: Strategies for qualitative research.* Chicago: Aldine.

Hashima, P. Y. & Amato, P. P. (1994). Poverty, social support, and parental behavior. *Child Development, 65*(2), 394-403.

Hawkins, J. D. & Lishner, D. M. (1987). Etiology and prevention of antisocial behavior in children and adolescents. In D. H. Crowell, I. M. Evans and C. R. O'Donnell (Eds.), *Childhood aggression and violence: Sources of influence, prevention and control* (pp. 263-282). New York: Plenum Press.

Hawkins, J. D., Lishner, D. M. & Catalano, R. F. (1985). Childhood predictors of adolescent substance abuse. *Journal of Children in Contemporary Society, 81*(1-2), 11-48.

Huston, A. (Ed.). (1991). *Children in poverty: Child development and public policy.* Cambridge:MA: Cambridge University Press.

Jackson, A. (1994). Psychological distress among single, employed, black mothers and their perceptions of their young children. *Journal of Social Service Research, 19*(3/4), 87-100.

Johnson, L. C., & Abramovitch, R. (1988). Paternal unemployment and family life. In Pence, A. R. (Ed.), *Ecological research with children and families: From concepts to methodology* (pp. 49-75). New York: Columbia University Press.

Lester, B., McGrath, M., Garcia-Coll, C., Brem, F., Sullivan, M. & Mattis, S. (1995). Relationship between risk and protective factors, developmental outcome, and the home environment at four years of age in term and preterm infants. In Fitzgerald, H., Lester, B. & Zuckerman, B. (Eds.), *Children Of Poverty: Research, Health, and Policy Issues* (pp. 197-226). New York: Garland Publishing.

McLoyd, V. C. (1990). The impact of economic hardship on black families and children: Psychological distress, parenting, and socioemotional development. *Child Development, 61,* 311-346.

McLoyd, V. C. (1998). Socioeconomic disadvantage and child development. *American Psychologist, 53,* 185-204.

Myers, H., Taylor, S., Alvy, K., Arrington, A. & Richardson, M. (1992). Parental and family predictors of behavior problems in inner-city black children. *American Journal of Community Psychology, 20(5)*, 557-576.

Pearlin, L. & Johnson, J. (1977). Marital status, life-strains and depression. *American Sociological Review, 42,* 704-715.

Ryan, W. (1971). *Blaming the victim.* New York: Random House.

Sameroff A., Seifer, R., Barocas, R., Zax, M. & Greenspan, S. (1987). Intelligence quotient scores of four year old children: Social environmental risk factors. *Pediatrics, 79,* 343-350.

Schorr, L. B. (1988). *Within our reach: Breaking the cycle of disadvantage.* New York: Doubleday.

Stevens, J. H. (1988). Social support, locus of control, and parenting in three low-income groups of mothers: Black teenagers, black adults and white adults. *Child Development, 59,* 635-642.

Werner, E. (1995). Resilience in development. *Current Directions in Psychological Science, 4,* 81-85.

Werner, E. & Smith, R. (1992). *Overcoming the Odds: High Risk Children from Birth to Adulthood.* New York: Cornell University Press.

Woodcock, R. W. & Johnson, M. B. (1990). *Woodcock-Johnson psycho-educational battery-revised.* Allen, TX: DLM Teaching Resources.

Enhancing Family Competence Through Literacy Activities

Judy Primavera

Fairfield University

SUMMARY. The present paper describes the range of positive family outcomes found when the parents of low-income preschoolers engage in literacy activities with their children. One hundred parents attended a series of family literacy workshops designed to instruct parents on the use of effective book sharing techniques to use with their children. The goal of the program was to increase the children's school readiness and emergent literacy skills by training parents to be more effective and self-confident "first teachers" of the type of literacy skills necessary for early school success. Parents reported that both the amount of parent-child book sharing increased and the time spent reading was more interesting and enjoyable. Children's language skills as well as their interest in books and learning increased. Personal benefits to the parent

---

Address correspondence to: Judy Primavera, Department of Psychology, Fairfield University, Fairfield, CT 06430 (E-mail jprimavera@fair1.fairfield.edu).

The author thanks Matthew Cook, Megan Connolly, Stephen Dwyer, Kathleen McGuigan, Anne O'Donnell, Erica Quinn, Nancy Bartlett, Donna Delpo, Kerrin Fenton, and Tara Fischetti for their assistance in data collection and analysis. Special gratitude and recognition is due to Parents as Partners fascilitators Thelma Peeples, Dorothy Spears, and Tomilyn Williams. The author also thanks Dr. Janet F. Gillespie for her generous support throughout the life of the project.

This work was supported by the F. M. Kirby Foundation, the Reader's Digest Foundation, Peoples' Bank, Inc., the Corporation for National Service, the College of Arts and Sciences of Fairfield University, and Action for Bridgeport Community Development, Inc.

[Haworth co-indexing entry note]: "Enhancing Family Competence Through Literacy Activities." Primavera, Judy. Co-published simultaneously in *Journal of Prevention & Intervention in the Community* (The Haworth Press, Inc.) Vol. 20, No. 1/2, 2000, pp. 85-101; and: *Diverse Families, Competent Families: Innovations in Research and Preventive Intervention Practice* (ed: Janet F. Gillespie, and Judy Primavera) The Haworth Press, Inc., 2000, pp. 85-101. Single or multiple copies of this article are available for a fee from The Haworth Document Delivery Service [1-800-342-9678, 9:00 a.m. - 5:00 p.m. (EST). E-mail address: getinfo@haworthpressinc.com].

included enhanced self-esteem and self confidence, increased knowledge of normative child development and sense of efficacy as a parent, heightened understanding of the importance of parental involvement, increased feeling of literacy competence and interest in improving their own education, and sense of increased social support. Other family members (spouses and siblings) also increased their literacy activities. Family relationships, communication, and feelings of togetherness were also enhanced. Implications for individual and family competency enhancing interventions are discussed. *[Article copies available for a fee from The Haworth Document Delivery Service: 1-800-342-9678. E-mail address: <getinfo@haworthpressinc.com> Website: <http://www.haworthpressinc.com>]*

KEYWORDS. Literacy, family literacy, family competency, school readiness, school success

Being literate is thought to be a significant factor in a person's ability to function successfully in society and thus, is perhaps the single most important skill a child can acquire (Dorotik & Betzold, 1992; Hess, Holloway, Price, & Dickson, 1982). The U.S. Department of Education's most recent national survey reported that nearly 25% of all Americans (more than 40 million adults) are functionally illiterate (National Center for Educational Statistics, 1993). These individuals have difficulty reading the safety labels on medications, filling out applications, following written instructions, writing a note to their child's teacher, and reading a newspaper. Low literacy negatively affects both the individual and society as a whole as it contributes to poor school achievement, high dropout rates, underemployment and unemployment, welfare dependence, crime and incarceration, and poverty (Sticht & McDonald, 1989). In a technologically advanced, print-dependent environment, the illiterate are often excluded from full and meaningful participation in society and are placed "at risk" as consumers, employees, tenants, and parents. At highest risk for inadequate literacy skill development are people of color and those from low-income backgrounds (National Center for Educational Statistics, 1993).

The acquisition of age-appropriate language skills is basic to a child's educational progress and achievement. Children from low-income, urban backgrounds are at high risk for underachievement, school adjustment problems, and dropping out (Children's Defense Fund, 1992; Raz & Bryant, 1990; Tuma, 1989). The Carnegie Foundation's report on school readiness found that as many as 35 percent of children entering kindergarten are unprepared for formal education with deficits in "language richness" rated as a "moderate-to-serious" problem for 88% of these unprepared youngsters (Boyer, 1991). In other words, significant numbers of children from low-income, urban areas enter school deficient in the necessary prerequisite skills for academic success and, once in school, engage in a perpetual game of academic "catch-up" which many eventually lose (Alexander & Entwistle, 1988; Morrison, McMahon, & Williamson, 1993). While functional literacy skills guarantee neither positive school adjustment as a child nor successful vocational achievement as an adult, without these skills such accomplishments are nearly impossible.

The need for preventive efforts during the preschool years focused on school readiness, in general, and language readiness, in particular, is clear. The importance and necessity of involving parents at this early stage is also clear. Parents are the child's first and perhaps their most influential teacher. Literacy development begins in early childhood within the context of looking at books and listening to stories being read or told to them by an adult. Parent-child storytelling activities encourage the development of rudimentary emergent literacy skills that are essential for successful mastery of more formal reading instruction (Teale & Sulzby, 1986). Research suggests that preschool-aged children whose parents read to them on a regular basis become more competent readers and are significantly more successful in school (Gottfried & Gottfried, 1984; Rich, 1985; Stevenson & Fredman, 1990; Teale & Sulzby, 1986; U.S. Department of Health & Human Services, 1991; Wells, 1985). Research also shows that one of the best predictors of a child's educational success is the parent's positive involvement in the educational process (Reynolds, 1991; Rich, 1985). Unfortunately, functional illiteracy and insecurity about their own reading competence discourage many low-income parents from engaging in both parent-child literacy activities and active involvement in their child's schooling.

Clearly, if low literacy and early school failure in high risk children is to be prevented, early intervention focused on developing or improving parent-child literacy activities before a child enters school would seem to be a most propitious place to begin. The existing literature includes examples of several different approaches to teaching effective parent-child literacy strategies (e.g., Arnold & Whitehurst, 1994; Cronan, Cruz, & Arriaga, 1996; Edwards, 1991; McCormick & Mason, 1986). The present study reports the results of a family literacy intervention that involved training parents to be more effective "first teachers" of the types of emergent literacy skills that are important factors in children's readiness for school, reading acquisition, and later school success. The evaluation will focus not only on the "intended" outcome of increased language skills in the target preschoolers but also on the "unintended" positive consequences at both the individual and the family systems levels.

METHOD

The Adrienne Kirby Family Literacy Project

The Adrienne Kirby Family Literacy Project is a competency-enhancing intervention program. Its goal is to increase low-income, preschool-age children's language and school readiness skills. The project is a "resource exchange" (Sarason & Lorentz, 1979) collaboration between an urban, non-profit family service agency and a private, suburban university (Primavera, 1999). The Family Literacy Project consists of a child and a parent component. The child component provides individual or small group language tutoring in the classrooms by over 200 undergraduate volunteers for nearly all of the 800 preschoolers enrolled in the agency's Head Start/Childcare program (Primavera, 1999; Primavera & Cook, 1997). The goal of the parent component is to enhance the children's emergent literacy skills by training parents to become more effective "first teachers" to their children and to increase the parents' sense of competence and involvement in their children's education. Parents attend an eight-session series of literacy workshops led by workshop facilitator who is a member of the Head Start staff. The literacy activities presented in the workshops are modeled after the "Parents as Partners in Reading" curriculum (Edwards, 1990) and are designed to instruct parents, regardless of their own literacy skills, in age-appropriate book-sharing techniques to use with their children. The lessons rely heavily upon modeling and role-playing. Each session consists of a full group meeting where formal instruction, video presentations, discussion, or activity preview takes place followed by more individualized practice of the particular book sharing/literacy skill(s) featured for that session. For example, one activity was designed to help parents develop effective book-reading techniques by showing how a child's attention might be increased by the use of different parent-child seating arrangements or different book-holding strategies or by changing voice tones and inflections. Another activity was designed to acquaint parents with the types of questions that they could ask their children during reading to stimulate the development of the more advanced of literacy skills utilized in formal schooling (e.g., answers that must be put together from different parts of the story or answers that cannot be found in the story and rely on the child's own experiences). Each week parents are provided with "homework" assignments that reinforce the concepts presented during the workshop session. The workshop series culminates with a parent book-making project where each parent authors their own book to become part of their child's home library.

Participants

From September 1994-June 1998 (four academic years), 100 parents/guardians (97 mothers and 3 fathers) of preschool-aged children (age 3-5 years; 52% male, 48% female) enrolled in an urban Head Start/Childcare program volunteered to participate in the parent workshop component of the Adrienne Kirby Family Literacy Project. The Project was advertised (i.e., via posted announcements in the Head Start classrooms and by direct invitation by the teacher) as one that would focus on helping parents help their children be successful in school. The participating families were representative of the demographics of the approximately 800 families serviced by the agency's Head Start/Childcare program: 48% were Black/Caribbean; 39% Hispanic/Latino; and 13% White. For 25% of these families, a language other than English was spoken in the home. Seventy-nine percent of the families were single parent, mother-headed households. All families were either receiving public assistance or had yearly family incomes of less than $20,000. Parents' educational level ranged from less than eighth grade to having some college experience. Thirty-seven percent of the parents did not have a high school diploma or its equivalent. Self-reported reading ability ranged from functionally illiterate to literate.

Procedure

The information gathered was derived from three sources: pre- and post-interviews with participating parents, journal entries of the workshop facilitators, and teacher assessments of the children's progress. To control for existing differences in participating parents' literacy levels, all assessments were conducted via semi-structured interviews with Project staff. Two raters conducted a content analysis of the interviews to identify the themes expressed in the participants' responses. A coding scheme was developed that defined each of these themes. Two other raters coded the participants' responses. The intercoder agreement was 95%. Coding differences were resolved by consensus.

Pre-Project Assessment. Before beginning the literacy workshop series, participating parents answered a series of questions (either open-ended or Likert-type ratings) related to: (1) their personal and parent-child reading activities (e.g., "In a typical week, how often do you read the newspaper? . . . read a magazine? . . . read a book?"; "When you read newspapers, magazines, or books for yourself, how much time do you spend reading?"; "In a typical week, how often do you and your child read or look at books?"; "When you read or look at books with your child, about how much time do you spend?"), (2) their level of satisfaction with both their own reading ability and their ability to share books with their children, and (3) the availability of reading material in the home.

Post-Project Assessment. At the conclusion of the parent workshop series and at the end of the academic year, parents answered a series of questions (either open-ended or Likert-type ratings) related to their perceptions of overall program success and, more specifically, how their participation in the literacy workshops had affected (1) the quality of parent-child book sharing, (2) their preschool-age child's language skills, (3) their feeling about themselves and about their own literacy skills, and (4) other family members (i.e., siblings, spouses). In addition, the teachers of the children of participating parents were asked to assess the children's language skill improvement and to indicate the type of language skills that had shown most improvement.

RESULTS

Pre-Program Literacy Behaviors and Satisfaction

The data suggested that prior to participating in the project, the majority of parents were sharing books with their children and reading on their own on a regular basis. Forty-one percent reported that they shared books or read to their child every day or nearly every day (5-6 times per week) and 17% reported a frequency of three or four times per week. Infrequent (1-2 times per week) parent-child book sharing was reported by 26% of the parents while 3% stated that they never shared books or read to their child. In terms of how much time they spend sharing books with their child, 40% of the parents said that their parent-child book sharing sessions typically lasted 15 minutes or less; 40% spent 15 to 30 minutes sharing books per session, and 20% spent 30 minutes or more.

Parents' reports of their own personal literacy behaviors revealed that a significant number were non-readers or infrequent readers. Overall, 20% percent reported that they never read books for pleasure and 12% never read newspapers or magazines. Fifty-two percent were infrequent (1-2 times per week) book, newspaper or magazine readers while only 26% read the newspaper and 12% read a book every day or nearly every day (5-6 times per week). The majority of parents (67%) reported that when they did read it was typically for 30 minutes or less.

Only a small percentage of parents reported that they were "very dissatisfied" or "somewhat dissatisfied" with their ability to share books with their child (10%) or their own reading skills (27%). The majority of parents categorized themselves as being "very satisfied" with parent-child book sharing skills (63%) and personal reading ability (51%).

The availability of children's books in the home varied considerably from no books to well over fifty. Fifty-eight percent of the homes had twenty or more children's books in the home while 14% had five or less.

Overall Program Success

When asked to rate the success of the program in meeting its goal of helping parents prepare their children for school by increasing their language skills, 97% of the parents gave the program the highest rating with the remaining 3% rating the program as "somewhat successful" (1 = not at all successful: 4 = very successful). One hundred percent of the parents said that the program was "helpful" in teaching them to more effectively share books with their children and that they would recommend the program to other parents.

> All parents should join the program. I always would read to my children a lot and I thought I knew how to do everything. But here [the program] I learned how to read to them better. They are more interested [in books] now. They ask me to read to them all the time. It changed everything. I feel more ready to help them in school. My kids learned so many new words. We have so much fun reading together!

The Quality of Parent-Child Book Sharing

Seventy-two percent of the parents said that they have learned how important reading to their child is to their child's future success in school. Eighty-nine percent of the parents said that, as a result of the program, they spend more time reading to their child. Most parents said that they learned how to make reading time more interesting for their child (82%) and that reading time was "more enjoyable" and "more fun" for both parent and child (75%). Many parents reported instituting some form of daily reading rituals (e.g., after dinner, before bed) and a decreased amount of television viewing. Over 1,000 books per year were borrowed from the Project lending library and nearly one-third (31%) of the families became new users of their local public library.

> I used to just read, read, read. And he used to wiggle around and not pay attention 'til I yelled at him. Now I know that it's not important to finish a book if he wants to talk about one page. I learned how to 'make funny voices' and give him hugs and kisses so we have more fun. Now instead of 'Mommy, stop!,' he say 'Mommy, more books!' I make time every day now to read to him no matter how busy I am.

> I read more to my children. I did not read enough before. I read to them every day now. And I read books that will help them learn.

> I learned how to pick books that will help them learn more. I took my children to the library and now they have their own cards. Now they can choose their own books.

Children's Language Skills

Both parents and classroom teachers indicated that the children made substantial gains in their language skills as a result of the home literacy activities. Using a 4-point Likert rating scale (1 = no improvement; 4 = significantly/greatly improved), 47% of the parents and 30% of the teachers rated the children's improvement language skills as "significantly improved," 43% of the parents and 42% of the teachers rated the language improvement as "moderately improved," and 10% of the parents and 28% of the teachers described the children's language skills as "a little improved." Parents and teachers noted increases in the children's vocabulary and that the children used more words and understood more words in conversation. They also noted that the children were able to express their ideas with greater detail and conceptual clarity and that their speech/pronunciation was more understandable. The children were also seen as being better able to use their imaginations and more interested in learning, in general, and in learning how to read and write, in particular.

Parent Outcome

The data suggested that parents reaped significant personal benefits through their participation in the parent literacy workshops including: enhanced self-esteem, self confidence, and pride; an increased knowledge of normative child development and sense of efficacy as a parent; a sense of empowerment in playing a crucial role in their child's education; an increased feeling of literacy competence and interest in improving their own education; and sense of increased social support and decreased feelings of isolation.

Seventy-one percent mentioned that they felt better about themselves, proud of themselves for how they are able to help their child learn, or more confident in what they do.

> Even though I did not receive my high school diploma I feel very good about myself. I see that I am helping my children. When I

> read the books they think I am so smart and so funny. When I read, it encourages them to be like Mommy 'a reader.' They are proud of me and that makes me proud of me too.
>
> Before I don't read books to my children because I [was] scared to say some of the words. Now I see how much they learn and how much I learn too. I can help them even if I don't read so good now. But I'm learning to read better too!

Sixty-eight percent said that they had achieved a greater understanding of their children's age-appropriate developmental needs and capabilities and that they had learned more creative and effective ways to parent their children.

> My daughter used to line up her dolls and open a book to 'read' to them. But she wasn't 'reading,' she was just making up stories in her head. I used to yell at her and tell her to stop making up stories. Now I know that it was good what she was doing. Now I know that I should praise her for trying to 'read' to her dolls. It's good for child to use make-believe.
>
> My older daughter always gave me such a problem with doing her homework. I usually ended up yelling at her or punishing her. Then I started using the things I learned here [the literacy workshops] about how to make reading more fun and I tried some of the things with my daughter's homework. Now it is more like a game. She does her homework every day and we don't have to fight as much.

Sixty-six percent mentioned that the program taught them how important a parent is to their child's school success. Seventy-one percent felt better able to help their child succeed in school.

> I had such a hard time in school when I was growing up that I pretty much stayed out of my older kids' school. I figured they're smart. They can do it. Now I know I need to be there every step of the way. I need to get in there and be a part of it. If I don't know something, we can learn together. I can help my older ones like I'm helping [my preschooler].

A little over one-half of the parents (51%) reported that as a result of their participation in the program they were thinking about returning to school themselves to further their education. Follow-up contacts by the Head Start staff revealed that 25% of the parents had returned to school ranging from general education studies to high school diploma equivalency programs to college courses.

> My mother didn't know how to read so I had to struggle more than the other kids in school. This group helped me to decide to do something about it. If I'm going to be able to help my kids, I have to be able to read better. I'm going back to school.

> I never told anyone before but I can't read. I'm smart so I learned the tricks to 'get by' and fool people. It's easy to fool people. I think bringing these books home is helping me. They're easy so I don't make too many mistakes. Pretty soon my kids will be using harder books in school and I won't be able to fool them. I need to go to school. Funny thing, I really think I can do it this time.

Perhaps the most striking example of personal empowerment was the professional advancement of one of the mothers who participated in the very first parent workshop series. After completing the program, this mother applied for a job as an Assistant Teacher at the agency. She matriculated at the local community college and received her Associates degreė in Early Childhood Education. She is now the Head Teacher of her Head Start classroom and has served as one of the three parent workshop facilitators for the Family Literacy Project for over two years.

Finally, 68% of the parents indicated that they benefited psychologically from the social support they received from the parents' group as they faced the difficult task of effective parenting within a stressful, sometimes dangerous urban environment. They reported that they felt less alone, less afraid, and better able to cope with the challenges of daily living.

Effects on Other Family Members and Family Functioning

Participants reported numerous positive consequences within their family and for other family members who did not directly participate in the Project. In the majority of the two parent households (65%), program parents indicated that their spouse also became more involved in sharing books with the children. Of the 84 families consisting of two or more children, 84% reported positive effects for the target preschooler's older or younger siblings. Younger siblings were included in parent-child reading time where they otherwise would have been excluded because they were "too young" and target preschoolers were apt to imitate the book sharing behaviors of their parents and "read" to their younger siblings. Older children were found to be reading more themselves, to model the behavior of their parents and become more involved in reading books to their younger siblings, to improve in their own reading skills due to increased practice, and to achieve higher grades. The most dramatic case was that of an 8-year-old girl whose mother was told that her daughter would be placed in a class for "slow learners" the following school year because of her poor language skills and difficulty mastering third grade material. The mother, who was functionally illiterate herself, began to use the strategies she had learned in the literacy workshops with both her 3-year-old and her 8-year-old. The television was turned off and, one hour each day was set aside as "reading time." The mother encouraged both girls to use their imagination and tell stories or to remember what they had done that day and relate the details in sequence. She made vocabulary games out of almost every commonplace daily routine (e.g., meals, shopping). The older child's reading skills quickly progressed using the easier preschool books as a starting level. By the end of that academic year (6 months later), the girl was performing at grade level in all areas including reading and the issue of placement in a remedial program was abandoned.

At a larger family systems level, parents frequently commented that the successful and enjoyable experience of reading together resulted in a more general improvement in both parent-child relationships and sibling relationships. Interactions within the family were seen as being more positive, communication between family members increased, and there was an increased sense of closeness and togetherness.

DISCUSSION

The present study found that, in addition to the "intended" outcome of increased emergent literacy and school readiness skills in the target preschoolers, the families that participated in the Family Literacy Project also displayed a host of positive "unintended" consequences as well. These positive outcomes included increases in multiple indices of well-being for individual family members as well as several positive changes at a family systems level.

Two of the most important protective factors that support the development of both literacy competence and social-emotional competency in low-income preschoolers are exposure to engaging, responsive, and cognitively challenging caregiver-child interactions and the caregiver's level of self-esteem (Brody, Stoneman, & McCoy, 1994). The data presented here suggests that even an eight-week intervention is capable of setting that protective process in motion. The data suggest that parents, regardless of their reading proficiency, were able to adopt interpersonally enjoyable, cognitively stimulating book sharing strategies that were appropriate for their child's interests and temperament. The parents' experience of success with the Project's literacy activities contributed to increased feelings of parental efficacy, self-confidence, and competence. Persons with a positive sense of self can be expected to cope in a planful, focused, and active way with the problems and challenges confronting them (Schier & Carver, 1992). This type of empowerment was well-documented by the workshop facilitators' journals. These parents began to take more risks while in the process of trying to help their children succeed in school. They volunteered more frequently in their child's classroom, they shared intimate details about their own literacy deficits, they secured information regarding the city's magnet programs and submitted applications for their children, they applied for employment, and they matriculated in school themselves. Clearly no single, short-term intervention is sufficient to combat the negative impact of intergenerational illiteracy or to offset the powerful deleterious influence of poverty, but interventions such as the one described here represent a powerful "first step."

Indeed, the families' positive experience with the Project seems to have set in motion a series of inter-related, mutually sustaining psychological and cognitive processes. For example, the gains in language skills exhibited by the children might serve to validate the parents' feelings of personal efficacy and self-confidence that they, indeed, do have the power to help their children be successful in school. These efficacy beliefs would support increased levels of parental involvement in the child's education, which, in turn, further fosters continued academic success (Eccles & Harold, 1996).

Low income children are considered to be at risk for early school failure and the blame is often placed on the inferior quality and quantity of parent-child literacy activities, especially book reading (Adams, 1990; Snow & Ninio, 1986; Teale, 1986). Clearly, no one factor leads to school success or failure and being poor in and of itself is not responsible for a lack of school readiness, deficient literacy skills, and poor achievement. It is not whether a child lives in a poor or middle class home or whether that home is in the city or the suburbs or whether the child's skin is dark or light. Rather, it is the kinds of literacy activities that are generated in the home (White, 1982). The data reported in this study echoes the claim of Delgado-Gaitan (1990) that low-income parents are very interested and concerned about their children's school success, but many lack the necessary skills and resources to effectively break the intergenerational cycle of illiteracy. The majority of parents in this study provided their children with an adequate home library and nearly one-half reported that they read to their children every day or nearly every day. Unfortunately, few parents were good models for voluntary reading in that most reported being infrequent readers themselves. What is perhaps most disconcerting is the fact that prior to participating in the program, most parents overestimated their reading and book sharing competence and reported that they were "very satisfied" with their skills. This fact mirrors the U.S. Department of Education's finding that the majority of functionally illiterate Americans do not perceive themselves as being "at risk" (National Center for Education Statistics, 1992). These findings have important implications for those providing family literacy services. That is, parents are more likely to volunteer for and commit to an intervention that is advertised as being related to enhancing their children's competencies than they might be if it is focused on their own literacy needs. In fact, the first time the present program was offered, it was called "The Family Literacy Project" and parent turnout was poor. Parents told Project staff that many of their friends refused to come because they did not think that they had any problems reading. A change in the Project's name to "Parents as Partners" as well as the addition of the two recruitment mottoes "Help your child get ready for kindergarten" and "Help your child succeed in school" solved the attendance problem.

This study provides evidence those early interventions that train parents, regardless of their reading proficiency, to use effective book sharing techniques with their children can improve children's language skills, enhance the parents' efficacy beliefs and self esteem, as well as have a positive impact on family functioning as a whole. Although longitudinal data for this study is not available to assess the longevity of the intervention's positive impact, the literature related to long term effects of early intervention programs suggests that it is important for early intervention programs to offer additional, post-intervention follow-through contact (Zigler, 1998). The provision of a series of follow-through literacy sessions would serve to either reinforce a previously learned skill, or to provide a boost to participants' investment in the intervention, or to teach new, more advanced skills to keep pace with the developmental needs and capabilities of the family members.

REFERENCES

Adams, M. J. (1990). *Learning to read: Thinking and learning about print.* Cambridge, MA: MIT Press.

Alexander, K. L., & Entwisle, D. R. (1988). Achievement in the first two years of school: Patterns and processes. *Monographs for the Society for Research in Child Development, 53,* (2, Serial No. 218).

Arnold, D. S., & Whitehurst, G. J. (1994). Accelerating language development through picture book reading: A summary of dialogic reading and effects. In D. K. Dickinson (Ed.), *Bridges to literacy: Children, families, and schools* (pp. 103-128). Cambridge, MA: Blackwell.

Boyer, E. L. (1991). *Ready to learn: A mandate for the nation.* Princeton, NJ: The Carnegie Foundation.

Brody, G. H., Staneman, Z., & McCoy, J. K. (1994). Contributions of protective and risk factors to literacy and socioemotional competency in former Head Start children attending kindergarten. *Early Childhood Research Quarterly, 9,* 407-426.

Children's Defense Fund. (1992). *The state of America's children: 1992.* Washington, D.C.: Children's Defense Fund.

Cronin, T. A., Cruz, S. G., & Arriaga, R. I. (1996). The effects of a community-based literacy program on young children's language and conceptual development. *American Journal of Community Psychology, 24,* 251-272.

Delgado-Gaitan, C. (1990). *Literacy for empowerment: The role of parents in children's education.* New York: Falmer Press.

Dorotik, M., & Betzold, M. R. (1992). Expanding literacy for all. *Reading Teacher, 48,* 574-578.

Eccles, J. S., & Harold, R. D. (1996). Family involvement in children's and adolescents' schooling. In A. Booth & J. F. Dunn (Eds.), *Family-school links: How they affect educational outcomes?* (pp. 3-34). Mahwah, NJ: Lawrence Erlbaum.

Edwards, P. A. (1990). *Parents as partners in reading: A family literacy training program.* Chicago: Children's Press.

Edwards, P. A. (1991). Fostering early literacy through parent coaching. In E. H.

Hiebert (Ed.), *Literacy for a diverse society: Perspectives, practice, and policies* (pp. 199-227). New York: Teachers College Press.

Gottfried, A. W. & Gottfried, A. E. (1984). Home environment and mental development in young children. In A. W. Gottfried (Ed.), *Home environment and early mental development: Longitudinal research.* New York: Academic Press.

Hess, R. D. Holloway, S., Price, G. G., & Dickson, W. P. (1982). Family environments and the acquisition of reading skills: Toward a more precise analysis. In L. M. Laosa & I. E. Sigel (Eds.), *Families as learning environments for children* (pp. 87-114). New York: Plenum.

Morrison, F., McMahon, E. H., & Williamson, G. A. (1993). Two strikes from the start: Individual differences in early literacy. *Society for Research in Child development Abstracts, 9,* 221.

McCormick, C. E., & Mason, J. M. (1986). Intervention procedures for increasing children's interest in and knowledge about reading. In W. H. Teale & E. Sulzby (Eds.), *Emergent literacy: Writing and reading* (pp. 90-115). Norwood, NJ: Ablex.

National Center for Educational Statistics. (1993). *Adult literacy in America.* Washington, DC: U.S. Department of Education, National Center for Educational Statistics.

Primavera, J. (1999, in press). The unintended consequences of volunteerism: Positive outcomes for those who serve. *Journal of Prevention & Intervention in the Community.*

Primavera, J. & Cook, M. J. (1997, May) *A successful university-community partnership: The Family Literacy Project.* Poster presented at the sixth biennial conference of the Society for Community Research and Action, Division 27 of the American Psychological Association, Columbia, SC.

Raz, I. S., & Bryant, P. (1990). Social background, phonological awareness, and children's reading. *British Journal of Developmental Psychology, 8,* 209-225.

Rich, D. (1985). *The forgotten factor in school success: The family.* Washington DC: Home and School Institute.

Reynolds, A. (1991). Early schooling of children at risk. *American Educational Research Journal, 28,* 392-422.

Sarason, S. B. & Lorentz, E. (1979). *The challenge of the resource exchange network.* San Francisco: Jossey-Bass.

Schier, M. F., & Carver, C. S. (1992). Effects of optimism on psychological and physical well-being: Theoretical overview and empirical update. *Cognitive Therapy and Research, 16,* 210-228.

Snow, C. & Ninio, A. (1986). The contract of literacy: What children learn from learning to read books. In W. H. Teale & E. Sulzsby (Eds.), *Emergent literacy: Writing and reading.* Norwood, NJ: Ablex Publishing.

Stevenson, J., & Fredman, G. (1990). The social environment correlates of reading ability. *Journal of Child Psychology and Psychiatry, 31,* 681-698.

Sticht, T., & McDonald, B. (1989). *Making the nation smarter: The intergenerational transfer of cognitive ability.* San Diego, CA: Applied Behavioral & Cognitive Sciences.

Teale, W. H. (1986). Home background and young children's literacy development.

In W. H. Teale & E. Sulzby (Eds.), *Emergent literacy: Writing and reading*. Norwood, NJ: Ablex Publishing.

Teale, W. H. & Sulzby, E. (1986). *Emergent literacy: Writing and reading*. Norwood, NJ: Ablex Publishing.

Tuma, J. M. (1989). Mental health services for children: The state of the art. *American Psychologist, 44,* 188-199.

U.S. Department of Health & Human Services. (1991). *Promoting family literacy through Head Start.* DHHS Publication No. (ACF) 91-31266. Washington, DC.

Wells, G. (1985). Preschool literacy-related activities and success in school. In O. R. Olson, N. Torrance, & A. Hildyard (Eds.), *Literacy, language, and learning: The nature and consequences of reading and writing* (pp. 229-255). New York: Cambridge University Press.

White, K. R. (1982). The relation between socioeconomic status and academic achievement. *Psychological Bulletin, 91,* 461-481.

Zigler, E. F. (1994). Reshaping early childhood intervention to be a more effective weapon against poverty. *American Journal of Community Psychology, 22*, 37-47.

Parents' Perceptions of Teacher Outreach and Parent Involvement in Children's Education

Evanthia N. Patrikakou
Roger P. Weissberg

The University of Illinois at Chicago

SUMMARY. The present study investigated associations between parents' perceptions of various teacher outreach practices and self-reported parent involvement both at home and at school. A survey was administered to 246 parents whose children attended one of three inner-city schools in a Midwestern city. Overall, large percentages of parents reported helping their children with schoolwork at home, whereas

---

Address correspondence to: Evanthia N. Patrikakou, Department of Psychology (M/C 285), The University of Illinois at Chicago, 1007 West Harrison Street, Chicago, IL 60607-7137.

For parent and teacher brochures on the topics of parent-teacher communication, report card sharing, and homework, please contact the LSS, 1301 Cecil B. Moore Ave, Philadelphia, PA 19122-6091; telephone: 800-892-5550, or visit the LSS website at <http://www.temple.edu.LSS>.

The authors wish to express their appreciation to Drs. Lascelles Anderson and Timothy Shanahan for their contributions with the design of the parent and teacher surveys, and the Technical Review Board of the Mid-Atlantic Laboratory of Student Success for their constructive and insightful suggestions.

This study was supported, in part, by the Office of Educational Research and Improvement of the U. S. Department of Education through a contract to the Mid-Atlantic Laboratory for Student Success (LSS) established at the Temple University Center for Research in Human Development and Education (CRHDE). The opinions expressed herein do not necessarily reflect the position of the supporting agencies.

[Haworth co-indexing entry note]: "Parents' Perceptions of Teacher Outreach and Parent Involvement in Children's Education." Patrikakou, Evanthia N., and Roger P. Weissberg. Co-published simultaneously in *Journal of Prevention & Intervention in the Community* (The Haworth Press, Inc.) Vol. 20, No. 1/2, 2000, pp. 103-119; and: *Diverse Families, Competent Families: Innovations in Research and Preventive Intervention Practice* (ed: Janet F. Gillespie, and Judy Primavera) The Haworth Press, Inc., 2000, pp. 103-119. Single or multiple copies of this article are available for a fee from The Haworth Document Delivery Service [1-800-342-9678, 9:00 a.m. - 5:00 p.m. (EST). E-mail address: getinfo@haworthpressinc.com].

smaller percentages reported engaging in ongoing school communication with classroom teachers. Results also indicated that, even after controlling for diverse sociodemographic variables (e.g., the educational and employment levels of both parents, child's grade, gender, and race) the strongest predictor of parent involvement was the parents' perceptions of teacher outreach. Specifically, the more parents perceived their child's teacher as valuing their contribution to their child's education, trying to keep them informed about their child's strengths and weaknesses, and providing them with specific suggestions to help their child, the higher the parents' involvement was both at home and at school. Implications for school-family partnership interventions are discussed. *[Article copies available for a fee from The Haworth Document Delivery Service: 1-800-342-9678. E-mail address: <getinfo@haworthpressinc.com> Website: <http://www.haworthpressinc.com>]*

KEYWORDS. Parent involvement, perceptions, teacher outreach, schools

The topic of parent involvement has recently been at the center of multidisciplinary research efforts that examine how parents influence their children's academic, social, and emotional development (Booth & Dunn, 1996). The parent-child relationship is a profound catalyst of social, emotional, and cognitive development (Parke & Buriel, 1998). Families are the first socialization system in which parenting styles interact with the child's development, and through this interaction children grow into social maturity (Santrock, 1996). Once children enter the stage of formal schooling, strong parental influences extend to the child's academic progress. Research has provided mounting evidence that parent involvement plays a crucial role in a child's school performance (Eccles & Harold, 1996; Patrikakou, 1996, 1997; Reynolds & Walberg, 1991). Parent attitudes and behaviors toward education continue to have a great impact when the individual progresses into adolescence (Patrikakou, 1997; Steinberg, Dornbusch, & Brown, 1992). Therefore, by developing interventions that empower parents and provide them with the necessary information and skills to be involved in their child's education, the chances for children's success can be increased.

Research has indicated that effective school-home relationships can be instrumental for student success by enhancing the skills that parents need in order to be involved in their child's education more effectively (Eccles & Harold, 1996; Epstein & Dauber, 1991). However, the majority of studies in the area of parent involvement have examined family influences on children's performance, whereas few have examined the effects that school experiences can have on families.

Different theoretical and empirical models have been developed or adapted from other areas in psychology and education to explain school-family relations. For example, using Bronfenbrenner's ecological theory (1979, 1986) one can illustrate the complexity of home-school relations. Once children begin formal schooling, two of the most important microsystems in a child's life, home and school, begin to interact. This interaction constitutes part of the mesosystem in which parents and teachers contribute to the child's academic and socioemotional development. School-family partnerships are not a static entity within the mesosystem. They can be affected by events taking place in higher systems, such as school policies (exosystem) or the globalization of the economy (macrosystem). While these settings do not include the child directly, events and decisions made within them may have a great impact on the child (Patrikakou, Weissberg, & Rubenstein, in press).

Eccles and Harold (1996) present a model of home-school relations that emphasizes the impact that parent and teacher beliefs and attitudes have on parent and teacher practices. The model includes various components ranging from general demographics to more specific parent, school, and community characteristics. Within this framework, Eccles and Harold describe relationships among teacher and parent beliefs and practices about the school and the roles that they can play. Such relationships include: (a) teacher beliefs and teacher practices; (b) parent beliefs and parent practices; (c) teacher and parent beliefs; and, (d) teacher and parent practices (see Figure 1). However, they do not sufficiently emphasize the link between teacher practices and parents' beliefs (dashed line in Figure 1). This link seems important because (a) studies which have examined this relationship between parent perceptions and teacher practices indicate that parent perceptions can be as critical for the levels of parent involvement as teacher practices per se (Eccles, 1983), and (b) it is possible to modify teacher practices and, through them, affect parent involvement. Initial evidence from correlational and qualitative studies, has indicated that parents are more likely to be actively involved in their child's education if they perceive schools to have strong parent outreach programs. When parents believe that their child's teacher is applying several

FIGURE 1. Effects of Parent and Teacher Beliefs and Practices

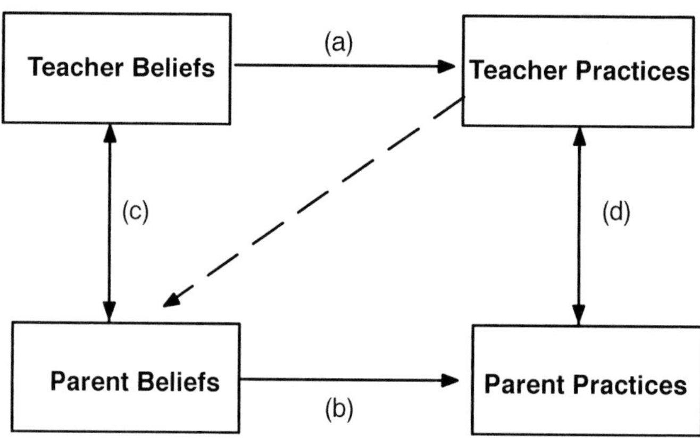

strategies to get them involved in their child's education, they tend to become more involved in the educational process (Dauber & Epstein, 1993). Initial evidence also indicated that parent perceptions were more influential on parent involvement than background variables, such as race, marital or work status (Dauber & Epstein, 1993; Epstein 1986).

Smith et al. (1997) provide qualitative evidence about the importance of parents' perceptions of teacher outreach practices and their effects on parent involvement. Specifically, parents' perceptions of involvement opportunities presented by their child's teacher significantly affected parent involvement both at school and at home. Parents who perceived that the school had a positive, inviting climate with teachers who were applying proactive strategies were less likely to report barriers to involvement.

The issue of parent perceptions and involvement is especially important in urban areas. A few studies have indicated that parent involvement in learning activities is low for public schools and low-income, least educated, minority parents (for example see Lichter, 1996). Often having limited education themselves, and also possibly having had negative personal experiences with the educational system, parents in inner-city environments may mistrust and feel uncomfortable with the school environment (Menacker, Hurwitz, & Weldon, 1988). Cultural and linguistic differences may also lead to additional problems such as paternalism and lower expectations for disadvantaged parents and their children on the part of school personnel (Moles, 1993). In such cases, teacher outreach and its perception by the parents may play a catalytic role in improving home-school relationships, parent participation, and ultimately enhancing the academic and social development of children.

In addition to perceptions, sociodemographic variables such as gender, grade level, family structure, etc., have been shown to affect parent involvement. For example, as children progress in school there is a decline of parent participation (Snodgrass, 1991). The gender of the child has also been found to relate to parent involvement. Specifically, parents of female students were shown to be more involved both in school and home activities (Hickman, Greenwood, & Miller, 1995). Finally, it has been shown that family structure plays an important role in parent involvement. Epstein (1990) found that although single parents reported that they spend more time more often than two-parent families assisting their children at home with schoolwork, they still believed that they did not have the "time and energy" to fulfill the teacher's expectations of them.

The present study builds on and combines information from initial findings that indicate the importance of parent perceptions of teacher outreach and the influence of sociodemographics on parent involvement. The focus of this study is on urban public schools in an effort to (a) gather further information about the nature and extent of parent-involvement attitudes and practices in public inner-city schools, and (b) investigate the relationships among sociodemographic factors, parent perceptions of teacher practices, and actual parent involvement. It was hypothesized that perceived teacher outreach has a stronger impact on parent involvement than sociodemographic variables. Specifically, the hypothesis was that the more teacher outreach parents perceive as taking place, the higher their involvement levels are both at home and at school.

METHOD

Participants

Participants of this study were parents from three inner-city elementary schools in a large Midwestern city. Two of the schools have a

100% African-American population, while in the third 96% of students are Latino. According to district reported data, the percentages for low-income students are as follows: 95% and 98% for the two African-American schools, and 96% for the Latino school. Summary information provided by the city's public school system indicated that only a minority of students in two of the schools scored at or above national norms in standardized tests (one of the two schools serving African-American students, and the one serving Latino students). For example, in reading, the percentage of eighth graders in one school and fifth graders in the other scoring at or above national norms was 7% and 9%, respectively. During the 1996-1997 school year, due to the low academic scores, the city school system placed the two schools on "academic probation," since fewer than 15% of the school's student population scored at or above state and national norms on standardized tests. The students at the third school performed better academically, with 24% of eighth graders performing at or above national norms in reading.

Parents were surveyed if they had a child attending a pre-kindergarten through third-grade classroom. A total of 385 questionnaires were distributed to the three schools and 246 were returned, a return rate of 64%. The majority of respondents (84%) were the mother or stepmother of the child. Fifty-two percent of the respondents said that the child's other parent was not living in the same home as the child. Overall, 20% of the parents in the sample had a child in pre-kindergarten, 23% had a kindergartner, 20% a first grader, 16% a second grader, and 21% a third grader. Fifty-eight percent of parent reports were for a female student and 42% for a male. Seventeen percent of the parents filling the questionnaire had grade school education, 27% some high school, 22% a high school diploma or GED, 20% some college or vocational training, and 4% held a college degree. The education reported for the child's other parent was 22% grade school, 29% some high school, 31% high school diploma or GED, 11% had some college experience or vocational training, and 7% held a college degree. Parents' employment status was as follows: 60% of parents completing the questionnaire were unemployed, 12% held part-time jobs, and 28% had a full-time job. Employment status reported for the child's other parent was 44% unemployed, 8% had a part-time job, and 48% held a full-time job.

Measure

The parent survey used in the present study was developed as a collaborative effort between the School-Family Partnership project at the University of Illinois at Chicago, a collaborative site of the Mid-Atlantic Laboratory of Student Success at Temple University, and personnel at the participating schools. Based on feedback from teachers and principals in participating schools, the measure underwent several revisions. English and Spanish versions of the survey were created. The four-page questionnaire consisted of 37 items and covered the following areas: demographics, parent involvement at home, parent involvement at school, parent perceptions about teacher outreach to parents, and parent willingness to expand his/her involvement in a variety of ways.

Variables

This study explored eight sociodemographic and background variables, a measure of parents' perception of student outreach, and two measures of actual parent involvement. The single-item sociodemographic variables included: (a) gender (*males* = 0 and *females* = 1); (b) grade level (from *pre-kindergarten* = 1 to *3rd grade* = 5); (c) parents' highest educational level (*grade school* = 1 to *college degree* = 5); (d) parents' employment status (*unemployed at the time* = 0, *employed part-time* = 1, and *employed full time* = 2); (e) ethnicity (*African-American* = 0 and *Latino* = 1); and (f) family structure (0 = if the child's *other parent was living in the same home,* 1 = if the child's *other parent did not live in the same home*).

Parent Involvement at Home. The scale of *Parent Involvement at Home* (PIH) was comprised by eight items that investigated various kinds of parent practices which contribute to the enhancement of academic and social development. Parents were asked how many days *during an average week* certain behaviors occurred. For example, parent involvement in homework was assessed using the following three items: "I make sure that my child has a quiet place to do homework," "I check that my child's homework is done on school nights," and "I help my child with homework (see Table 1 for item information). The Cronbach's α of the PIH scale was .77.

Parent Involvement at School. The *Parent Involvement at School* (PISC) scale, which was the dependent variable in the second equation, consisted of six items that measured various ways in which parents are involved in their child's education at school (α = .71). Parents were asked how often certain parent involvement behaviors occurred *during the current academic year*. Items on this scale measured parent participation both in policy-dictated activities (e.g., picking up the child's report-card) and in voluntary activities (e.g., volunteering to help in the child's classroom). Table 2 summarizes information about the items in the PISC scale.

Parent Perceived Teacher Outreach. The scale of *Parent Perceived Teacher Outreach* (PPTO) includes ten items that measured the parents' perceptions of various teacher outreach behaviors and practices that encourage and reinforce parent involvement (α = .87). Parents were asked to consider how often certain types of teacher outreach took place *during the current academic year (never, sometimes,* or *usually)*. Items on the perception of both the climate that the teacher creates for parents (e.g., Does your child's teacher share information with you in a positive way?) and the level of information the teacher relays to parents (e.g., Does the teacher tell you specific ways that you could help your child do better?) were included. Table 3 presents information about the items in this scale.

Procedure

Surveys were distributed in the Spring of 1997. Classroom teachers handed every child the questionnaire along with a cover letter. In the case of the Latino school both English and Spanish versions of the cover letter and the questionnaire were included in the packets. The cover letter informed parents about the purpose of the survey and the school's partnership with UIC. Parents who chose to participate were encouraged to return the surveys within a week. The majority of the surveys were returned within the first two weeks following distribution. The follow-up process, which was conducted in classrooms where the response rate was below 30%, included sending a second questionnaire to parents who did not respond. This process yielded some additional completed questionnaires placing the return rate at 64%.

RESULTS

The results section is divided into two parts. The first presents descriptive findings for parent involvement at home, parent involvement at school, and perceived teacher outreach. The second part includes results from the regression analyses.

Descriptive Findings

Parent involvement at home (see Table 1). The most common forms of parent involvement at home were checking to see that the child's homework was completed (74%) and actively helping the child with homework (68%). The behavior that parents reported as occurring least frequently was reading to their child (26%).

Parent involvement at school (see Table 2). Parents reported that their most frequent type of involvement at school was a visit for picking up their child's report card (71%). Forms of involvement in which parents were never or rarely (1-2 times a year) engaged were volunteering in the child's classroom (81%) and going to parent-teacher conferences (71%). In addition, parents reported that they never or rarely called or went to see their child's teacher (53%), or asked the teacher how they could help their child at home (69%).

Parents' perceptions of teacher outreach (see Table 3). Regarding teacher outreach practices, 80% of parents reported that the teacher notified them when their child was "in trouble" at school and 71% said that the teacher let them know when the child was doing something well at school. Most of the parents (74%) felt that it was easy to talk or meet with their child's teacher and that the teacher answered their questions in a helpful way (77%). Ways of parent outreach that were reported as applied less frequently include teacher encouraging parents to come to school (55%), and offering specific suggestions to parents to help their child do better (63%).

Regression Analysis

The process followed for each of the two dependent variables (parent involvement at home and at school) included two steps. First, each outcome was regressed on sociodemographic factors. Second, the variable of Parent Perception of Teacher Outreach (PPTO) entered the equation. Analyses examined whether including the PPTO variable significantly changed the R^2, which would suggest that these perceptions add statistically significant explanatory power to the model.

The eight sociodemographic variables did not significantly predict

TABLE 1. Percentages of Items on the Parent Involvement at Home Scale

Items	Less than 1 day	1 day	2-4 days	5-7 days
I talk to my child about what he or she is learning at school	1%	6%	33%	60%
I read with my child	3%	17%	54%	26%
I help my child with homework	6%	4%	22%	68%
I have my child in bed by 9:00 pm	3%	4%	30%	63%
I check that my child's homework is done on school nights	5%	3%	18%	74%
I make sure that my child has a quiet place to do homework	6%	3%	28%	63%
I talk to my child about getting along with his or her friends	2%	4%	26%	68%
I arrange for my child to play with other children of his or her age	14%	11%	31%	44%

TABLE 2. Percentages of Items on the Parent Involvement at School Scale

Items	Never	1-2 times	Several times
Called or went to see my child's teacher	17%	36%	47%
I asked the teacher how I can help my child with school work	32%	37%	31%
I visited my child's classroom	8%	26%	66%
I volunteered to help in my child's classroom	59%	22%	19%
I went to parent-teacher conferences	36%	35%	29%
I picked up my child's report card	6%	23%	71%

parent involvement at home ($F = 1.49$; $p = .17$). However, when PPTO variable entered the equation in the second step, the F was statistically significant ($F = 3.62$; $p = .0006$) and the R^2 accounted for 25% of the variance in parent involvement at home. As expected, the ΔF was statistically significant ($p < .0001$). Adding the PPTO variable more than doubled the magnitude of R^2, a 127% increase from the R^2 of the first

TABLE 3. Percentages of Items on the Perceived Teacher Outreach Scale

Items	Never	Sometimes	Usually
Does your child's teacher share information with you in a positive way?	2%	33%	65%
Does the teacher answer your questions in a helpful way?	3%	20%	77%
Does the teacher try to make you feel comfortable when you meet?	3%	15%	82%
Does the teacher greet you in the morning when you take your child to school?	8%	21%	71%
Is it easy to talk to or meet with your child's teacher?	4%	22%	74%
Does the teacher encourage you to come to school to visit or help?	15%	30%	55%
Does the teacher let you know when your child is having trouble at school?	3%	17%	80%
Does the teacher let you know when your child is doing something well at school?	4%	25%	71%
Does the teacher tell you specific ways that you could help your child do better?	10%	27%	63%
Do the teacher's suggestions work in helping your child?	5%	29%	66%

Note: A does not apply choice was also provided to respondents. For the purposes of the present study doesn't apply was set as missing values.

step. The only two variables that significantly affected home involvement were ethnicity (where African-Americans were more involved than Latino parents) and PPTO (see Table 4).

The eight sociodemographic variables also failed to predict parent involvement at school ($F = 1.77$; $p = .09$). Once more, however, when the variable of parent perceptions of teacher outreach entered the equation in the second step, the F became statistically significant ($F = 2.80$; $p = .006$) and the R^2 accounted for 20% of the variance in parent involvement at school (see Table 4). As expected, the ΔF was statistically significant ($p < .005$). With the PPTO variable included in the equation the R^2 increased by 67%. The PPTO variable was once again statistically significant ($b = .37$; $p < .005$). The only sociodemographic variable that reached statistical significance was family structure for which two-parent households were more involved in school activities than their single-parent counterparts.

DISCUSSION

The present study gathered data on parent-involvement attitudes and practices in inner-city schools, and explored the relationship between perceived teacher outreach and parent involvement at home and at school. Findings indicate that parents whose children attend inner-

TABLE 4. Coefficients of Parent Involvement at Home and Parent Involvement at School Full-Model Regression Equations

Variables	PIH	PISC
Gender	.042 (.043)	–.105 (–.115)
Grade Level	.013 (.040)	–.030 (–.097)
Parent's Education	–.051 (–.107)	–.008 (–.020)
Other Parent's Education	.010 (.024)	.095 (.240)
Parent's Employment Status	.082 (.154)	.061 (.124)
Other Parent's Employment Status	–.039 (–.078)	–.076 (–.163)
Race	–.286* (–.293)	.032 (.036)
Family Structure	–.000 (–.001)	.251* (.282)
Perceived Teacher Outreach	.596*** (.391)	.367** (.289)
R^2	.25	.20

Note: Standardized coefficients are in parentheses.
*$p < .05$. **$p < .01$. ***$p < .0001$.

city public schools make significant efforts to be involved in their child's education both at home and at school in spite of adverse conditions such as low education and SES. As Bronfenbrenner (1979; p. 849) noted, "whatever the socioeconomic level, ethnic group, or type of family structure, we have yet to meet a parent who is not deeply committed to ensuring the well-being of his or her child. Most families are doing the best they can under difficult circumstances." This evidence is in accordance with that of previous studies which have also found that parents in the inner city generally display positive attitudes toward their children's education (Reynolds & Gill, 1994).

However, it must be noted that certain parent practices which have been shown to be extremely important for children's cognitive and academic development were not as widely practiced as expected. For example, reading to their child was something that few parents (26%) practiced regularly at home. This finding points to the need to increase our efforts in informing parents about different ways they can contribute to their child's education and, therefore, extend classroom learning to the home environment. As Walberg (1984) noted the "curriculum of the home" is alterable and can lead to enormous benefits in academic achievement. Parents who are aware of the benefits of improved learning conditions at home, as well as willing to learn specific ways in which they can implement such changes, can have large positive effects on their children's education (Eccles & Harold, 1996).

Schools can play an instrumental role in disseminating to parents meaningful strategies with which they can be involved in their child's education. This goal can be achieved if there is proactive, regular, and persistent communication between home and school, and a partnership between parents and teachers is established and maintained. Specifically, in order for parents to be involved in meaningful ways, they should be kept informed regularly about class rules, expectations, and current activities. Letting parents know about classroom routines, such as quizzes and homework, involves parents in the educational process and provides them with a structured opportunity to be involved in their child's education (School-Family Partnership Project, 1998).

Home-school communications can become even more effective if parents and teachers communicate with each other using the best ways (phone calls, notes, home-school journal, etc.) they can be reached. The survey's 64% return rate was an adequate one for research purposes and it also indicated that the majority of the parents in these urban schools were sufficiently interested in parent involvement to contribute their opinion on the matter. On the other hand, for the remaining 36% of parents who did not respond, the written form may not have been the optimal way for them to be reached for several reasons such as literacy level, regardless of their primary language (English or Spanish). If parents and teachers inform each other about the best ways they can be reached, the frustration of not reaching each other can be minimized, and, most importantly, the message can go through.

Findings also indicated that several forms of school involvement did not occur frequently. For example, 59% of parents reported that they had never volunteered in their child's classroom. In addition, 45% of them stated that the teacher had never or seldom encouraged them to volunteer at school. Given the fact that volunteering is not an uncommon practice for early grades, one wonders why this behavior was not more extensively applied in these inner-city schools. Although involving parents as classroom volunteers may seem desirable in theory, fostering high quality participation that benefits students, parents, and teachers requires considerable time, effort, and skill on the teacher's part. With more support and training, it would be possible to increase teacher outreach and constructive parent volunteerism in the classroom.

Other behaviors of parent involvement at school pointed to less communication between home and school. For example, 36% of parents reported that they had never participated in a parent-teacher conference and 32% had never asked the teacher how they could help their child with schoolwork. When one combines these findings with results from the regression analysis, which indicated that perceptions of teacher outreach are crucial for parent involvement, the importance of reaching out to parents becomes even more pronounced. A teacher from one of the participating inner-city schools described the solution best: "Our school can extend itself more to the parent. Sometimes the parents need a little push or motivation. If a parent can't come to the school to support their child, we must go to them."

Parent perception of teacher outreach was the only variable that was statistically significant in predicting parent involvement both at home and at school. This finding is important because it emphasizes once again how crucial school factors are as reinforcing agents of parents' behavior. In agreement with previous studies (Dauber & Epstein,

1993), parent perceptions were found to be more influential than sociodemographic and background variables. In the case of parent involvement at home, the only variable other than parent perceptions that was statistically significant was race. This finding indicated that, in our sample, African-American parents had higher levels of involvement than Latino parents. One possible explanation for this phenomenon is the language factor. When asked what language they speak, half of the parents from the predominantly Latino school checked the Spanish only option. Without knowing the language and, therefore, the demands of the task sent home, Latino parents face an additional obstacle in their effort to get involved in their child's learning at home. On the other hand, since the current study involved three schools, it is difficult to disentangle whether this finding is actually due to a school effect. Future research might explore the issue using a larger sample of schools.

When predicting parent involvement at school, parent perception of teacher outreach was once again the most influential variable. Parents who perceived teachers as extending a helpful hand, as well as encouraging parents to visit the school, were more likely to participate in a variety of school activities. The only other variable that had statistically significant effects on parent involvement at school was family structure. Specifically, if the child's other parent was living at home, parents were more likely to participate in school activities. It may be difficult for a single parent who cannot share parenting responsibilities with a spouse to participate in activities that take them out of the home. It seems important to identify and offer supports, such as child care, to single parents so it will be easier for them to connect more with schools.

In agreement with previous findings (Smith et al., 1997) the present study provides evidence that parent perceptions of teacher outreach is an important contributing factor to parent involvement. The more parents perceived that teachers extended a partnership to them by keeping them informed and providing them with the necessary information to maximize participation in learning activities, the higher their involvement with their children's schooling. Therefore, it should be included in models investigating the issue of parent participation both in home and school activities.

Although the current results identify an important predictor of parent involvement, they do not directly contribute to an explanation of it.

Interviewing parents on the issue of teacher outreach will provide insights about why parents are so influenced by their perceptions of teacher outreach, as well as illuminate specific teacher behaviors parents consider as crucial motivation for their participation. Future research should further explore the specifics of relationships among parent and teacher beliefs and practices. In this way, existing assessment tools can be further refined and interventions to enhance home-school relationships can be more successful.

REFERENCES

Booth, A., & Dunn, J. F. (Eds.) (1996). *Family-school links.* Mahwah, NJ: Lawrence Erlbaum.

Bronfenbrenner, U. (1979). Contexts of child rearing. *American Psychologist, 34,* 844-850.

Bronfenbrenner, U. (1986). Ecology of the family as a context for human development: Research perspectives. *Developmental Psychology, 22,* 723-742.

Dauber, S. L., & Epstein, J. L. (1993). Parents' attitudes and practices of involvement in inner-city elementary and middle schools. In N. F. Chavkin (Ed.), *Families and schools in a pluralistic society* (pp. 53-71). Albany, NY: State University of New York Press.

Eccles, J. (1983). Expectancies, values, and academic behaviors. In J. T. Spence (Ed.), *Achievement and achievement motives* (pp. 75-145). San Francisco: Freeman.

Eccles, J., & Harold, R. D. (1996). Family involvement in children's and adolescents' schooling. In A. Booth, & J. F. Dunn (Eds.), *Family-school links* (pp. 3-34). Mahwah, NJ: Lawrence Erlbaum.

Epstein, J. L. (1986). Parents' reactions to teacher practices of parent involvement. *Elementary School Journal, 86,* 277-294.

Epstein, J. L. (1990). Single parents and the schools. In M. T. Hallinan, D. M. Klein, & J. Glass (Eds.), *Change in societal institutions* (pp. 91-121). New York: Plenum Press.

Epstein, J. L., & Dauber, S. L. (1991). School programs and teacher practices of parent involvement in inner-city elementary and middle schools. *Elementary School Journal, 91,* 288-304.

Hickman, C. W., Greenwood, G., & Miller, M. D. (1995). High school parent involvement: Relationships with achievement, grade level, SES, and gender. *Journal of Research and Development in Education, 28,* 125-134.

Lichter, D. T. (1996). Family diversity, intellectual inequality, and academic achievement among American children. In A. Booth, & J. F. Dunn (Eds.) *Family-school links* (pp. 265-274). Mahwah, NJ: Lawrence Erlbaum.

Menacker, J., Hurwitz, E., & Weldon, W. (1988). Parent-teacher cooperation in schools serving the urban poor. *The Clearing House, 62,* 108-112.

Moles, O. C. (1993). Collaboration between schools and disadvantaged parents:

Obstacles and openings. In N. F. Chavkin (Ed.), *Families and schools in a pluralistic society* (pp. 21-49). Albany, NY: State University of New York Press.

Parke, R. D., & Buriel, R. (1998). Socialization in the family: Ethnic and ecological perspectives. In W. Damon (Series Ed.) & I. E. Sigel & K. A. Renninger (Vol. Eds.). *Handbook of child psychology: Vol. 4. Child psychology in practice* (5th ed., pp. 463-552). New York: Wiley.

Patrikakou, E. N. (1996). Investigating the academic achievement of adolescents with learning disabilities: A structural model approach. *Journal of Educational Psychology, 88,* 435-450.

Patrikakou, E. N. (1997). A model of parental attitudes and the academic achievement of adolescents. *Journal of Research and Development in Education, 31,* 7-26.

Patrikakou, E. N., Weissberg, R. P., & Rubenstein, M. I. (in ress). School-family partnerships. In A. J. Reynolds, H. J. Walberg, & R. P. Weissberg (Eds.) *Promoting positive outcomes in children and youth.* Washington, DC: Child Welfare League of America.

Reynolds, A. J., & Gill, S. (1994). The role of parents' perspectives in the school adjustment of inner-city black children. *Journal of Youth and Adolescence, 23,* 671-694.

Reynolds, A. J., & Walberg, H. J. (1991). A structural model of science achievement. *Journal of Educational Psychology, 83,* 97-107.

Santrock, J. W. (1996). *Child development.* Chicago: Brown & Benchmark.

School-Family Partnership Project (1998). *The School-Family Partnership training manual.* University of Illinois at Chicago.

Smith, E. P., Connell, C. M., Wright, G., Sizer, M., & Norman, J. M., Hurley, A., & Walker, S. N. (1997). An ecological model of home, school, and community partnerships: Implications for research and practice. *Journal of Educational and Psychological Consultation, 8,* 339-360.

Snodgrass, D. M. (1991). The parent connection. *Adolescence, 26,* 83-87.

Steinberg, L., Dornbusch, S. M., & Brown, B. B. (1992). Ethnic differences in adolescent achievement. *American Psychologist, 47,* 723-729.

Walberg, H. J. (1984). Improving the productivity of America's schools. *Educational Leadership, 41,* 19-30.

Toward a Model of Latino Parent Advocacy for Educational Change

Eliot B. Levine
Harvard University

Edison J. Trickett
University of Maryland

SUMMARY. Parent involvement in children's education has increasingly become a focus of research, policy, and practice that offers evidence of diverse benefits for families. A theoretical framework for understanding involvement of Latino parents was developed based on interviews with 14 Spanish-speaking parents from low-income backgrounds. Parent strategies for addressing school-related concerns emerged as a critical component of that theoretical framework. Discussion of individual and collective strategies and their contexts leads to suggestions for promoting effective engagement of parents from low-income, immigrant, and limited English proficiency groups.

Address correspondence to: Eliot B. Levine, Harvard Children's Initiative, 126 Mount Auburn Street, Cambridge, MA 02138 (E-mail: clevin@alum.mit.edu).

The authors are indebted to Marcela Betzer, Wendy Burk, Silvia Petuchowski, and Ana Raffo for their skilled research assistance.

This research was conducted for the first author's dissertation, which was supported by grants from the Society for the Psychological Study of Social Issues, the Department of Psychology at the University of Maryland, the Spencer Foundation, and the Honor Society of Phi Kappa Phi. The work itself and the conclusions reached are solely the responsibility of the investigators.

[Haworth co-indexing entry note]: "Toward a Model of Latino Parent Advocacy for Educational Change." Levine, Eliot B., and Edison J. Trickett. Co-published simultaneously in *Journal of Prevention & Intervention in the Community* (The Haworth Press, Inc.) Vol. 20, No. 1/2, 2000, pp. 121-137; and: *Diverse Families, Competent Families: Innovations in Research and Preventive Intervention Practice* (ed: Janet F. Gillespie, and Judy Primavera) The Haworth Press, Inc., 2000, pp. 121-137. Single or multiple copies of this article are available for a fee from The Haworth Document Delivery Service [1-800-342-9678, 9:00 a.m. - 5:00 p.m. (EST). E-mail address: getinfo@haworthpressinc.com].

KEYWORDS. Parent involvement, parent participation, parent advocacy, elementary education, multicultural education, Latinos

Parent involvement in children's education has increasingly become a focus of research, policy, and practice that offers evidence of diverse benefits for families (Epstein, 1996). These benefits include increasing children's academic achievement (Henderson & Berla, 1994), strengthening parental control over their children's education (Delgado-Gaitan, 1991; Fine, 1993), building family social networks in the school and community (Epstein, 1996), and fostering parent empowerment (Winters, 1993). The research literature on this topic has not focused sufficiently on Latino families, a rapidly growing population in the United States. The sociocultural characteristics of these families might mediate the development and evaluation of effective programs for strengthening families through collaboration with schools.

Latino parents are less involved with their children's schools than majority group parents (Delgado-Gaitan, 1991) despite their eagerness to participate in a range of activities and their potential for productive involvement (Chavkin & Williams, 1989). Obstacles include limited English proficiency, employment demands, limited understanding of local educational systems, mistrust and misunderstanding between parents and educators, and fear of the discovery of undocumented immigrant status (Chavkin & Williams, 1989; Harry, 1992). Strategies proposed to surmount these barriers have included providing bilingual school personnel, promoting cultural sensitivity, arranging meetings during evenings and weekends, etc. (Lewis, 1993; Nicolau & Ramos, 1990).

A recent review of factors influencing parent involvement suggested that understanding parent strategies for solving school-related concerns is a fruitful route for understanding how parents influence their children's academic achievement (Hoover-Dempsey & Sandler, 1997). Few studies have explored such parent strategies, particularly for immigrant parents who face language barriers and limited familiarity with the local educational system.

The current study reports on the development of a theoretical framework for understanding involvement of low-income Latino parents with their children's schools. Guiding research questions were as follows: (1) What are participants' goals for their children's school experiences and what strategies do they use in service of these goals? (2) What have been participants' experiences with school involvement? (3) Have participants worked with other parents or with community organizations as part of their involvement in their children's education? (4) What contextual factors and personal characteristics influence their involvement in their children's education?

Parent strategies for addressing school-related concerns, hereafter referred to as parent advocacy, emerged as a critical component of the emergent theoretical framework. The current article explores these strategies in an attempt to facilitate development and evaluation of appropriate parent involvement program models for low-income Latinos, and for other low-income, immigrant, and limited English proficiency groups who experience obstacles to interacting with the public education system.

METHOD

Participants

Participants were 14 low-income Latino and Latina parents in the Boston area. Parents included eight females and six males ranging in age from 29 to 57 (mean = 39). Thirteen were married and one was divorced. They had immigrated from Bolivia, Colombia (2), the Dominican Republic (4), El Salvador (2), Guatemala (2), Mexico, Puerto Rico, and Venezuela. Recency of immigration ranged from 7 months to 21 years (mean = 11 years). Four participants had immigrated during the past 5 years, seven had immigrated within 8-14 years, and three had immigrated within 20-21 years. Children per family ranged from 1 to 7 (mean = 2.8), and the children ranged in age from 1 to 26 years (mean = 10). All participants had at least one child in elementary school, and the proportion of Latinos in these schools (N = 6) ranged from 23% to 67% (mean = 42%). Seventy-nine percent of parents graduated from high school in their countries-of-origin, and none had obtained additional formal schooling in the United States.

To document low-income status, study participants (N = 14) were asked about their own occupations as well as the occupations of their spouses (N = 13). Participants and spouses were either unemployed (N = 7, 26%) or employed in service, repair, and laborer positions (N = 20,

74%). A combination of occupational data, informal assessments of living space during interviews, and feedback from referral sources suggested that all participants were from low-income families. Hereafter we consider only the 14 study participants and not their spouses.

Recruitment

Initial recruitment was carried out through contacts in community agencies, health and mental health centers, and schools. Subsequent recruitment was carried out through these same contacts, and also by asking study participants to suggest additional parents to contact. Level of school involvement was assessed briefly during initial phone contacts to ensure diversity across participants on this dimension. To overcome potential obstacles for low-income parents, participants were paid thirty dollars, reimbursed for hiring babysitters, offered evening and weekend interviews, and offered transportation to the interview location if they chose not to complete it in their home.

Parent Interviews

The guiding research questions listed above were developed from a literature review and then transformed into a semi-structured interview protocol. This protocol was then revised by a process of consultation and piloting with experts in cross-cultural research, qualitative interviewing, and issues of Latino parents. Consultants included university faculty, three Latina health and human service professionals who worked closely with low-income Latino parents, and a Latina parent who was actively involved in the Boston schools. All consultants provided feedback about the tone, content, and clarity of the interview, and the parent completed a pilot interview prior to offering feedback. The protocol was then finalized for use with study participants.

Interviews lasted 90-120 minutes and were conducted in Spanish by the first author. Bilingual research assistants attended all interviews to help with translation of nuance and unfamiliar vocabulary, to resolve miscommunications, and to ask questions or offer comments that supported data collection. Subsequently, these same research assistants transcribed and then translated interview audiotapes.

Consistent with principles of qualitative interviewing (Weiss,

1994), interview questions were addressed with some flexibility allowed. All questions were addressed during every interview, but their order and exact phrasing varied depending on each participant's individualized responses. Inquiries were sufficiently circumscribed to elicit material of direct relevance to each research question, but sufficiently open-ended to encourage elaboration based on the respondent's unique experiences. Such individualized elaboration is essential to the theory-building process discussed below.

Data Analysis

Transcripts were analyzed using the grounded theory method (Glaser & Strauss, 1967; Strauss & Corbin, 1990), a model that advocates building theory from rich, narrative data in the voices of study participants. In the first stage of analysis, called open coding, transcripts are subdivided into text segments (e.g., phrases, sentences, or paragraphs) that embody discrete aspects of each participant's reported experience. The researcher conducting the analysis then assigns each segment a fitting conceptual label or code (e.g., "attending school activities" or "seeking better future for child"). In the second stage of analysis, called axial coding, conceptually related codes from the open coding phase are grouped into higher order conceptual categories (e.g., "monitoring child's performance" or "school responsiveness"). In the third and final stage of analysis, called selective coding, the categories from axial coding are organized conceptually in relation to each other and to a core category that best summarizes the data. The theoretical model in the current study is built around the core category of "parent advocacy," and its principal categories are detailed below. Specialized software (ATLAS/ti) was utilized to organize the data and to create graphic displays of the relationships among codes (Muhr, 1995).

The present study utilized a team analysis approach that has been advocated and utilized by the founders of grounded theory. This approach has been used to reduce bias and increase openness to emergent theoretical constructs (e.g., Strauss, 1987). The analysis team consisted of two European-American male psychologists (the authors) and an Argentinean-American female psychologist (who was recruited at the analysis stage of the study but had not participated in earlier stages). At each level of coding (open, axial, and selective), one team member conducted preliminary coding that was then supplemented and modified based on feedback from the other team members. Coding differences were resolved among team members through discussion and reaching consensus about the meaning of particular narrative segments or higher level codes.

To quantify participant responses while maintaining the narrative quality of the findings, a system modeled after Richie et al. (1997) was used: (a) The words "most," "often," "usually," and "typically," indicate the characteristic response of more than 50% of participants; (b) the words "some," "several," and "sometimes" indicate responses from 25% to 50% of participants; and (c) the words "a few" indicate responses from fewer than 25% of participants.

RESULTS

The three sets of principal phenomena that emerged as relevant to the core category of "parent advocacy" are summarized in Figure 1. These phenomena are grouped under the summary labels of "parent contexts," "school contexts," and "associated involvement processes."

Parent Contexts

Advocacy efforts were influenced by numerous aspects of parents' contexts. These aspects included motivations for parent involvement, cross-cultural factors, life demands, and specific parent attributes. Most parents were motivated to become involved in their children's education because they believed such involvement would improve their children's future. They wanted their children to become economically successful, morally upright, socially conscious adults with happy families, and several parents viewed schools and teachers as resources that could facilitate such life success for children.

Participants' advocacy efforts were hindered by cross-cultural factors including language barriers and lack of familiarity with the local education system. One parent remarked "I was very involved with the school when my son was in first grade because the professor was Latina . . . today I hardly keep in touch because my son's teacher speaks only English." In addition, differences between education systems in the United States versus the country-of-origin sometimes led

FIGURE 1. Parent Advocacy Contexts and Processes

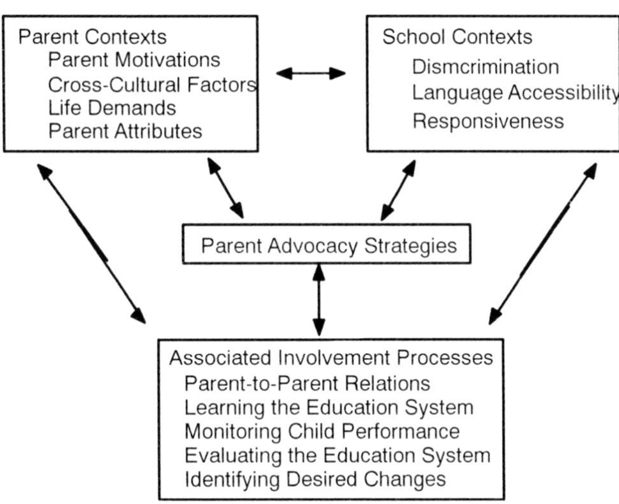

to parent dissatisfaction with school procedures. For example, several parents wanted stricter dress codes, discipline, and grade-level promotion standards. Finally, immigrant status reduced involvement of a few parents who feared discovery of their undocumented status or who felt minimal commitment to local schools because they planned to repatriate as soon as economically feasible.

Involvement for most parents was limited by numerous life demands, especially employment and child care, and, to a lesser extent, health and housing problems, lack of transportation, and conflicts between church and school commitments. In some families, parent involvement was achieved despite such demands via a division of labor among multiple caregivers, or because the parents had decided to forego additional income in exchange for the perceived benefits of engagement in parent involvement activities. These families did not appear to have more money or family support than others, but they had arranged their lives to permit a higher level of parent involvement.

Diverse attributes of individual parents often emerged as influences on advocacy, including assertiveness, confidence, desire to be helpful, dissatisfaction with existing conditions, persistence, a sense of entitlement to desired changes, and consciousness of the possibility of engaging in advocacy. For example, assertiveness and persistence were essential to the success of one mother's response to perceived harassment of her daughter by the daughter's bus driver. The mother approached the principal, who initially minimized her complaints and reinterpreted the driver's actions as benign. However, when she reiterated her position politely but firmly, the principal changed the driver to another route.

Another attribute strongly related to advocacy was parent efficacy expectations–their assessment of whether their advocacy would be successful. Multiple determinants of efficacy expectations were apparent. First, several parents believed that their status as a small, minority constituency reduced their potential influence. This belief led some parents to avoid activism because they felt that minority status doomed them to ineffectiveness, while others decided to form groups and work collectively. Second, efficacy expectations were bolstered for some parents by evidence of past successes, although others sustained a sense of futility despite such evidence. Last, efficacy expectations were influenced by aspects of school context, discussed next.

School Contexts

Parents' desire to engage in school-based advocacy was influenced by aspects of school context including perceived discrimination, language accessibility, and school responsiveness. Discrimination was mentioned by several parents despite its absence from the interview protocol. These parents reported that Latino students were given an inadequate share of school resources and that school personnel considered Latino parents lacking intellectual capacity for meaningful school involvement. Consequences of perceived discrimination for parents included resentment, distrust, and feelings of helplessness to intervene. While some parents responded by reducing their advocacy efforts, others pursued desired changes despite repeated failures attributed to discrimination.

Language accessibility, such as the availability of a translator or a bilingual teacher, influenced the advocacy efforts of most parents. One parent mentioned that the school had promised but then failed to provide a translator for a school-sponsored meeting about the bilingual program. This resulted in parent discouragement, anger, and diminished subsequent participation by parents whose attendance reflected vigorous outreach efforts by activist Latino parents. In contrast, language accessibility sometimes opened otherwise blocked avenues for advocacy, as with one mother whose productive interactions with a bilingual principal apparently relied on their sharing a common language.

School responsiveness encompasses both teacher and school variables that influenced parent perceptions that their advocacy was welcomed and supported. Typical circumstances that made parents feel welcome included being invited to school events, feeling that the principal had listened and offered plausible avenues for change, being treated respectfully by school personnel, being asked for their opinion, or having a teacher who was readily accessible, Spanish-speaking, or outspokenly grateful for parent input. In contrast, several parents found the school unwelcoming, reporting that they had been ignored, treated disrespectfully, or offered what felt like token gestures designed to dispatch them without addressing their concerns adequately. In response to such incidents, some parents became demoralized and resigned to the status quo, while others increased their advocacy for desired school changes. Finally, a few parents avoided advocacy because they feared reprisals, such as the teacher disliking their child if they sought classroom changes.

Involvement Processes Associated with Advocacy

Parent advocacy influenced and was influenced by several parent involvement processes, including parent-to-parent relations, monitoring children's school performance, learning the education system, evaluating the education system, and identifying desired changes. For most participants, parent-to-parent relations were complicated by barriers including mistrust and lack of time. Despite these barriers, some parents made time-consuming outreach efforts to other parents in order to provide encouragement and problem-solving assistance, establish trust and friendship, share perspectives on school-related issues, and urge greater involvement in their child's education.

Monitoring a child's academic and behavioral performance was also important for most parents in their attempts to foster their child's educational success. Monitoring strategies included questioning the child, checking grades, obtaining feedback from school personnel, and making comparisons with other children. Monitoring and advocacy were sometimes related, such as when a parent reviewed her child's assignment, disputed the grade, and succeeded in having it increased.

Parent advocacy was also facilitated by "learning the system"–increasing their understanding of school processes relevant to achieving goals for their children. For most parents, this learning was achieved via participation in school activities, obtaining school-based employment, targeting questions to a knowledgeable Latino parent, accessing bilingual school personnel, learning basic English, or utilizing information provided by the school. Participants varied widely in their level of school knowledge and the speed with which they gained that knowledge. The participant who had immigrated most recently had, in just seven months, achieved an apparently greater understanding of the school system than most other participants, and was actively involved in school-based advocacy. A few other parents displayed minimal knowledge of their child's school and minimal desire to increase that knowledge.

Last, evaluating the educational system and identifying desired changes were essential precursors to advocacy for most parents. While some parents identified numerous problems and blamed the school, several others were satisfied and could identify few desired changes. For parents seeking change, target areas included physical facilities, curriculum, school procedures, resource provision for children and parents, safety of school grounds, and the aspects of school context discussed above.

Parent Advocacy

Once parents decided to engage in advocacy, they utilized numerous strategies. Preparatory strategies for most parents included gathering information (e.g., unannounced classroom visits), seeking advice (e.g., consulting a teacher), and discussing issues with other parents (e.g., sharing ideas about how to establish school dress codes). An important dimension of preparation was deciding whether to intervene individually or in cooperation with other parents or parent groups. This dimension characterized both the types of problems facing parents and the level of response they selected. Table 1 facilitates conceptualization of diverse parent advocacy strategies by offering a classification based on this individual versus collective dimension.

Individual action was usually associated with a parent addressing circumscribed problems related to his or her own child, such as contesting a grade or resolving a discipline problem. Typical individual advocacy strategies included calling or meeting with the teacher or

TABLE 1. Advocacy Strategies by Levels of Problem and Response

Level of Problem	Level of Response: Individual	Level of Response: Collective
Individual	Meet with school personnel to discuss, complain, make demands	Participate in informal discussions with other parents
	Collaborate with teacher to make custom work plan for child's individual needs	Community advocacy group helps parent who has been unsuccessful addressing problem as an individual
	Enlist child or neighbor to serve as translator	
Collective	Parent becomes secret conduit for teacher's complaints to administration	Conduct advocacy meetings and political lobbying
	Parent facilitates school-based parent support activity unrelated to his/her own children	Maximize power via litigation and hiring experts
		Minimize *appearance* of power by posing as "just parents"

principal to complain, discuss, or make demands. A few parents worked collaboratively with teachers to create the resources they felt were needed (e.g., schoolwork schedules tailored to their child's individual needs) or else arranged for the needed resources themselves (e.g., having their own child provide translation at parent-teacher conferences).

A few parents also reported advocacy efforts that were carried out by individuals but targeted at collective problems. In a fascinating example of parent-teacher collaboration, teachers made secret calls to one parent, a well-known Latina activist, to report problems such as an unheated classroom or an overly punitive cafeteria monitor. The parent reported that teachers feared administrative reprisals for raising such complaints themselves, but they knew that the parent would confront the situation directly.

Collective action strategies were sometimes as simple as an informal meeting between two parents, but usually involved complex activities such as political organizing or collaboration with auxiliary participants in the school (e.g., parent coordinators) or community (e.g., lawyers, construction experts). The main supports for collective action mentioned by participants were a Latino parent coordinator hired by a local school system and a local coalition of bilingual parent action committees.

Collective action was most often associated with issues relevant to an entire classroom or school, such as health risks in school buildings or inequitable resource provision to bilingual classrooms. However, collective action was also brought to bear on individual-level problems, with a few participants reporting that advocacy groups had made themselves available to parents who had been unable to address their personal concerns without assistance. For example, a parent advocacy group helped one parent to overturn the school's exclusion of her child from the sixth-grade graduation ceremony, a disciplinary measure that some parents had perceived as unfair.

Several parents utilized collective action strategies that included recruitment of additional Latino parent activists, demonstrating a Latino political presence via meetings with school administrators or rallies at government offices, and, when unsuccessful, threatening litigation or bringing in experts (e.g., hiring construction experts in response to a facility problem). One participant reported a form of collective political maneuvering opposite to the preceding examples. He urged parents to *avoid* the appearance of having power, believing that politicians treat parents less favorably when they display political power than when they are just being "simple parents struggling for the rights of their children."

Participants' advocacy efforts led to diverse school responses. A few parents were satisfied, reporting that the school had affirmed their efforts, provided convincing plans for change, apologized for inappropriate actions, or utilized the interaction to build stronger relationships with parents. Typically, however, parents were dissatisfied or even outraged. Some felt that the school had offered ineffective solutions or attempted to silence them by offering special treatment to their children without addressing the underlying problem. Several parents also felt that their requests had been ignored or minimized, such as when school administrators failed to investigate facility problems implicated in an outbreak of student illnesses. Parent reactions to perceived school unresponsiveness ranged from disengagement to increased motivation for participation in school-based advocacy.

DISCUSSION

The current study developed a theoretical model of Latino parent strategies for addressing school-related concerns about their children's education. This model can inform the development of programs that strengthen families by building contexts and processes for effective collaboration among families, schools, and communities. Such collaboration will require recognition and valuing of the mutually enhancing human and organizational resources that each partner can contribute to the attainment of common goals, as well as recognition of the potential stresses arising from such collaborations (Sarason & Lorentz, 1998; Trickett & Birman, 1989).

The principal influences on parent advocacy suggested by the current findings are summarized in Figure 1 as parent contexts, school contexts, and associated parent involvement processes. Each of these domains offers numerous pathways for promoting family competence by strengthening parent involvement. Many programmatic implications related to parent and school contexts have already been discussed amply in the literature–for example, offering child care, transportation, and evening times for parent-teacher conferences; providing translators and bilingual school personnel; and enhancing cultural sensitivity of school personnel through professional development activities. Unfortunately, such efforts strain school resources and have not been readily implemented despite a clear need. The present findings suggest that programs should foster collaboration between parents and schools directed toward finding solutions–whether by mobilizing to advocate for systemic changes in resource allocation or governance structures (Sarason, 1995; Shirley, 1997) or by seeking creative alternatives to current utilization of existing family, school, and community resources (e.g., altering school schedules so that teachers are available periodically for evening meetings with parents, fostering child care networks among parents, encouraging employers to release parents for daytime school events, enlisting bilingual parent groups to provide translators in exchange for off-hours use of school facilities, etc.).

Coordinated efforts such as these require active engagement of parents, so programs for strengthening families through parent involvement must foster the parent and school attributes that lead to such engagement. The current findings suggest that parent interventions should seek to foster and build upon those qualities that, in response to formidable barriers, lead to parent feelings of motivation and engagement, rather than discouragement and passivity. The desired personal qualities are well-described by Kobasa's (1979) hardiness construct, which refers to individuals that have "the belief that they can control or influence the events of their experience, an ability to feel deeply involved in or committed to the activities of their lives, and the anticipation of change as an exciting challenge to further development" (p. 3). Efficacious parent advocates in the current study also displayed assertiveness, persistence, a sense of entitlement to high quality schooling, and, most basically, an awareness that desired outcomes can and should be actively pursued. This pursuit can be facilitated by helping parents to understand the processes by which schools function and change, to build skills for monitoring these processes, and to articulate goals for their children's education as a basis for evaluating schools and identifying desired changes.

Individual hardiness, efficacy, and school knowledge must arise not in a vacuum, but in partnership with schools and communities. Schools need to foster an organizational culture that welcomes meaningful parent involvement and encourages development of parent qualities needed for effective involvement. The current findings suggest that such a culture should actively solicit, listen to, and respectfully address parent opinions and concerns, with explicit attention to cultural minority group parents such as Latinos who may feel alienated, undervalued, distrustful, and fearful of discrimination. When parent requests cannot be fulfilled, a forthright and detailed discussion of relevant constraints on the school may result in additional debate, but, over time, appears likely to build parent trust and stronger parent-school relationships. Such effective collaboration with parents requires complex skills for which school personnel require specific training beyond what is typically provided in teacher education programs (Shartrand, Weiss, Kreider, & Lopez, 1997). These data also suggest that parent involvement can be strengthened by a school-based Latino parent coordinator who fosters the development of parent social networks, initiates activities for Latino parents, and facilitates their participation. The presence of such a trusted insider may be particularly important for building involvement of undocumented immigrant parents who are understandably wary about public engagement.

These data remind us that improving home-school relations requires not only the presence of supportive, accessible people, but also the creation of supportive, accessible settings (Barker, 1968; Sarason, 1972). Most notably in the current study, this included a community-based coalition of bilingual parent action groups located outside the school. Parent involvement programs both inside and outside of schools should work with existing community-based groups, understand the processes by which such groups evolve, and support the development of community-based structures and processes for parent advocacy (e.g., Shirley, 1997).

Study participants appeared to have little knowledge of, and few opinions about, higher-order ecological structures such as educational bureaucracies. However, transforming these settings has been identified as essential to effective home-school collaboration (Fine, 1993; Sarason, 1995). Parents' minimal knowledge of the educational exosystem raises two key issues. First, with respect to program development, it suggests the utility of consciousness-raising approaches (e.g., Freire, 1970) to help parents learn about their sociopolitical context and how to influence that context in service of educational goals for their children. Second, it suggests a methodological limitation of the grounded theory approach–that theoretical frameworks constructed exclusively from the perspectives of informants will omit phenomena with which the informants are unfamiliar. Hence the theory presented here is limited with regard to understanding the potentially powerful influences of larger systemic efforts.

The uncommon resilience of common folks is reaffirmed by these parents. With few external resources, many showed ingenuity, creativity, savvy, and persistence in assessing and mobilizing relevant resources and creating favorable conditions for their children. Future research should confirm the findings from this small sample with larger surveys. However, the rich specifications of important constructs permitted by this method suggest that future investigations should utilize a similar method both with this population and with other immigrant and refugee groups. In this way both the individual and environmental aspects of immigrant parent involvement can be studied and linked to the varying personal qualities and social contexts of these parents. Such investigations are needed to continue building our understanding of factors associated with the emergence, implementation, sustenance, and efficacy of parent advocacy efforts for strengthening family-school collaboration.

REFERENCES

Barker, R. G. (1968). *Ecological psychology: Concepts and methods for studying the environment of human behavior.* Stanford, CA: Stanford University Press.

Chavkin, N. F. & Williams, D. L. (1989). Low-income parents' attitudes toward parent involvement in education. *Journal of Sociology and Social Welfare, 16(3),* 17-28.

Delgado-Gaitan, C. (1991). Involving parents in the schools: A process of empowerment. *American Journal of Education, 100(1),* 20-46.

Epstein, J. L. (1996). Advances in family, community, and school partnerships. *New Schools, New Communities, 12(3),* 5-13.

Fine, M. (1993). [Ap]parent involvement: Reflections on parents, power, and urban public schools. *Teachers College Record, 94(4),* 682-710.

Freire, P. (1970). *Pedagogy of the oppressed.* New York: Continuum Books.

Glaser, B. G., & Strauss, A. L. (1967). *The discovery of grounded theory: Strategies for qualitative research.* Chicago: Aldine.

Harry, B. (1992). An ethnographic study of cross-cultural communication with Puerto Rican-American families in the special education system. *American Educational Research Journal, 29(3),* 471-494.

Henderson, A., & Berla, N. (Eds.) (1994). *A new generation of evidence: The family is critical to student achievement.* Washington, DC: National Committee for Citizens in Education.

Hoover-Dempsey, K. & Sandler, H. M. (1997). Why do parents become involved in their children's education? *Review of Educational Research, 67(1),* 3-42.

Kobasa, S. C. (1979). Stressful live events, personality, and health: An inquiry into hardiness. *Journal of Personality and Social Psychology, 37(4),* 1-11.

Lewis, M. C. (1993). *Beyond barriers: Involving Hispanic families in the education process.* Washington, DC: National Committee for Citizens in Education.

Muhr, T. (1995). *ATLAS/ti. Computer-aided text interpretation and theory building. Release 1.1E User's Manual (2nd ed.).* Berlin, Germany: Author.

Nicolau, S., & Ramos, C. L. (1990). *Together is better: Building strong partnerships between schools and Hispanic parents.* New York: Hispanic Policy Development Project.

Richie, B. S., Fassinger, R. E., Linn, S. G., Johnson, J., Prosser, J., & Robinson, S. (1997). Persistence, connection, and passion: A qualitative study of the career development of highly achieving African American-Black and White women. *Journal of Counseling Psychology, 44(2),* 133-148.

Sarason, S. B. (1972). *The creation of settings and the future societies.* San Francisco, CA: Jossey-Bass.

Sarason, S. B. (1995). *Parent involvement and the political principle: Why the existing governance structure of schools should be abolished.* San Francisco: Jossey-Bass.

Sarason, S. B., & Lorentz, E. M. (1998). *Crossing boundaries: Collaboration, coordination, and the redefinition of resources.* San Francisco: Jossey-Bass.

Shartrand, A. M., Weiss, H. B., Kreider, H. M., & Lopez, M. E. (1997). *New skills for new schools: Preparing teachers in family involvement.* Cambridge, MA: Harvard Family Research Project.

Shirley, D. (1997). *Community organizing for urban school reform.* Austin, TX: University of Texas Press.

Strauss, A. L. (1987). *Qualitative analysis for social scientists.* New York: Cambridge University Press.

Strauss, A. L., & Corbin, J. (1990). *Basics of qualitative research: Grounded theory procedures and techniques.* Newbury Park, CA: Sage.

Trickett, E. J., & Birman, D. (1989). Taking ecology seriously: A community development approach to individually-based interventions in schools. In L. A. Bond & B. E. Compas (Eds.), *Primary prevention and promotion in the schools. Primary prevention of psychopathology, Vol. 12* (pp. 361-390). Newbury Park, CA: Sage.

Weiss, R. S. (1994). *Learning from strangers: The art and method of qualitative interview studies.* New York: The Free Press.

Winters, W. G. (1993). *African American mothers and urban schools: The power of participation.* New York: Lexington Books.

Promoting Resilience Among Children of Sandwiched Generation Caregiving Women Through Caregiver Mutual Help

Jacob Kraemer Tebes
Julie T. Irish
Yale University School of Medicine

SUMMARY. Women who care for an older family member while also caring for a child under 18 years old living at home are known as sandwiched generation caregivers. These caregivers are at risk for health and psychosocial problems due to competing family role demands, and their children are at risk for poor adaptive outcomes due to their mothers' risk status. Mutual help was hypothesized to reduce caregiver risk, and thus, to promote resilience among caregivers' children. Eighty-seven caregivers were randomized into two, time-limited, mutual help conditions and a no-intervention control condition, and then one child from each family was assessed at posttest and at a 6-month follow-up. At posttest, children of caregivers participating in a mutual help group reported a significant decrease in depressive symp-

---

Address correspondence to: Jacob Kraemer Tebes, PhD, Division of Prevention and Community Research and The Consultation Center, Yale University School of Medicine, 389 Whitney Avenue, New Haven, CT 06511. (E-mail: jacob. tebes@yale.edu).

The authors gratefully acknowledge the contributions of Diane Puterski, Julia C. Levy, Linette P. Norboe, and Elizabeth G. Ricksecker in the completion of this study. They also wish to thank Deborah Tebes Kraemer and the Editors of the Special Issue for their thoughtful comments on the manuscript.

This paper was supported by a grant from the Prevention Research Branch of the National Institute of Mental Health (R01MH47310).

[Haworth co-indexing entry note]: "Promoting Resilience Among Children of Sandwiched Generation Caregiving Women Through Caregiver Mutual Help." Tebes, Jacob Kraemer, and Julie T. Irish. Co-published simultaneously in *Journal of Prevention & Intervention in the Community* (The Haworth Press, Inc.) Vol. 20, No. 1/2, 2000, pp. 139-158; and: *Diverse Families, Competent Families: Innovations in Research and Preventive Intervention Practice* (ed: Janet F. Gillespie, and Judy Primavera) The Haworth Press, Inc., 2000, pp. 139-158. Single or multiple copies of this article are available for a fee from The Haworth Document Delivery Service [1-800-342-9678, 9:00 a.m. - 5:00 p.m. (EST). E-mail address: getinfo@haworthpressinc.com].

toms and the negative impact of caregiving, and were found to exhibit increases in global functioning and social competence. In addition, the effects for social competence and the negative impact of caregiving were sustained at follow-up. These results are discussed in terms of their implications for theory and research in family caregiving, mutual help, and resilience promotion. *[Article copies available for a fee from The Haworth Document Delivery Service: 1-800-342-9678. E-mail address: <getinfo@haworthpressinc.com> Website: <http://www.haworthpressinc.com>]*

KEYWORDS. Resilience, mutual help, caregiving, women, children, grandchildren, mothers

A caregiver is someone who provides informal care for an individual who requires some form of assistance due to illness, injury, or disability (Horowitz, 1985). Family caregivers render care and assistance to a family member in one or more activities of daily living, such as grooming, dressing, bathing, feeding, toileting, transportation, managing a household, or dealing with personal finances (Horowitz, 1985; Tebes, 1998). According to a recent national survey, approximately 23% of all U.S. households–or about 22 million families–have at least one person who is a caregiver for an older family member (National Alliance for Caregiving and the American Association for Retired Persons, 1997). In this survey, approximately 75 percent of caregivers were women, 66 percent married, 52 percent employed, and over 62 percent under the age of 50. In addition, over 40 percent of all caregivers provided care to at least one child under 18 years of age living at home. These figures are comparable to others found in the literature (American Association for Retired Persons, 1986, 1988; National Alliance for Caregiving, 1997), and reflect demographic and societal trends over the past several decades which indicate that family caregiving is becoming a normative family life event (Brody, 1985; Singer & Irvin, 1991).

As a group, family caregivers are at risk for a range of health and psychosocial problems–including depression, anxiety-related disorders, and health problems–due to the increased stress and role demands engendered by this family circumstance (Cattanach & Tebes, 1991; Pearlin, Mullan, Semple, & Skaff, 1990). One subgroup of caregivers who may be at particular risk for such problems are women who provide assistance to an older family member while also parenting a child who lives at home (Tebes, 1999). Brody (1981) has described these women as caught "in the middle"–between two generations of family members, between competing caregiving demands, and often, between competing pressures of work and family. The outcome for many of these caregivers with children under 18 years of age is increased caregiver stress (Brody, 1981; Brody, Hoffman, Kleban, & Schoonover, 1989; Hamill, 1994; Tebes, 1999), heightened intergenerational conflict (Hamill, 1994; Pett, Caserta, Hutton, & Lund, 1988), diminished caregiver health (Pett et al., 1988; Tebes, 1999), increased marital conflict (Tebes, 1999), and reduced caregiver coping effectiveness (Pett et al., 1988). Drawing on previous literature as well as caregivers' own words, Tebes (1998) has described these women as "sandwiched generation" caregivers; a term that is intended to acknowledge caregivers' demographic position in American society as well as their lived experience within their own family. This term draws on, yet is distinct from, the related term "sandwich generation" which refers to middle-aged adults caring for aging parents who have *adult children* (Miller, 1981; Raphael & Schlesinger, 1994; Schlesinger, 1989; Zal, 1992).

The increased difficulties experienced by sandwiched generation caregivers poses a substantial risk to adaptation for caregivers' children. In the only study to examine explicitly the risk impact of caregiving on these grandchildren of the elder care recipient, Tebes (1999) found that children were at increased risk for depression, problem behaviors, and diminished functioning, and that the negative impact of this experience was significantly correlated with increased risk. These findings are consistent with related research which has shown that parental stress is associated with increased problem behaviors in children and families (Abidin, 1990; Institute of Medicine, 1994).

RESILIENCE PROMOTION THROUGH MUTUAL HELP

It is widely accepted that individuals faced with challenging, threatening, or otherwise adverse circumstances are at risk for poor adaptive outcomes. However, research over the past 25 years has also shown that some individuals remain resilient despite adversity (Masten & Coatsworth, 1998). This capacity for resilience involves individual variation in response to risk such that poor outcomes are reduced or good outcomes are enhanced beyond previous levels (Garmezy, 1985;

Rutter, 1987). As a result, resilience has been defined as successful adaptation despite adverse circumstances (Tebes, Irish, Vasquez, & Perkins, in press). Preventive or promotive interventions may be understood as fostering resilience when they enhance adaptation despite adversity–either through the reduction of risk or through the promotion of competence. It is in this context that resilience has been described as a multidimensional construct that involves assessments of both positive and negative indicators of individual adaptation (Luthar, Doernberger, & Zigler, 1993).

Over the past two decades, evidence from many sources has suggested that mutual help (i.e., self-help, mutual support) may foster resilience either by reducing risk or promoting competence among individuals coping with stressful, threatening, or adverse circumstances (Humphreys & Rappaport, 1995; Institute of Medicine, 1994). Mutual-help is an activity in which participants share a number of characteristics: (a) they have a common problem, focus, or status usually based on personal experience; (b) they seek personal and/or societal change in relation to that problem, focus, or status; (c) they interact as peers, usually face-to-face, in small groups; (d) they function both as providers and recipients of help; and, (e) they attend groups or other shared activities voluntarily and without remuneration (Humphreys & Rappaport, 1995; Gartner & Reissman, 1977; Katz & Bender, 1976).

Thus far, no studies have reported on the impact of mutual help interventions specifically targeted at sandwiched generation caregivers or their children. Nevertheless, evidence from related studies of caregivers suggest that mutual help which involves some combination of group education and support focused on the caregiving experience may promote successful adaptation, and thus, foster resilience (Toseland & Rossiter, 1989).

HYPOTHESES

This paper reports findings from a randomized, longitudinal trial of the effectiveness of family-focused mutual help on the promotion of resilience among children of sandwiched generation caregiving women. The study comprises three conditions: two mutual help interventions ("conventional" and "cognitive adaptation") and a delayed intervention control. Both mutual help interventions consisted of a short-term group intended to provide caregiving women with mutual support, a reduced sense of isolation, and practical assistance to meet the familial role demands of being a dual primary caregiver. In addition, the explicit family focus of mutual help was expected to promote resilience in the children of sandwiched generation caregivers. Specifically, children of caregivers who participated in either mutual help condition were expected to report reductions in depressive symptoms, problem behaviors, and the negative impact of the caregiving experience, as well as increases in social and self-esteem competence and global psychological functioning. Since the effects of mutual help were expected to be indirect and small, there were no specific hypotheses of differential effectiveness for the two mutual help conditions.

METHOD

Participants

Children of caregivers were invited into the study after caregivers were found to meet study eligibility criteria. To be eligible for the study, caregivers must have been women who provided at least 10 hours per week of care to an elder relative living in the surrounding community, *and* be the mother of a child between the ages of 6-18 living in the caregiver's home. Participants must also have identified themselves as the primary caregiver of both the child and the elder.

A total of 87 children of sandwiched generation caregiving women completed all three study interviews at baseline, posttest, and follow-up. These children were drawn from a total of 120 children, over 6 years of age, who assented to participate in the study and whose mother completed all three interviews. For the 87 children included in the study, 33 had mothers enrolled in the conventional condition, 25 in the cognitive adaptation condition, and 29 in the control condition. The were no significant differences in attrition across the three conditions, and no differences in baseline demographic and dependent variables were found between children who completed all three assessments and those available for only one or two assessments.

Demographic characteristics of caregivers and their children did not differ significantly by condition. Overall, the mean age for caregiving mothers was 44.1 years (range, 28-59 years) and for participating children 12.4 years (range, 6-18 years). Fifty-one percent of the children were female. Ninety-three percent of children were Caucasian, 4% African-American, 2% Latino/Hispanic, and 1% percent Native American. These figures were generally representative of Connecticut in terms of race/ethnicity. A total of 74% of caregivers were married for the first time, 17% were remarried, and 9% were separated, divorced, widowed, or single. In addition, social class was assessed using the Hollingshead measure of social position (Hollingshead, 1975); with 10.2% of caregivers identified as in the highest social class category (Level I), 3.1% in the lowest category (Level V), and 16.5%, 52%, and 18.1%, in categories II, III, and IV, respectively. Finally, participants reported having been caregivers a mean of 2.4 years (range, 4 months-7 years).

Interventions

Each of the two interventions consisted of 10 sessions facilitated by a caregiver–five weekly 2-hour meetings followed by five monthly 2-hour meetings. One group of caregivers were assigned to the "conventional" mutual help condition in which members shared information and concerns as they saw fit in a group context. No explicit structure for group interaction occurred other than that introduced by the members themselves.

A second group of caregivers were assigned to the "cognitive adaptation" condition in which members were encouraged to share information and concerns as they wished, but were also asked to participate in activities believed to foster cognitive adaptation. According to Taylor's (1983) theory of cognitive adaptation, individuals engage in three relatively distinct social cognitive processes to restore self-esteem and self-efficacy threatened by highly stressful experiences: finding meaning in the experience, making attempts at mastering its challenges, and engaging in downward social comparisons. Downward social comparisons are cognitions in which individuals view their coping efforts favorably as compared to similar others or consider themselves fortunate that the adverse circumstances with which they are faced are not worse (Taylor, 1983; Wills, 1987). To promote cognitive adaptation, caregivers were asked to: (1) report one caregiving "challenge and success" they had experienced since the previous meeting, and (2) to share what they had learned from their caregiving experiences since the previous meeting. Sharing one "challenge and success" was intended to make attempts at mastery an explicit aspect of the group process; while sharing a learning experience was intended to help caregivers find meaning in the caregiving experience. Furthermore, the explicit introduction of these shared activities into each group was believed to enhance opportunities for downward comparison as members learned about the details of each other's experiences. Caregivers from both intervention conditions also were provided with handouts relevant to caring for an elderly family member that were distributed by the group facilitator at the conclusion of each of the 10 scheduled meetings. Finally, caregiver facilitators for the group meetings were trained in listening, facilitation, group management, and crisis intervention skills by members of the research management team in two 3-hour training sessions with individual follow-up contacts.

In the third study condition, caregivers did not participate in any mutual help group through the study follow-up period, but were referred to existing groups once the study was completed. Further details about the mutual help interventions is available elsewhere (Tebes & Irish, 1999).

Measures

Interviews were conducted with caregiving women and their children to obtain family and child demographic information as well as to assess children's adaptation. Measures of child maladaptation included assessments of child depression, global psychological functioning, clinical problem behaviors, and the negative impact of caregiving, while positive adaptation was assessed through the measurement of social and self-esteem competence.

Children's Depression Inventory. Child depression was assessed through administration of the Children's Depression Inventory, or CDI (Kovacs, 1982). The CDI is a 27-item measure in which the child is asked to indicate which of three sentences best describes their "feelings or ideas" during the past two weeks. The CDI is a widely used measure of child depression.

Child Behavior Checklist. Child problem behaviors were assessed with the Child Behavior Checklist, or CBCL (Achenbach & Edelbrock, 1983). The CBCL is a 113-item, norm-referenced measure in which a parent is asked to indicate how well a given statement is true of their child within the past six months. The parent version of the

CBCL was used to assess problem behaviors for children under 12 years of age, and the Youth Self-Report version was used to assess problem behaviors for children 12 years of age and older. The overall problem behavior score of the CBCL was used in the present study.

Child-Global Assessment of Functioning Scale. Children's global psychological functioning was assessed through interviewer ratings of the child Global Assessment of Functioning Scale, or C-GAS (Shaffer et al., 1983). The C-GAS is a clinical rating procedure that provides a single overall rating of impairment and functioning, and is used extensively in clinical and epidemiological contexts (Shaffer et al., 1983). C-GAS ratings were made by trained research interviewers after all child measures were administered.

Self-Esteem and Social Competence Scales for Children. Ratings of children's perceived self-competence were obtained through administration of the self-esteem and social competence subscales of the Perceived Competence Scale for Children (Harter, 1982). These 12-items assess children's self-esteem and social competence by asking children to indicate which of two statements is true for them.

Impact of Caregiving on the Family and Child. The impact of caregiving on the family and child, or ICFC, was assessed with a measure developed for this study. This measure was adapted from a scale to assess behavioral problems for caregivers of elders developed by Scott, Wiegand, and Niederehe (1984). The ICFC consists of 43 items in which the child is asked to indicate the frequency from 1 (Never) to 5 (Very much or always) a given statement pertains to them individually or their family since their mother began caring for their elderly family member. The ICFC has two subscales, one consisting of 22 items which assess the personal impact of caregiving on the child (e.g., "I get upset with grandfather/grandmother." "It's nice that grandfather/grandmother likes my help."), and another consisting of 21 items which assess the family impact of caregiving as perceived by the child ("My family complains about my grandmother/grandfather." "Helping grandfather/grandmother has made my family close."). For both subscales, the ICFC was coded to provide a measure of *negative* impact of the caregiving experience as perceived by the child. The final 43 items which the two subscales were drawn from a total of 91 original items administered as part of the study. Final items selected for both the family and personal subscales were required to have an item-subscale Pearson correlation of .40 or higher.

Reliabilities for each subscale were good: Cronbach's alpha for the ICFC personal impact subscale was .92, and .88 for the family impact subscale; and, six-month test-retest reliabilities for each subscale for the control sample was .69 and .74, respectively. Finally, correlations of each subscale with other measures of child functioning assessed, such as the CDI, C-GAS, CBCL, and Harter social competence ranged from .18 to .41 in the expected direction, indicating satisfactory content validity.

Procedure

Prior to the recruitment of participants, 51 Connecticut towns were divided into matched groups of three for randomization. These towns were demographically representative of Connecticut in terms of: total population, household income, household education, urbanicity, race/ethnicity, and Spanish-speaking household status. Caregivers were recruited through direct mail announcements of the study sent to the homes of women in a given town selected by the randomization procedure. To supplement recruitment of caregivers through direct mail, caregivers were also recruited through advertisements placed in town newspapers and through letters sent to adult day centers in a given community. Children were invited to participate and asked for their assent after their mother was determined to have met study eligibility criteria and had provided consent.

Assessments were made through interviews conducted at participants' homes at study entry (pretest), immediately after completion of the intervention or approximately 6.5 months after study entry (posttest), and 6.5-months later (follow-up). When there was more than one child eligible for the study, children were randomly selected for invitation with a priority given to children 6-12 years old. Caregivers were paid a total of $50 per assessment, and at the conclusion of the baseline interview, were provided with a list of caregiver resources.

RESULTS

An initial multivariate analysis of variance (MANOVA) was conducted using the two independent variables (Intervention Condition and Time of Testing–pretest/posttest/follow-up) to predict individual dependent measures. This MANOVA was used to identify anticipated Condition × Time interactions at posttest and follow-up. Planned contrasts were then conducted to assess differential effectiveness. To facilitate analyses, a log transformation was conducted for measures whose scores indicated substantial skewness.

Table 1 depicts means and standard deviations for each measure of child adaptation by condition at baseline, posttest, and follow-up.

Depression and Global Psychological Functioning. The pattern of findings for children's depression and global psychological functioning exhibited remarkable similarity and consistency even though they were obtained through different data sources. For children's self-reported depression as assessed by the CDI, there was a significant Condition × Time interaction effect for the MANOVA: Wilks lambda = .88, $F(4,166) = 2.65$, $p < .04$, and the univariate F for this interaction revealed a significant curvilinear relationship, $F(2,84) = 4.38$, $p < .02$. As is shown in Figure 1, simple contrasts indicated a significant positive impact of the cognitive adaptation and conventional conditions, respectively, on child depression at the posttest, but a return to previous levels of depressive symptoms at the follow-up, $t = 2.17$, $p < .04$ and $t = 2.82$, $p < .01$, respectively. Repeated contrasts revealed no significant differences in effect between the two conditions.

For children's global functioning as rated by interviewers using the C-GAS, there was a significant Condition × Time interaction effect for the MANOVA: Wilks lambda = .87, $F(4,166) = 2.96$, $p < .03$, and the univariate F for this interaction revealed a significant curvilinear relationship, $F(2,84) = 5.28$, $p < .01$. As depicted in Figure 2, simple contrasts indicated that children of caregivers in the conventional and cognitive adaptation conditions, respectively, were rated as having increased their global psychological functioning at the posttest, compared with children in the control condition, but then were rated as returning to baseline levels of functioning at the follow-up, $t = 3.20$, $p < .002$ and $t = 2.07$, $p < .05$. Repeated contrasts revealed no significant differences in effect between the two conditions.

Total Problem Behaviors. For the total problem behavior score of the CBCL, there was no significant Condition × Time interaction effect for the MANOVA, indicating the absence of an intervention effect. However, all three groups of caregivers' children reported significant reductions in total problem behaviors over time, with the MANOVA for the time effect highly significant: Wilks lambda = .72,

TABLE 1. Means and Standard Deviations for Child Measures of Adaptation by Caregiver Condition at Baseline, Posttest, and Follow-Up (N = 87)

	Conventional		Cognitive Adaptation		Control	
	M	SD	M	SD	M	SD
Depression						
Baseline	6.67	3.49	6.00	4.13	6.10	3.27
Posttest	5.06	3.03	3.92	2.60	6.66	4.17
Follow-Up	6.42	4.56	6.65	3.28	6.55	3.59
Total Problem Behaviors						
Baseline	51.27	10.85	51.68	12.04	52.05	11.64
Posttest	44.30	9.91	47.39	11.92	49.46	11.16
Follow-Up	45.84	10.30	46.75	12.63	48.86	11.27
Global Psychological Functioning						
Baseline	85.47	7.96	83.81	10.76	83.86	8.50
Posttest	90.06	6.02	88.00	7.23	82.70	8.69
Follow-Up	84.53	10.11	86.19	10.60	84.40	9.42
Social Competence						
Baseline	3.26	.47	3.27	.53	3.38	.57
Posttest	3.43	.52	3.55	.52	3.26	.56
Follow-Up	3.51	.43	3.63	.45	3.46	.50
Self-Esteem Competence						
Baseline	3.44	.55	3.51	.57	3.42	.46
Posttest	3.47	.48	3.61	.38	3.50	.46
Follow-Up	3.46	.58	3.59	.45	3.46	.50
Personal Caregiving Impact						
Baseline	38.86	12.93	39.75	8.93	37.68	11.20
Posttest	35.64	10.06	35.74	9.32	38.77	8.36
Follow-Up	33.82	9.65	35.02	7.80	38.94	10.24
Family Caregiving Impact						
Baseline	48.62	12.43	49.18	11.68	47.15	8.48
Posttest	46.86	11.52	47.08	13.32	50.46	9.12
Follow-Up	45.26	10.12	45.71	11.59	50.20	9.33

The hypothetical range for each measure was as follows: Depression (CDI): 0-54; Total Problem Behaviors (CBCL): 0-226 (raw scores); Global Psychological Functioning (C-GAS): 1-100; Social Competence: 0-12; Self-Esteem Competence: 0-12; Personal Caregiving Impact: 22-110; Family Caregiving Impact: 21-105.

FIGURE 1. Plot of Baseline, Posttest, and Follow-Up Means on Children's Depression for the Conventional, Cognitive Adaptation, and Control Conditions (n = 87)

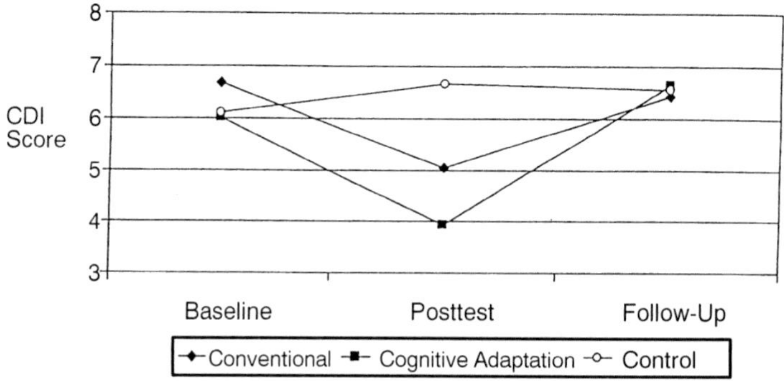

FIGURE 2. Plot of Baseline, Posttest, and Follow-Up Means on Children's Global Functioning for the Conventional, Cognitive Adaptation, and Control Conditions (n = 87)

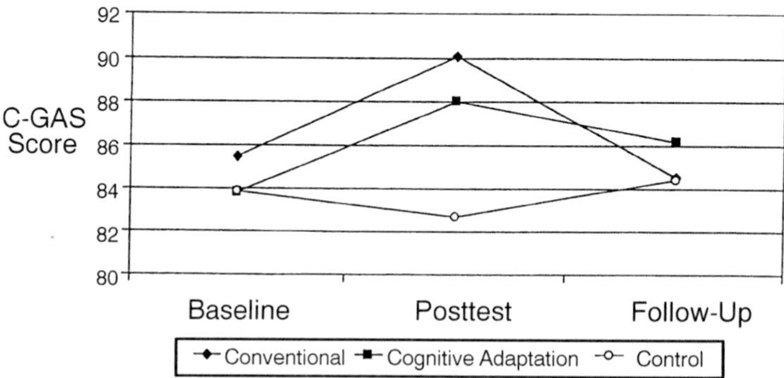

$F(2,83) = 18.82$, $p < .001$. The univariate F for time revealed a significant linear effect, $F(1,84) = 31.76$, $p < .0001$.

Self-Esteem and Social Competence. For children's social competence as assessed by the Perceived Competence Scale, the MANOVA revealed a significant Condition × Time interaction: Wilks lambda = .87, $F(4,166) = 2.95$, $p < .03$, and the univariate F for this interaction demonstrated a significant linear relationship, $F(2,84) = 4.85$, $p < .01$, and a curvilinear relationship that was significant at a trend level of significance, $F(2,84) = 2.76$, $p < .07$. As is shown in Figure 3, simple contrasts indicated that children of caregivers in the conventional and cognitive adaptation conditions, respectively, reported increasing levels of social competence, $t = 2.25$, $p < .03$ and $t = 2.98$, $p < .01$, while those with parents in the control condition reported competence scores that remain relatively comparable over time. Repeated contrasts revealed no significant differences in effect between the two conditions. No significant Condition × Time interaction effects or main effects for self-esteem competence was observed.

Negative Impact of Caregiving. Findings for both the negative personal and familial impact of caregiving were also strikingly similar and consistent to each other. For the negative personal impact of caregiving on the child, there was a significant Condition × Time interaction effect for the MANOVA: Wilks lambda = .88, $F(4,166) = 2.62$, $p < .04$, and the univariate F for this interaction revealed a significant linear relationship, $F(2,84) = 4.61$, $p < .02$. As shown in Figure 4, simple contrasts indicated that the negative personal impact of caregiving on children in the conventional and cognitive adaptation conditions, respectively, decreased over time, $t = 2.75$, $p < .01$ and $t = 2.50$, $p < .02$, while the negative caregiving impact for children of

FIGURE 3. Plot of Baseline, Posttest, and Follow-Up Means on Children's Perceived Social Competence for the Conventional, Cognitive Adaptation, and Control Conditions (n = 87)

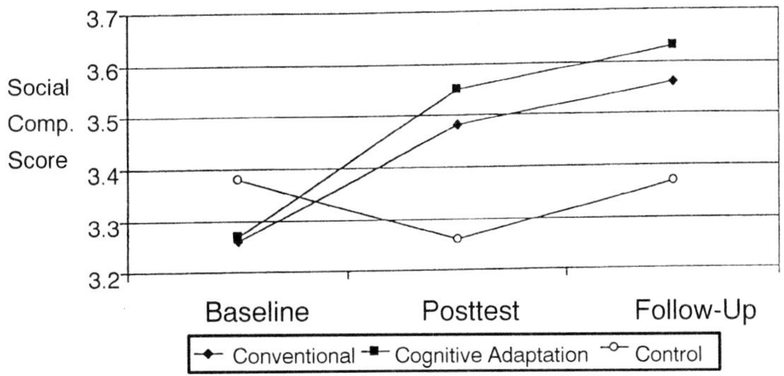

FIGURE 4. Plot of Baseline, Posttest, and Follow-Up Means on Children's Perceived Personal Impact of Caregiving for the Conventional, Cognitive Adaptation, and Control Conditions (n = 87)

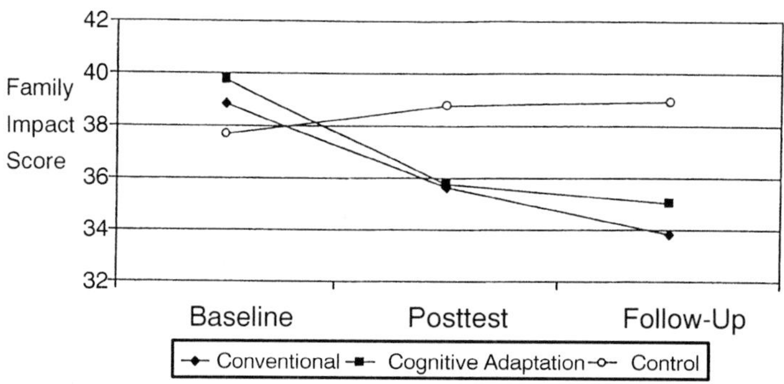

parents in the control condition remained relatively unchanged. Repeated contrasts revealed no significant differences in effect between the two conditions.

For the family impact of caregiving on the child, there was a significant Condition × Time interaction effect for the MANOVA: Wilks lambda = .86, $F(4,166) = 3.09$, $p < .02$, and the univariate F for this interaction revealed a significant linear relationship, $F(2,84) = 5.34$, $p < .01$. As depicted in Figure 5, simple contrasts indicated that the impact of caregiving on the family of caregivers in both the conventional and cognitive adaptation conditions, respectively, was reduced over time, $t = 2.90$, $p < .01$ and $t = 2.76$, $p < .01$, as compared to that observed for children of parents in the control condition. Repeated contrasts revealed no significant differences in effect between the two conditions.

DISCUSSION

These results support this study's primary hypothesis: that a family-focused mutual help intervention for sandwiched generation caregiving women promotes resilience among their children. Children of mutual help group participants exhibited reduced depressive symptoms, enhanced global functioning, reduced negative personal and

FIGURE 5. Plot of Baseline, Posttest, and Follow-Up Means on Children's Perceived Family Impact of Caregiving for the Conventional, Cognitive Adaptation, and Control Conditions (n = 87)

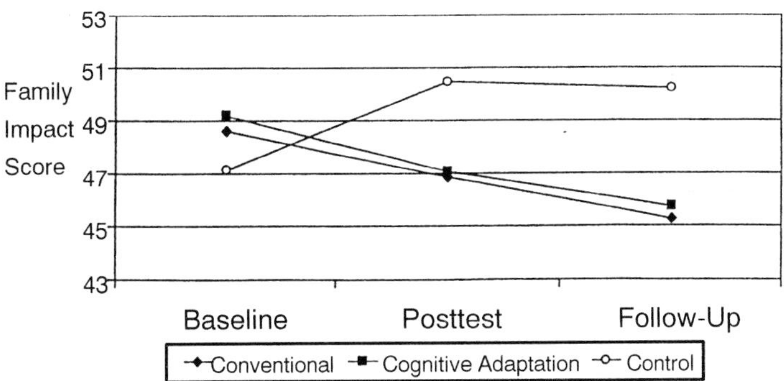

family impacts of caregiving, and increased social competence. Effects were observed for all of these measures at the posttest, and were sustained for an additional 6-7 months at the follow-up for social competence, personal caregiving impact, and family caregiving impact. No posttest or follow-up effects were observed for children's clinical problem behaviors and for self-esteem competence. Finally, no differences were observed between the two mutual help conditions on measures of child adaptation. A strength of this study was that several data sources were used to assess child adaptation. Ratings were obtained from parents (problem behaviors), children (depression, personal and family impact, social and self-esteem competence), and independent interviewers (global functioning). Importantly, the pattern of findings observed did not appear to be related to the data source obtained, providing further evidence for confidence in the findings. To the extent possible, future research should continue to use multiple data sources to examine risks and intervention impact among more developmentally-homogeneous groupings of caregiver children randomized and analyzed at the level of the town.

One limitation of this study was that, for practical reasons having to do with the feasibility of starting time-limited mutual help groups within local communities, randomization took place at the level of the town/group, and not at the individual level. As a result, analyses of individual scores across conditions do not represent results from a true experimental design because various internal validity threats (e.g., history, maturation) were uncontrolled by random assignment. For example, despite matching towns on several key sociodemographic indicators–total population, household income, household education, urbanicity, race/ethnicity, and Spanish-speaking household status–caregivers who agreed to participate in the study may have differed systematically in terms of the quality or quantity of caregiver resources available to them within their town or in the unequal distribution of adverse circumstances associated with caregiving within given localities. Another limitation was that the study involved comparisons across a wide age range–children 6 to 18 years old. This age range may have obscured actual differences in household caregiving demands experienced by children at varying developmental levels, such as children in primary grades vs. adolescents in high school. The sample age heterogeneity, however, likely made it *more* difficult to obtain differences among conditions, suggesting that the observed findings may have been even more robust than reported here.

Implications for Theory and Research

These findings have significant implications for theory and research in the area of resilience, mutual help, and caregiving. Rutter (1987) has hypothesized four processes which promote resilience following exposure to a risk factor: (1) reduction of the risk impact; (2) reduction of negative chain reactions; (3) promotion of self-esteem and self-efficacy; and, (4) opening up of opportunities. Each of these represents one type of protective process which may alter an individual's risk trajectory following exposure to risk so as to promote adaptation, and thus, resilience (Rutter, 1987). Specifically, one's risk trajectory may be altered directly by transforming or modifying the risk factor's meaning or by modulating one's exposure to, or involvement in, the risk factor. Resilience may also be promoted if the cascade of negative chain reactions that represent the hallmark of exposure are blocked, redirected, or reduced. Self-esteem and self-efficacy may also promote resilience through successful task accomplishment or through the availability of secure and supportive personal relationships. And finally, resilience may be promoted if, as a result of exposure to the risk factor, one's opportunities for successful adaptation are amplified, strengthened, or enhanced.

The present study indicates that participation by sandwiched generation caregiving women in a 6-month mutual help group likely reduces negative chain reactions and modulates children's exposure to risk associated with this family circumstance. Evidence for these effects is found in children's reports of change in the negative impact of caregiving on themselves and their family. Children whose mothers were enrolled in either mutual help condition reported *decreases* in negative impact while those in the control condition reported essentially no change or slight increases in negative impact. Even though close inspection of the impact scales indicates that such changes reveal generally low to moderate levels of negative impact, such stressors experienced for prolonged periods are likely to increase children's overall risk for poor adaptation. Mutual help for these children's mothers also fostered children's longer-term social competence and led to more positive and effective means of dealing with the caregiving situation, providing evidence of successful task accomplishment. Future research should include more developmentally-relevant indicators of risk exposure, negative chain reactions, and social competence for specific age groups of children of sandwiched generation caregiving women.

Another important implication of the present study is that it provides clear evidence of the preventive impact of mutual help. A growing body of research over the past two decades has shown that mutual help groups may be effective in reducing risk, enhancing competence, or preventing specific types of problems in living (Humphreys & Rappaport, 1995). In this connection, an important contribution of the present study is the finding of a positive indirect effect for mutual help for an at risk group not directly receiving an intervention. To our knowledge, such a finding has not been reported in the mutual help literature, indicating that some mutual help interventions may be more potent than previously believed. Future research should examine both direct and indirect effects of mutual help on individual adaptation among caregiver at risk groups.

Finally, this study provided a window into aspects of the caregiving experience of particular relevance to children of sandwiched generation caregiving women. The findings indicate that many children's lives are affected by having a grandparent cared for nearby or in the home, and that these impacts may be reduced significantly through a family-focused, parental intervention which emphasizes caregiver needs related to caring for both elders and children. Future research should examine more closely the qualitative experiences of these caregivers and their children so that interventions may be developed to better address the individual and family developmental needs of both groups.

REFERENCES

Abidin, R. (1990). *Parenting Stress Index: Short Form.* Charlottesville, VA: Pediatric Psychology Press.

Achenbach, T. M., & Edelbrock, C. S. (1983). *Manual for the Revised Child Behavior Checklist and Profile.* Burlington, VT: University Associates in Psychiatry.

American Association for Retired Persons. (1986). *A profile of older persons: 1986.* Washington, D.C.: Author.

American Association for Retired Persons and The Travelers Foundation of Hartford, CT. (1988). *A National Survey of Caregivers.* Washington, D.C.: Author.

Brody, E. M. (1981). "Women in the middle" and family help to older people. *The Gerontologist, 2,* 471-479.

Brody, E. M. (1985). Parent care as a normative family stress. *The Gerontologist, 25,* 19-29.

Brody, E. M., Hoffman, C., Kleban, M. H., & Schoonover, C. B. (1989). Caregiving daughters and their local siblings: Perceptions, strains, and interactions. *The Gerontologist, 3,* 529-538.

Cattanach, L., & Tebes, J. K. (1991). The nature of elder impairment and its impact on family caregivers' health and psychosocial functioning. *The Gerontologist, 31,* 246-255.

Garmezy, N. (1985). Stress-resistant children: The search for protective factors. In J. E. Stevenson (Ed.) *Recent Research in Developmental Psychopathology.* J Child Psychol Psychiatry Book Supplement 4, (pp. 213-233) London: Pergamon.

Gartner, A., & Reissman, F. (1977). *Self-help in human services.* San Francisco: Jossey-Bass.

Hamill, S. B. (1994). Parent-adolescent communication in sandwich generation families. *Journal of Adolescent Research, 9,* 458-482.

Harter, S. (1982). The Perceived Competence Scale for Children. *Child Development, 53,* 87-97.

Horowitz, A. (1985). Family caregiving to the frail elderly. In C. Eisdorfer (Ed.), *Annual review of gerontology and geriatrics*: Vol 5. (pp. 195-246). New York: Springer.

Humphreys, K., & Rappaport, J. (1995). Researching self-help/mutual aid groups and organizations: Many roads, one journey. *Applied and Preventive Psychology, 3,* 217-231.

Institute of Medicine. (1994). *Reducing risk for mental disorders: Frontiers for Preventive intervention research.* Washington, D.C.: National Academy Press.

Katz, A. H., & Bender, E. I. (1976). Self-help groups in western society: History and prospects. *Journal of Applied Behavioral Science, 12,* 265-282.

Kovacs, M. (1982). *The Children's Depression Inventory: A self-rated depression scale for school-aged youngsters.* Unpublished manuscript, University of Pittsburgh.

Luthar, S. S., Doernberger, C. H., & Zigler, E. S. (1993). Resilience is not a unidimensional construct: Insights from a prospective study of inner-city adolescents. *Development and Psychopathology, 5,* 707-717.

Masten, A. S., & Coatsworth, J. D. (1998). The development of competence in favorable and unfavorable environments: Lessons from research on successful children. *American Psychologist, 53,* 205-220.

Miller, D. A. (1981). The 'sandwich' generation: Adult children of the aging. *Social Work, 26,* 419-423.

National Alliance for Caregiving. (1997). *Comparative analysis of caregiver data for caregivers to the elderly 1987 and 1997.* Bethesda, MD: Author.

National Alliance for Caregiving and the American Association of Retired Persons. (1997). *Family Caregiving in the U.S.: Findings from a national survey.* Bethesda, MD: Author.

Pearlin, L. I., Mullan, J. T., Semple, S. J., & Skaff, M. M. (1990). Caregiving and the stress process: An overview of concepts and their measures. *The Gerontologist, 30,* 583-591.

Pett, M. A., Caserta, M. S., Hutton, A. P., & Lund, D. A. (1988). Intergenerational conflict: Middle-aged women caring for demented older relatives. *American Journal of Orthopsychiatry, 58,* 405-417.

Raphael, D., & Schlesinger, B. (1994). Women in the sandwich generation: Do adult children living at home help? *Journal of Women & Aging, 6,* 21-45.

Rutter, M. (1987). Psychosocial resilience and protective mechanisms. *American Journal of Orthopsychiatry, 57,* 316-331.

Schlesinger, B. (1989). The "sandwich generation": Middle-aged families under stress. *Canada's Mental Health, 37,* 11-14.

Scott, J., Wiegand, G., & Niederehe, G. (November, 1984). *Measuring behavioral problems and dimensions of family caregiving in senile dementia.* Poster presented at the Annual Scientific Meeting of the Gerontological Society of America. San Antonio, TX.

Shaffer, D., Gould, M. S., Brasic, J., Ambrosini, P., Fisher, P., Bird, H., & Aluwalhli, S. (1983). A children's global assessment scale. *Archives of General Psychiatry, 40,* 1228-1231.

Singer, G. H. S., & Irvin, L. K. (1991). Supporting families of persons with severe disabilities: Emerging findings, practices, and questions. In L. H. Meyer, C. A. Peck, & L. Brown (Eds.), *Critical issues in the lives of people with severe disabilities* (pp. 271-312). Baltimore: Brookes.

Taylor, S. E. (1983). Adjustment to threatening events: A theory of cognitive adaptation. *American Psychologist, 38,* 1161-1171.

Tebes, J. K. (1998). Reducing risk for "sandwiched generation" caregiving women. *Yale Psychiatry Bulletin,* 7(2), 14-15.

Tebes, J. K. (1999). A risk profile of "sandwiched generation" caregiving women and their children. Unpublished manuscript.

Tebes, J. K., & Irish, J. T. (1999). Impact of mutual help on the adaptation of "sandwiched generation" caregiving women. Manuscript in preparation.

Tebes, J. K., Irish, J. T., Vasquez, M. J. P., & Perkins, D. V. (in press). Cognitive transformation as a marker for resilience. *Substance Use and Misuse.*

Toseland, R. W., & Rossiter, C. M. (1989). Group interventions to support family caregivers: A review and analysis. *Gerontologist, 29,* 438-448.

Wills, T. A. (1987). Downward comparison as a coping mechanism. In C. R. Snyder & C. E. Ford (Eds.). *Coping with negative life events.* New York: Plenum Press.

Zal, H. M. (1992). *The sandwich generation: Caught between growing children and aging parents.* New York: Plenum Press.

"You Have to Be Real Strong": Parenting Goals and Strategies of Resilient, Urban, African American, Single Mothers

Anne E. Brodsky

University of Maryland Baltimore County
Department of Psychology

Katherine A. DeVet

Johns Hopkins University
School of Public Health

SUMMARY. This study explored the range of parenting goals and strategies in a sample of resilient, urban, poor, African American, single mothers. Transcripts of semi-structured interviews with 10 mothers were analyzed using a standard qualitative data analysis technique. Contrary to the negative stereotypes held about the parenting skills of

---

Address correspondence to: Anne E. Brodsky, UMBC, Department of Psychology, 1000 Hilltop Circle, Baltimore, MD 21250.

The authors thank the community members and families who participated in this study and Raymond P. Lorion, Henry Ireys, Douglas Teti, Judy Primavera and Janet F. Gillespie for their assistance.

Data for this study was collected as part of the first author's dissertation. This study was funded in part by the Society for the Psychological Study of Social Issues and the University of Maryland Department of Psychology. The writing of this paper was supported in part by NIMH grant MH18834-09.

[Haworth co-indexing entry note]: "'You Have to Be Real Strong': Parenting Goals and Strategies of Resilient, Urban, African American, Single Mothers." Brodsky, Anne E., and Katherine A. DeVet. Co-published simultaneously in *Journal of Prevention & Intervention in the Community* (The Haworth Press, Inc.) Vol. 20, No. 1/2, 2000, pp. 159-178; and: *Diverse Families, Competent Families: Innovations in Research and Preventive Intervention Practice* (ed: Janet F. Gillespie, and Judy Primavera) The Haworth Press, Inc., 2000, pp. 159-178. Single or multiple copies of this article are available for a fee from The Haworth Document Delivery Service [1-800-342-9678, 9:00 a.m. - 5:00 p.m. (EST). E-mail address: getinfo@haworthpressinc.com].

poor, single mothers, these resilient mothers described a range of planfully implemented parenting strategies designed to respond to a variety of parenting goals, including protecting their children, instilling values, and disciplining misbehavior. Mothers used parenting strategies that were congruent with their goals, the neighborhood context, and particular child behaviors. Mothers primarily used verbal instruction to instill values, but utilized a wider range of strategies, including instruction, loss of privileges, and physical punishment to correct misbehavior and protect their children. *[Article copies available for a fee from The Haworth Document Delivery Service: 1-800-342-9678. E-mail address: <getinfo@haworthpressinc.com> Website: <http://www.haworthpressinc.com>]*

KEYWORDS. Risk, resilience, single mothers, parenting practices, qualitative

Although there have been many studies of parenting failures or weaknesses among "at-risk" parents (e.g., Kellam, Ensminger, & Turner, 1977; Lindblad-Goldberg, Dukes, & Lasley, 1988; Rodgers, 1986), not much is known about the range of parenting strategies used by non-abusive, non-system involved, and furthermore, successful, urban, poor, African-American, single mothers. Poverty and ethnicity have often been suggested as risk factors for poor parenting and physical abuse (Boyd-Franklin, 1988; Kelley, Power, & Wimbush, 1992; Knutson & DeVet, 1995). Despite the fact that multiple findings of significant within-group variability suggest that variables other than ethnicity and poverty influence abuse risk (e.g., White & Cornely, 1991), variation within so-called "at-risk" samples has often not been explored. The current study of resilient, poor, African-American single mothers seeks to address this need.

The variability reported above suggests the need for studies of resilience and also highlights the fact that risk represents an elevated potential for some outcome, but by no means represents a certainty for that outcome. The study of resilience (i.e., successful outcomes which occur in individuals designated "at-risk" for bad outcome) seeks to identify those factors which mediate and moderate the relationship between risk and negative outcomes (Anthony, 1987; Brodsky, in press; Rutter, 1979). Exploration of resilience is important because the successes of resilient individuals are usually the rule and not the exception (Werner, 1986). For example, while the finding that approximately one third of abused children go on to abuse their own children suggests a risk of intergeneration abuse (Kaufman & Zigler, 1987), this finding also means that the majority of abused children do *not* go on to abuse their own children despite the elevated risk.

Because risk is not absolute and little is known about successful, poor, urban parents, study of this study of resilient parents is an important next step. This line of research allows for more accurate identification of particular stresses and risks, and thus, a more targeted delineation of the components and processes of risk and is crucial to the design of targeted and effective preventive and promotive interventions (Brodsky, in press; Masten & Garmezy, 1985; Rutter, 1979).

A recent special edition of *Pediatrics* suggested the gaps in our understanding of parenting could be addressed by exploration of the ecological, inter-individual, and intra-individual context of parenting and parental discipline strategies–physical and nonphysical (e.g., Socolar, 1996; see also: Baumrind, 1996a, 1996b; Bronfenbrenner & Crouter, 1983; Kelly, 1986).

Embedded in the discussion of parenting, context, risk, and resilience is the controversy over physical punishment (Larzelere, Klein, Schumm, & Alibrando, 1989; Polite, 1996). Prior research on physical punishment has varied from that which labeled all physical punishment as violent parental behavior associated with negative outcomes (Strassberg, Dodge, Pettit, & Bates, 1994; Straus, 1996) to research which found physical punishment to be a common occurrence not necessarily leading to serious adverse outcomes (Baumrind, 1996b; Knutson & Selner, 1994). The general impression has been that parents who use physical punishment do not use other strategies, or that other strategies are unimportant if physical punishment is used (Friedman & Schonberg, 1996; Socolar, 1996). However, Wissow (1996) points out that the extent to which families using physical punishment do or do not use other disciplinary strategies is unknown. Thus, we need to move beyond dichotomous questions of use and non-use of physical punishment to better understand parenting practices and outcomes.

One particular approach to studying parenting in context has been to examine the meaning, intention, and perception of parenting practices in the context of parenting style, child behavior, parent child relationships, family atmosphere, environmental risks, and cultural values (Darling and Steinberg, 1993; DeVet, 1997; McLoyd, 1990). Darling and Steinberg (1993) propose that parenting styles act as a context in which parenting practices are carried out. Baumrind's (1991) differentiation of authoritative and authoritarian parenting styles is among the best known examples of this approach. Baumrind focuses on parenting styles as context rather than focusing solely on specific parenting behaviors. In this typology, authoritative parents demand adherence to parental rules, values and norms, within a supportive, warm atmosphere. In contrast, authoritarian parents are restrictive, and expect strict obedience to rules without the affective responsiveness and interaction that might enhance such behavior. Recent studies have found a social and emotional advantage for children and adolescents living in authoritative rather than authoritarian homes (e.g., Maccoby & Martin, 1983; Steinberg et al., 1994). This may result because these two parenting styles produce different contexts in which time-out, yelling, or even spanking may have quite a different intent, meaning, perception and outcomes.

Randolph (1995) stated that qualitative research is needed to explore adaptive strengths of single-mother families within a family-environment transactional context. This paper qualitatively explored the *range* of parenting and disciplinary techniques, physical and nonphysical, utilized by a sample of successful, urban, poor, African-American, single mothers to meet a variety of parenting goals. Our goal was to explore the parenting strategies of successful, urban, single mothers, to contextualize mothers' parenting techniques within their community context, and to explore the interplay of parenting goals with parenting strategies.

METHOD

This study presents the content analysis of 18 semi-structured interviews conducted with single mothers raising daughters in high-risk neighborhoods as part of a larger study (Brodsky, in press). The larger study was designed to identify the stresses, resources, parenting techniques, definition and processes of resilience among single mothers raising children in high-risk neighborhoods. This paper will focus solely on the findings related to parenting.

Setting

The families lived in 7 census tracts located within 1.5 miles of each other in a predominately residential section of Washington, DC. Statistics from the 1990 Census (District of Columbia Government, 1992b) were used to identify the neighborhoods as high risk. Local published reports, key informants, community members, and observation corroborated this data. The neighborhoods were characterized by a high incidence of crime, violence, drug abuse, poverty, inadequate prenatal care and overcrowding as well as low high school graduation rates. Observationally, public housing was in disrepair, commercial establishments had heavily barred windows and doors, and gang graffiti was evident on homes, businesses and schools.

Participants

The director of an afterschool program and an elementary school principal served as key informants and recommended resilient participants. These key informants defined maternal resilience as successful parenting, ability to identify and utilize resources, successful, positive goal attainment, and positive social and emotional adjustment of both mother and daughter. The key informants knew both parent and child, and their judgements were confirmed by transcript analysis (Brodsky, in press).

The ten, African American, single mother participants were the biological mothers of a 4th, 5th, or 6th grade daughter who attended one of the key informants' elementary schools. Participants were the sole parent, but not necessarily the sole adult in the home. The mothers ranged in age from 26 to 46 (M = 34). Age at the birth of their first child ranged from 14 to 24, (M = 18.5). Family size ranged from one to four children and children's ages ranged from 3 to 26. Participants had been single mothers from between 6 and 26 years (M = 12.5). Six had never been married, while four were divorced. Three left school before completing high school; one of these women was currently working on her GED. One participant stopped school after high school graduation, one completed trade school, five attended some college, one of these women completed an associate's degree and two were still working on their college degrees. Four of the ten participants received some form of public assistance and of these four, three also had part time jobs and one was in a job/school program. The remaining six women had full time jobs, and two of these also had part time jobs. Three women received some form of child support; two had taken the fathers to court but did not receive child support. Seven of the ten reported having male 'friends' involved in their lives and of these; two lived with the women at least part time. Six of the ten women lived with family or had family living with them at least temporarily. In two cases, living with family was integral to childcare and financial stability. In three cases, participants provided care for the family members in their home and did not receive any help from these extra adults.

Procedure

Participants were recruited in two waves with new recruitment ending when redundancy in responses occurred, response sets could be accurately predicted, and "breakdown" (i.e., the ability to find evidence to the contrary of working hypotheses) no longer occurred (Agar, 1986). Eight of ten mothers participated in two, 2 hour long, audio-taped interviews; the remaining two women participated in one interview. All ten completed a short demographic survey. Participants received a $25 gift certificate to a restaurant of her choice and were entered in a drawing to win dinner for four at a local restaurant. A semi-structured, open-ended interview was used to learn how participants defined and described their lives as single mothers in high-risk neighborhoods. After obtaining a general description of their lives, four underlying questions were asked (1) what issues do you have to cope with (stresses)?, (2) what and who helps you cope (resources)?, (3) do you consider yourself successful, and (4) how do you define success? In all of these questions, parenting concerns, strategies and goals were often a primary focus. Interviews with nine of 10 target daughters corroborated mother's responses and second interviews with mothers helped to clarify themes, gain more details, check researcher understanding, and compare and contrast themes across all of the interviews. Interviews with mothers resulted in 169 examples of the interaction of parenting goal and parenting strategy.

Data Analysis

Interview transcripts were coded by the authors using template analysis style (Crabtree & Miller, 1992). In this method, initial coding categories derived from the literature on parenting were modified and expanded as they were applied to the text. In this iterative process, the text informs the coding process and coding continues until a set coding format has been applied to all text and discrepancies between text and codes have been resolved (Agar, 1986). The authors performed separate, concurrent coding application and revision, followed by conjoint review in which coding was compared and any differences in coding were aligned by consensus (see Hill, Thompson, & Williams, 1997). The final codes included the categories and exemplars of parenting goals (see Table 1), the categories of parenting strategies and exemplars (see Table 2). The interaction of goal and strategy codes was then examined in order to learn what particular strategies were used for what particular goals (see Table 2).

RESULTS

Parenting Goals

Participants described a hierarchy of parenting concerns and goals that were shaped by their experiences as mothers raising children in difficult economic circumstances and in high-risk neighborhoods. Their goal included not only correcting children's current behavior, but also protecting their children and preventing future harm, and instilling essential values (see Table 1).

Nearly all of the women mentioned that before they worry about future goals for their children, they had to meet current basic needs

TABLE 1. Three Parenting Goals After Providing the Basics

Protect from Current & Prevent Future Harm	Teach Values	Correct Current Behavior
1. Neighborhood Danger	1. To distinguish between wants and needs	1. Annoying behavior
2. Sexual Assault	2. To appreciate what they have	2. Not listening
3. Negative Peers	3. To respect parents and home	3. Not doing what told
4. Teen Pregnacy	4. To care for siblings	4. Having too many wants
5. Drugs	5. To avoid being teenage mothers	5. Acting too grown-up
6. Hanging Out	6. To value education	6. Doing poorly in school
7. Dropping Out	7. To be independent	7. Publicly embarrassing parents
8. Giving Up	8. To strive to reach goals which will better their lives	8. Having negative peers
		9. Hanging out on the streets

TABLE 2. Parenting Strategies and Reasons Used

Parenting Strategy	Goals					
	Teach Values		Correct Behavior		Prevent/Protect	
	# of Reports[1]	% of Mothers[2]	# of Reports	% of Mothers	# of Reports	% of Mothers
Instructive/Verbal						
Lecture/Explain	18	60%	12	50%	21	80%
Use Stories & Examples	3	20%	2	10%	5	30%
Positive Strategies	9	40%	1	10%	9	60%
Read from Bible/Pray	3	30%	3	30%	2	20%
Read/Write Essays	1	10%	1	10%	0	0%
Active						
Monitor/Set Limits	2	20%	8	50%	14	70%
Take Things Away	0	0%	6	30%	0	0%
Time Out	0	0%	1	10%	0	0%
Ground	1	10%	5	30%	0	0%
Ignore	0	0%	2	20%	0	0%
Fuss	1	10%	2	20%	2	20%
Holler	0	0%	4	40%	0	0%
Physical						
Tell Teacher OK to Hit	0	0%	1	10%	0	0%
Spank	0	0%	9	50%	0	0%
Threaten to Leave	0	0%	1	10%	0	0%
Send Away/Threaten to	1	10%	1	10%	2	20%
Threaten Death	0	0%	2	10%	8	20%
Threaten Another Child	0	0%	0	0%	3	30%

[1] Number of times strategy was reported to be applied to this goal.
[2] Percent of mothers reporting use of this strategy for this goal.

such as providing a roof, food and clothing. These basic parenting activities do not depend on children's behavior, and are the sole responsibility of mothers in single mother families. After providing the basics, three parenting goals were identified. The first goal, protecting their children's current and future safety, was mentioned by all of the participants. Although many mothers worry about their children's safety, this first parenting goal was a particularly serious concern for these urban mothers due to the number and severity of the risks present in their neighborhoods. Mothers in this neighborhood worried about both *protecting* their children from immediate risks (e.g., being hit by a stray bullet) and *preventing* future risks (e.g., acquiring attitudes and behaviors from gang related peers which might lead to future dangerous situations and behaviors). Teresa Brown,[1] having provided a roof, described protecting her 3 children from neighborhood risks that were close to home:

> I have my own roof over my head, but . . . somebody could come through my door any day . . . there a lot of different traffic in our hallway . . . Some people was in my hall doing a little thing that they shouldn't of been doing and the kids was walking up the steps. I took it upon myself and said, "no, ya'll getting out of my hall doing that. . . . don't come back in the hallway no more selling drugs in our hallway". . . . But I took that chance. See they could have rebelled on me and did anything to me . . . I was just saying respect the kids . . .

Grace Roberts, worried about her adult son as well as her 12 year old daughter, Marie, and described the current and future risks she saw Marie facing and how she attempted to protect her:

> OK, now as far as the neighborhood, you can't escape crime. It's everywhere. It's just more prevalent . . . in this particular neighborhood, you have so many drug dealers. . . . You have so many young guys standing on the corners. . . . (and) there is . . . one crack house. Around here. . . you just got to worry. Not only that, I worry because by her being big for her age. She's only 11 . . . but she look like she's 14 or 15. I worry about young guys approaching her or saying something to her. . . I worry about her getting hooked up with the wrong people. . . . And you've got shootings all the time. Shootings. Well she's not out after night anyway unless she's going somewhere or she's in the car or we're going across the street to her . . . brother's girlfriend's mother's house but that's as far as she goes.

Beyond protecting their children, each of the mothers described a second parenting goal: teaching their children the values, morals, and behaviors that they need to survive and to succeed. There were eight major values that were common to participants and comprised the essence of parenting for these mothers (see Table 1). Teaching these values was both a preventive measure, giving children the skills and morals that would hopefully keep them from future harm, and the basis of the behavioral code that parents expected their children to follow.

Candy Johnson described the interconnection of the values in her goals for her children:

> I want 'em to finish high school and . . . go to college and just make something of themselves and . . . I mean it's all right to have a little boyfriend . . . but not get so involved . . . that school and education . . . comes second. So . . . I'm stressing . . . them keeping their legs closed and not having babies and not getting caught up in the system and stuff like that. I don't want them to be on welfare. . . . I just want them to be something. I want them to be happy. Mainly I don't want them to have to depend on anyone else. I mean it's alright to ask somebody for help but I want them to be able to put forth the . . . most effort they can on doing it themselves. . . . I want 'em to fear God too. I think they will be OK.

Kristina Stuart described the value of appreciation she tries to instill in her daughter, Keona:

> As long as my kids are being fed and we have a roof over our head, we have a bed to sleep in, um, I have a job to go to, I can provide for my kids, everything's okay. You're living. And . . . I . . . talk to Keona. And I say, "let's look at our situation. Now let's look at someone else. There are. . .kids who don't have mothers. There are kids that are not being fed. Kids . . . (whose) parents . . . don't spend time with them. They don't take them out. They don't cook for them. They don't go over their homework. They don't do their hair in the morning. . .Those things should mean a lot to you, Keona, you have a lot". . . . So much for her to be thankful for. There's some families that don't have homes. Some families with their parents are on drugs. . ."Look at that, Keona–and then you look at your situation. You have a lot to be thankful for."

The third parenting goal was to correct current behavior. Some of the behaviors these parents correct are those points of contention in most parent-child relationship: annoying behavior (e.g., whining, teasing siblings, staying on the telephone too long, having an "attitude"), not listening, not doing what told, and publicly embarrassing parents. For example, Sonya Thomas, the mother of 10 year old Talamika, described:

> . . . my biggest problem with my daughter right now. . . . attitude . . . And a lot of people say, oh, she's growing up, you're gonna

> get that. And I just keep saying I'm ready. I can deal with this. . . but I keep trying to tell her, if you read the Bible it says do unto others as you would have them do unto you. . . . And I keep telling her that every day.

Many of the other behaviors that concerned these mothers: acting too grown-up (e.g., wearing makeup, dressing seductively, wanting grown-up things), having too many wants, having negative peers, doing poorly in school, and hanging out on the streets were related to the other two goals as well. Acting too grown-up, for instance, was of concern to mothers who saw their children growing up in a setting where childhood was often prematurely short, and early involvement with older peers could put children at risk for involvement with negative peers, teen pregnancy, distraction from their future goals and dropping out of school. Diane Martin worried about her mature looking, 12-year-old daughter and tried to make sure Kenya's behavior and dress did not accentuate this physical maturity:

> But . . . you see how big Kenya is. . . her body is more mature than her mind. And I don't wanna focus on the body so much. I wanna focus on the mind. So . . . she needs conservative-type [clothing] . . . where my daughter doesn't look like a slut. When she walks outside . . . she'll get respect. They won't be like, "hey girl," they won't be on her behind so much. They'll be like . . . "I gotta talk to this girl first. See where she's coming from." Cause . . . what you wear reflects how a person approaches you in our community.

Parenting Strategies

When participants talked about the strategies they used to raise their children, to protect them, to teach them values, and to correct their misbehavior, they first talked about the importance of having a strong parent-child relationship. They characterized a strong relationship as being built on two-way communication, an emphasis on trying to understand their child's point of view, and time spent together. Yolanda Williams described this:

> I touch my kids. I hug them. . . . Um, I try to talk to them. . . . Because if you keep telling a child to shut up . . . they're goin' a

> keep it inside and. . . . They're going to go talk to somebody else. And that might be that drug dealer down the street . . . or you don't know. . . . So you have to let the kids know that you're behind them.

As predicted, mothers described a range of parenting strategies including the use of positive strategies (e.g., keeping children busy, setting an example by going back to school), using stories and examples (e.g., talking about someone who had made the same mistake), grounding, "fussing" (ongoing, low level complaints and corrections), spanking, and threatening to send them away. Table 2 presents the complete list of parenting strategies discussed by participants. At the top of the column are more instructive verbal responses, next come action oriented responses from specifically targeted (e.g., take away a specific item, ground) to more general (e.g., ignore, holler), toward the bottom of the column are physical responses and threats.

These mothers chose their parenting strategies planfully. The simplest example of this was Teresa's explanation for why she yells: "Because I know my temper and I don't want to wait until I'm real frustrated and try to beat one of them so I do more hollering." Kristina gave an even more specific explanation of the choice of strategies:

> (I) give her all kinds of examples. But the best kinds of examples are the ones that you're actually faced with . . . now. . . . Hands on things . . . . So she can see and get a better understanding or feel . . . . Those are the best ones. I mean you can talk all you want to a child. You tell them. They forget. . . . Show me, I'll remember.

As another example of planful parenting, Catherine Clark described how her current parenting decisions will impact her ability to parent when 8 year old Precious becomes a teenager:

> You know as teenagers um, they tend to do what they want to do regardless of what you say. . . . that's why I try to develop the relationship that her and I have now. It's so that . . . when she get older . . . she can still feel free to come and talk to me about anything.

Interaction of Goals and Strategies

Planful parenting includes applying particular strategies to particular parenting goals. As Table 2 indicates, different types and strengths of parenting strategies were used to respond to different types of parenting goals. Verbal and instructive strategies were unique in their nearly equal use across all three goals and lecture/explain, in particular, was the most frequently used strategy overall. Active methods were used most often to correct misbehavior and monitor/set limits, in particular, was the second most often reported strategy overall. It was also often applied to the goal of prevent/protect. Finally, physical responses and threats were used to correct behavior and to prevent and protect. Of the physical punishment strategies, spanking was most often reported.

Within the goals in Table 2 the hierarchical application of strategies to parenting goals becomes clear. Severe strategies were rarely used for the goal of teaching values. Verbal and instructive strategies were often used to teach values. Lecture/explain, for example, was the most frequent strategy for teaching values. Sonya described this as follows:

> And I keep telling her that every day. . . . trying to teach her everything in life is not free. . . . You have to work for what you want if you want a good life. . . . When you get grown, if you want to go to college, get a good degree, get a good job. . . . You're not going to sit home twenty-four hours a day layin' on welfare . . . or thinkin' somebody's gonna knock on the door and say hey, you won a million dollars. . . . Uh-uh. Work for what you want. Strive for the best.

To meet the goal of correcting current misbehavior, mothers relied on the full range of parenting strategies, and especially lecturing, monitor/set limits and spanking. For this goal, monitor/set limits was the third most often used strategy, reported by 5 mothers, while spanking, also reported by 5 mothers, was the second most frequently used strategy to correct behavior. Grace described her use of physical punishment, drawing a distinction between spanking and abuse, and explained the progression of punishment from verbally correcting, to warning, setting limits, taking away a privilege-like the telephone, to finally using physical punishment:

> . . . I've had to whip her behind a couple of time but . . . not to hurt her or kill her . . . You know and she'll straighten up and I won't have any problem out of her for 3 or 4 months. Then she knows I'm very, very angry. . . . So yes I've smacked her behind . . . I say "Marie . . . don't let me get on you." "OK, alright." "Marie." "Man!" "No telephone," whatever, you know. . . . She has to let it build up for 3, 4 and 5 months then I (hit her) and she'll know. So, I'll hit her about 3 or 4 times on her behind or her legs and she knows.

Preventing future harm and protecting from current harm, was most often addressed by a range of verbal/instructive strategies, monitoring/setting limits, and threats of physical action including against other children who posed a risk to their own children.

Kristina gave an example of using positive strategies both to teach values and prevent future negative behavior:

> We walking down the street and I see . . . a group of teenagers and . . . if they're . . . carrying themselves in a way that I know they wouldn't act in front of their mother, I'll point it out to her. And I'll say Keona, . . . that isn't cute. . . . If you want attention be yourself. You don't have to be loud. . . .just show yourself in a–in appropriate way. You don't have to do that. Be yourself.

Catherine, below, gave a representative description of why monitoring and setting limits are necessary strategies to protect children:

> I . . . keep her on that block, you know. A lot of the children's mother may even let them go down to the end of the corner. . . . I don't like her to go that far away. . . . I am a very protective mother . . . there's so much that's going on . . . out here in the streets, that you can never be too careful. And . . . when she's outside playing, I'm sitting in the living room and . . . I look right out my window and be looking at TV–back and forth at the TV and her. . . As I say, it's . . . sad when you have to live that way to where you can't let your child go out and without you having to worry.

Threatening to harm their child was an infrequent strategy, but when used was most commonly mentioned as a way of preventing harm. Diane gave the best example of this:

> And my . . . baby son . . . he knows everything that's going on out there in the streets. And he was getting very disrespectful. . . . And . . . I was mad at his report card and I told him . . ."I will kill you." . . . I not gonna take, go and do that act. But I was letting him know, don't push me to that point. I will kill you. Be waiting on (the police) to come. Get locked up and take the death penalty before I see you standing on that corner being another Black statistic. . . . I had to say it like that . . . . because he's a Black male. Okay? In our community. . . . They're either dying or they're incarcerated.

For these successful parents, the use of physical punishment did not preclude the use of other parenting strategies, even to correct misbehavior. Fifty percent of participants reported that they used physical punishment to respond to misbehavior. These parents also reported a greater number of techniques other than physical punishment than did the mothers who didn't report the use of physical punishment. While this could mean that those parents who mentioned physical punishment merely talked more about parenting strategies overall, this nonetheless supports the hypothesis that parents who use *any* physical punishment do not use *only* physical punishment.

DISCUSSION

A common finding in resilience research is that the ability to use multiple strategies and resources is an effective means of successful coping (e.g., Anthony, 1987; Rutter, 1979; Werner, 1986). The multiple parenting strategies and goals reported by these successful mothers is in keeping with this past research. Although this group of urban, poor, African-American, single mothers would be considered at high risk for the use of poor parenting strategies, physical punishment, and physical abuse, based on some extant literature (see Knutson & DeVet, 1995 for review), they reported a range of parenting strategies, many of which are those that clinicians and researchers would recommend (e.g., monitoring; time-out; response-cost) (Braswell, 1991; Kazdin, 1988). Overall, these mothers described 14 parenting strategies that did not involve the use or threat of physical force, and the use of these positive strategies was reported much more frequently than strategies involving the use or threat of physical force. Only 50% of the mothers interviewed used physical punishment, and the use of physical punishment as a parenting strategy did not preclude the use of other parenting strategies. It is important to note that none of the mothers who reported using physical punishment are known by the key informants or interviewer to have applied punishment that would be considered abusive. These findings suggest the need for future research to move beyond questions of mere use and nonuse of physical strategies.

This is not meant to condone the use of physical punishment, or to recommend it as an effective or optimum parenting strategy. The findings, however, lend support to the literature that suggests that all forms or applications of physical punishment may not result from poor parenting strategies (Baumrind, 1996a; Larzelere, 1996). Nor is there evidence that the physical punishment used by these five mothers was having a negative effect on the children at this time. All of the target daughters identified in this study were doing well, as judging by report of the school-based key informants, mothers, and the children themselves. Participating mothers stated that they used physical punishment as a last resort and it was used narrowly to address only one type of parenting goal, misbehavior. It also appears possible that the context in which parenting occurs, as Baumrind (1991) and others have pointed out, affects the meaning, use and effect of physical punishment in the families involved in this study. Parenting in participant families was described as taking place within parent-child relationships built around talking and doing things together, listening to one another, and teaching the values that underlie the behavioral rules. This context may be important for the meaning that it lends to parenting strategies, including physical punishment. In a different context, one, for example where the only time the parent talks to the child is to correct behavior, the parent doesn't listen to the child's thoughts or feelings, or the parent is inconsistent or hypocritical, even the strategy of lecturing and explaining can be ineffective and offensive.

One important aspect of the parenting context for these ten mothers was the clear set of values and moral in which they believed, and which they thought crucial to their children's future. The goals they set and worked towards with their children were based on these values. Thus, their children begin to build not only a set of values and goals, but also a code of behavior that will help them live those values and reach those goals. And when these parents chose a particular parenting strategy, they did so planfully, thinking about the impact on their child and the goal that they had in mind. This far sightedness is also different from the view that often stereotypes poor, urban, families as reactive and shortsighted.

These mothers spent more of their parenting energy and attention teaching values and protecting their children than on correcting current misbehavior. This parenting pattern may fit the demands of the neighborhood context and the risks they saw their children facing. Current risks, such as random violence, combined with future threats, such as involvement with negative peers, and pregnancy, kept these parents ever wary. In addition, there was the fear that the stress or distraction of either of these risks could keep their children from striving to reach their full potential in school and in life. Preventing current harm and protecting from future harm was as immediate and perhaps even more frightening than confronting current misbehavior for these parents. When Diane threatened to kill her son, the immediate stimulus may have been a current behavior, but this exceptional response was motivated by fear of the future. In the larger study, (Brodsky, in press), these mothers described their resilience, not in terms of something they were, but in terms of something they were constantly striving for. The same is true of parenting. These mothers never relax, even when their children are behaving well. They remain constantly vigilant to the harm that might be around the corner, just as Catherine was constantly glancing out the window to watch as Precious played. As Carolyn Small, the mother of a grown son and 12 year old daughter explained:

> I used to think that if you raised your children right they wouldn't stray far . . . But I've seen different now so I'm not too certain about that . . . I just know that to a degree you can only do so much for 'em. Once they grown and can think a minute, or can't think a minute, you never know what will happen.

It is, perhaps, this need to be wary that also makes them such thoughtful and planful mothers. As parents who have heard that their children are at-risk for any number of reasons–for being African American, poor, from their neighborhood, the children of single mothers–these mothers work extra hard at parenting. As Tina Jordan said: "You really truly have to be strong because it's a lot out there that can harm you and your family . . . you have to be real strong."

One limitation of this study is that direct observation of parenting strategies was not included. While social desirability may have played a role in mothers' reports of sensitive behavior regarding parenting, their candor in discussing threats and examples of the use of physical punishment suggests otherwise. Supporting interviews with the children and key informants corroborated mothers' reports. Lack of a comparison sample also limits the ability to conclude that these mothers do things that are similar or different from unsuccessful mothers, parents of less successful children, or mothers in other neighborhoods. However, the goal of this qualitative study was to describe what a sample of successful mothers do and what successful parenting looks like in a group often assumed to be poor parents.

The mothers interviewed here teach us something about the natural process of successful parenting and about the range of good parenting which occurs in families described by a variety of negative labels such as "high-risk," "low-income," "single parent" and "living in a risky neighborhood." They inform us about the role of community stresses, the goals they have set for their children's success, the range of strategies they use to parent, and how all of these things interact. By increasing our understanding of the successes that occur despite risk, we will be better prepared to design and implement interventions to aid children and parents in similar situations. In this way, study of successful participants contributes to our knowledge of the natural variability of risk and resilience as well as contributing to our ability to help others reach for success.

NOTE

1. Mothers' and daughters' names are pseudonyms, most of which were chosen by participants themselves.

REFERENCES

Agar, M. H. (1986). *Speaking of ethnography.* Beverly Hills, CA: Sage.

Anthony, E. J. (1987). Risk, vulnerability, and resilience: An overview. In E. J. Anthony & B. J. Cohler (Eds.) *The invulnerable child.* New York: Guilford.

Baumrind, D. (1991). Effective parenting during the early adolescent transition. In P. A. Cowan & E. M. Hetherington (Eds). *Family transitions.* Hillsdale, NJ: Lawrence Erlbaum Associates.

Baumrind, D. (1996a). A blanket injunction against disciplinary use of spanking is not warranted by the data. *Pediatrics, 98* (Suppl. 4), 828-831.

Baumrind, D. (1996b). Personal statement. *Pediatrics, 98* (Suppl. 4), 857.

Boyd-Franklin, N. (1989). *Black Families in Therapy.* New York: Guilford.

Braswell, L. (1991). Involving parents in cognitive behavioral therapy with children and adolescents. In P. C. Kendall (Ed.), *Child and adolescent therapy,* (pp. 316-351). New York: Guilford.

Brodsky, A. E. (in press). Making it: The components and process of resilience among urban, African-American, single mothers. *American Journal of Orthopsychiatry.*

Bronfenbrenner, U. & Crouter, A. C. (1983). The evolution of environmental models in developmental research. In P. H. Mussen (Series Ed.) & W. Kessen (Vol. Ed.), *(Handbook of child psychology): Vol. 1. History, theory and methods* (4th ed., pp. 357-414.)

Crabtree, B. F. & Miller W. L., (Eds.). (1992). *Doing qualitative research: Research methods for primary care. Vol. 3.* Newbury Park, CA: Sage.

Darling, N. & Steinberg, L. (1993). Parenting style as context: An integrative model. *Psychological Bulletin, 113,* 487-496.

DeVet, K. A. (1997). Parent-adolescent relationships, physical disciplinary history, and adjustment in adolescents. *Family Process, 36,* 311-322.

District of Columbia Government. (1992b, December.) District of Columbia Socio-Economic indicators by census tract.

Friedman, S. B. & Schonberg, S. K. (1996). Personal statement. *Pediatrics (Suppl.) 98*(4), 857-858.

Hill, C. E., Thompson, B. J., & Williams, E. N. (1997). A guide to conducting consensual qualitative research. *The Counseling Psychologist, 25*(4), 517-572.

Kaufman, J. & Zigler, E. (1987). Do abused children become abusive parents? *American Journal of Orthopsychiatry, 57,* 186-192.

Kazdin, A. E., (1988) Child psychotherapy: Developing and identifying effective treatments. NY: Pergamon Press.

Kellam, S. G., Ensminger, M. R., & Turner, J. (1977). Family structure and the mental health of children. *Archives of General Psychiatry, 34,* 1012-1022.

Kelley, M. L., Power, T. G., Wimbish, D. D. (1992). Determinants of disciplinary practices in low-income Black mothers, *Child Development, 63,* 573-582.

Kelly, J. G. (1986). Context and process. An ecological view of the interdependence of practice and research. *American Journal of Community Psychology, 14*(6), 581-589.

Knutson, J. F. & DeVet, K. A. (1995). Physical abuse, sexual abuse and neglect. In M. C. Roberts (Ed.) *Handbook of pediatric psychology.* New York: Guilford.

Knutson, J. F. & Selner, M. B. (1994). Punitive childhood experiences reported by young adults over a ten-year period. *Child Abuse and Neglect, 18,* 155-166.

Larzelere, R. E. (1996). A review of the outcomes of parental use of nonabusive or customary physical punishment. *Pediatrics, 98* (Suppl. 4), 824-828.

Larzelere, R. E., Klein, M., Schumm, W. R., Alibrando, Jr., S. A. (1989). Relations of spanking and other parenting characteristics to self-esteem and perceived fairness of parental discipline. *Psychological Reports, 64,* 1140-1142.

Lindblad-Goldberg, M., Dukes, J. L. & Lasley, J. H. (1988). Stress in Black, low-income, single-parent families: Normative and dysfunctional patterns. *American Journal of Orthopsychiatry, 58*(1), 104-120.

Maccoby, E. E. & Martin, J. A. (1983). Socialization in the context of the family: Parent-child interaction. In P. H. Mussen (Series Ed.) & E. M. Hetherington (Vol. Ed.), *Handbook of child psychology: Vol. 4. Socialization, personality, and social development* (4th ed., pp. 1-101). New York: Wiley.

McLoyd, V. C. (1990). The impact of economic hardship on Black families and children: Psychological distress, parenting, and socioemotional development. *Child Development, 61,* 311-346.

Masten, A. S. & Garmezy, N. (1985). Risk, vulnerability, and protective factors in developmental psychopathology. In B. Lahey and A. E. Kazdin (Eds.) *Advances in clinical child psychology* (pp. 1-52). New York: Plenum.

Murray, B. (1996). Judges, courts get tough on spanking. *APA Monitor 27*(11).

Polite, K. (1996). The medium/the message: Corporal punishment, an empirical critique. *Pediatrics, 98* (Suppl. 4), 849-851.

Randolph, S. M. (1995). African-American children in single-mother families. In B. J. Dickerson (Ed.) *African-American single mothers: Understanding their lives and families,* pp. 117-145. Thousand Oaks, CA: Sage Publications.

Rodgers, H. R., Jr. (1986). *Poor women, poor families: The economic plight of America's Female headed households.* London: M. E. Sharpe, Inc.

Rutter, M. (1979). Protective factors in children's responses to stress and disadvantage. In M. W. Kent and J. E. Rolf (Eds.) *Social competence in children* (pp. 49-74). Hanover, N.H.: University Press of New England.

Socolar, R. (1996). Personal statement. *Pediatrics, 98* (Suppl. 4), 859-860.

Straus, M. A. (1996). Spanking and the making of a violent society. *Pediatrics, 98* (Suppl. 4), 837-842.

Steinberg, L., Lamborn, S. D., Darling, N., Monts, N. S., & Dornbusch, S. M. (1994). Over-time changes in adjustment and competence among adolescents from authoritative, authoritarian, indulgent, and neglectful families. *Child Development, 65,* 754-770.

Strassberg, Z., Dodge, K. A., Pettit, G. S., & Bates, J. E. (1994). Spanking in the home and children's subsequent aggression toward kindergarten peers. *Development and Psychopathology, 6,* 445-461.

Werner, E. E. (1986). The concept of risk from a developmental perspective. *Advances in Special Education, 5,* 1-23.

White, R. B. & Cornely, D. A. (1981). Navajo child abuse and neglect study: A comparison group examination of abuse and neglect of Navajo children. *Child Abuse and Neglect, 5,* 9-17.

Wissow, L. S. (1996). What clinicians want to know about teaching families new disciplinary tools. *Pediatrics, 98* (Suppl. 4), 815-817.

Competent Families, Collaborative Professionals: Empowered Parent Education for Low Income, African American Families

Sally Schwer Canning
John W. Fantuzzo

University of Pennsylvania

ABSTRACT. A brief empowered parent education strategy was developed and evaluated on African American, Head Start parents against a conventional parent education approach. Parents who participated in this unique approach to parent education critiqued the content and process of a conventional parent education strategy and collaborated with professionals to design and conduct their own culturally relevant parent workshop. Engagement for parents who participated in the em-

---

Address correspondence to: Sally Schwer Canning, Department of Psychology, Wheaton College, 501 College Avenue, Wheaton, IL 60187 (E-mail: Sally.S.Canning @wheaton.edu).

This paper presents results from the first author's dissertation and was funded by a grant from the National Center for Child Abuse and Neglect. It was conducted as part of The Play Buddy Project directed by the second author and funded by the Head Start Bureau and the National Center for Child Abuse and Neglect. We gratefully acknowledge support from Philadelphia Head Start and the Philadelphia Public Schools as well as the invaluable contributions of parent and professional workshop leaders Saburah Abdul Kabir, Wanda Watson, Colleen Sherman and Kristen McKee Gay.

[Haworth co-indexing entry note]: "Competent Families, Collaborative Professionals: Empowered Parent Education for Low Income, African American Families." Canning, Sally Schwer, and John W. Fantuzzo. Co-published simultaneously in *Journal of Prevention & Intervention in the Community* (The Haworth Press, Inc.) Vol. 20, No. 1/2, 2000, pp. 179-196; and: *Diverse Families, Competent Families: Innovations in Research and Preventive Intervention Practice* (ed: Janet F. Gillespie, and Judy Primavera) The Haworth Press, Inc., 2000, pp. 179-196. Single or multiple copies of this article are available for a fee from The Haworth Document Delivery Service [1-800-342-9678, 9:00 a.m. - 5:00 p.m. (EST). E-mail address: getinfo@haworthpressinc.com].

powered strategy was significantly greater than parents who participated in the conventional one. Content was judged as more relevant and presenter behavior was judged as more respectful than in the conventional approach. Ninety percent of participants queried preferred empowered parent education when asked which workshop they would attend if given the choice. Implications for our understanding of the construct of empowerment as well as for the design and implementation of parent education strategies with low-income and minority parents are discussed. *[Article copies available for a fee from The Haworth Document Delivery Service: 1-800-342-9678. E-mail address: <getinfo@haworthpressinc.com> Website: <http://www.haworthpressinc.com>]*

KEYWORDS. Parent education, parent training, empowerment, cultural relevance

Low-income, urban, minority families are faced with considerable difficulties as they raise children in contexts exposing them to the multiple risk factors associated with poverty (Garbarino, 1995). Parent education represents one line of approach taken by professionals to support families facing these challenges. Although positive outcomes from these interventions (such as decreases in children's externalizing behavior) have been reported over the last three decades (e.g., Barkley, 1987; Graziano & Diament, 1992; Patterson, 1976;) significant limitations persist in parent training with low-income families who are members of ethnic minority groups.

Problems attracting and retaining participants, achieving comprehensive treatment gains, and maintaining desired outcomes over time have been consistently reported when targeted parents are poor (Dumas, 1984; Israel, Silverman, & Solotar, 1986; Kitzman, Cole, Yoos, & Olds, 1997; McMahon, Forehand, Griest, & Wells, 1981), of single-parent status (Clark & Baker, 1983; Webster-Stratton, 1985), or of minority group status (Holden, Lavigne, & Cameron, 1990; Myers et al., 1992). Investigations of impediments to the success of parent education have tended to focus on these parent status variables along with other participant-related factors such as parental intelligence, psychopathology, level of distress before parent training, social isolation, and negative expectations of training (e.g., Patterson & Chamberlain, 1994; Wahler, 1980; Webster-Stratton, 1992).

An alternative to this focus on participant characteristics has been taken by those who have examined the content of parent education itself for clues as to why previous strategies have been less successful with some families. One clear factor was that culture was not attended to. As early as 1984, Lieh-Mak, Lee and Luk noted the impact of cultural differences in child rearing beliefs between Chinese parents and their parent trainers. More recently Forehand and Kotchick (1996) have issued a "wake-up call" for parent trainers to more seriously examine the role cultural values and practices play in shaping the content of effective parent education. Most attempts at culturally sensitive parent education have involved language translation only, or represent "cultural adaptations" which do not substantially transform the essential content of traditional parent education programs (Gorman & Balter, 1997). "Culturally-specific" programs which are "not merely derivations of traditional programs, but are formatted to be relevant to the target ethnic group" (Gorman & Balter, 1997, p. 343) are rare.

Culture has important implications not only for the content of parent education efforts, but for the process as well. Although mistrust toward professional helpers on the part of poor and minority consumers has been highlighted in recent research on a variety of interventions (Harris, Gorelick, Samuels, & Bempong, 1996; Nickerson, Helms, & Terrell, 1994; Pakman, 1995), it has received only minimal attention within parent education (Ayoub & Jacewitz, 1982). Engagement and training processes will need to be designed to actively foster trust and counter experiences of exploitation in the helping context.

Despite the minimal direction provided by studies specifically evaluating parent education, the literature on empowerment may be drawn upon to formulate and test more culturally congruent models for these interventions. The concept of empowerment has been viewed as both a means and an end state (Kieffer, 1984). It has been assessed at individual and group levels (Wallerstein, 1992) and it has been considered as both a psychological and political phenomenon (Rappaport, 1987). Regardless, discussions of empowerment usually incorporate the concepts of self-efficacy and self-determination, in which individuals or groups gain control over meaningful events, are able to share power in decision making, and have the ability to participate in changing the status quo and make new realities (Rappaport, 1987; Zimmerman, Israel, Schulz, & Checkoway, 1992).

Empowerment theory has obvious implications for the way in which helping strategies should be configured, particularly those that target poor and ethnically diverse families. Collaboration and partnership replace the more hierarchically structured conventional approaches which emphasize the contribution of an expert to a recipient (Riessman, 1990). Distinct cultural norms and expectations can be considered and incorporated within such a process. The application of empowerment theory to intervention strategies has been broadly described in a number of published accounts (e.g., Dunst & Trivette, 1987; Gruber & Trickett, 1987; Kalyanpur & Rao, 1991). More recently, advances have been made in the empirical study of empowerment as a more precise guide for conducting interventions (Cherniss, 1997; Heflinger, Bickman, Northrup, & Sonnichsen, 1997).

Following in this vein, the study presented here was an attempt to apply empowerment principles to parent education in order to increase the engagement of a group of low-income, African American parents and to enhance their perceptions of the content and process. To address the serious mismatch between the content and process of conventional parent education strategies and the culturally shaped competencies and needs of targeted parents, the investigators had three primary aims: (1) to examine how translating empowerment concepts into intervention methods would modify the conventional structure of parent education, (2) to test whether operationalized empowerment principles could be detected by consumers and, if so, (3) whether a strategy employing operationalized empowerment strategies would make a meaningful difference in their experience of the process. An empowered parent education strategy was developed, implemented and evaluated by comparing it with an approach based on conventional parent education methods. It was expected that the empowered parent education technique would be superior to the conventional method in its ability to involve low-income, African American parents and convey a sense of relevance and respect to its participants. Concurrently, an assessment device capable of capturing salient features of empowered parent education was designed and tested.

METHOD

Participants

One hundred twenty-six parents or guardians of preschoolers in a large urban Head Start program participated in the study. Participants were predominantly African American (95%) females (92%) of low socio-economic status by virtue of their children's Head Start eligibility. Participants' ages ranged from 20 to 64 with a mean age of 31 years. The majority were single (59%), unemployed (70%), and had some educational experience beyond high school (44%). While all participants in the study were parenting at least one preschool-aged child, the ages of all children in the families studied ranged from three months to 29 years old. The youngest children in the families studied had an average age of 3.3 years and the average age of their oldest children was 8.1 years.

Participants were recruited in the context of a series of ongoing, collaborative evaluation projects between a large private university and the public school district of a major urban center in the Northeast. The projects were conducted in the highest-risk neighborhoods for preschoolers. The communities served by these Head Start centers accounted for over 85% of the city's physically abused children, were disproportionately represented by families on public assistance, and had a mean family income below the poverty line (Fantuzzo, Weiss, & Coolahan, 1998).

Measures

Empowered Parent Education Scale (EPES). The 10-item EPES scale was designed by the authors in close collaboration with Head Start parents to tap perceptions about the nature and degree of participants' and presenters' involvement in parent education workshops. (While evaluations of parent training and other interventions have used traditional consumer satisfaction scales to measure participant responses, no measures tapping empowering features of parent training strategies could be identified at the time of the study.) EPES items were developed based on concepts from the empowerment literature and parent collaborators' observations from participation in parent education workshops. Items relate to a variety of workshop features such as (a) the degree to which parents spoke, shared personal material and displayed emotion, (b) the relevance of material presented, (c) the amount of interest shown in parents' lives by the presenter, and (d) whether or not the role of expert was assigned to parents or presenters. The forced-choice item format was taken from The Perceived Competence Scale for Children (Harter, 1983). Respondents endorse one of two statements best describing a workshop they just experienced, for example, "In some workshops parents talk a lot" versus "In other workshops parents talk a little." The scale is scored by assigning a point value of 0 or 1 to each item. A 15-item version of the EPES was piloted on a group of 51 parents for clarity, ease of completion and culturally-sensitive wording. Scale analyses yielded consistent item skews, adequate variability in responses (*SD*s = .25 to .33) and good reliability (α = .83). An oblique principal components cluster analysis was performed to examine the scale's dimensionality (Canning, 1994). Two reliable dimensions comprising 10 items of the original scale were identified: Parent Involvement (α = .72) and Presenter Respect for Parents (α = .70). Total scale scores were computed by summing item scores within each dimension. (A copy of the scale and individual item cluster loadings are available from the first author.)

Procedure

To carry out the study's objectives a three-stage process of intervention and assessment was devised in which (1) a group of parents participated in either empowered or conventional parent education sessions, (2) prototypical videotapes were developed and (3) a second group of parents rated the prototypical videotapes.

Stage I: Workshop Development and Participation. During the first part of the study, two parent education conditions were developed by the authors: an empowered parent education condition and a conventional one. Two-session workshop series were designed for each condition and were conducted with 43 parents from four Head Start centers. Participants were randomly assigned to either experimental or control conditions. The setting for both approaches was the parents' Head Start center and workshops were delivered to parents in a group format. All sessions were held at the start of the school day and lasted approximately 90 minutes. The conditions were facilitated by two teams of workshop leaders each consisting of one White professional (doctoral students in psychology) and one African American para-professional (parents from the Head Start community).

The *Empowered Parent Education* condition (EPE) was designed to operationalize such empowerment concepts as partnership (e.g., flexibility, decentralization of authority), critique (e.g., evaluation of the status quo), co-construction (e.g., participant involvement, compatibility with the needs, values, and past experiences of the community), and mastery (e.g., the ability to effect real change in a system). Partnership principles guided entry and recruitment procedures and the structure of facilitator roles. The choice of setting prioritized participant convenience and comfort and recruitment activities were carried out in close collaboration with Head Start parent consultants, as well as Head Start teachers, Parent Education Coordinators and school principals. Parent and professional workshop leaders were assigned equal roles in conducting the sessions, distributing power evenly and reflecting the assumption that each brought distinct resources and limitations to a mutually valued goal.

In the first session, parents were given the opportunity to critique the sort of parent education opportunities which have been a long standing tradition in Head Start. Parents were shown the "Typical Parenting Workshop" videotape, created by the authors, simulating characteristics of local Head Start parenting workshops. In the tape, an African American professional discusses common preschool child problems in a lecture format. Parents were asked to imagine they were participants in the taped workshop and were told they would be asked their opinions about the workshop after viewing the tape. Group discussion followed with questions about features of the content and process of the workshop such as need, relevancy, interest, enjoyment, and desire for involvement.

After some initial caution, parents voiced numerous negative responses to the taped workshop as well as other experiences with professionals. Criticisms related to the presenter's expertise and motivation (e.g., "doesn't sound like she's a parent," "doesn't seem like she really cares, she's just doing it because it's a job"), as well as the content ("black children don't have temper tantrums," "that sounds like the Cosby way") and the format ("boring," "like she's reading from a book") of the workshop itself.

Workshop leaders recorded parent reactions, then revisited them, this time asking parents to generate alternatives which would improve the workshop. Brainstorming culminated in the opportunity for parents to create their own workshop, incorporating the ideas just generated. The rest of Session I was devoted to planning a workshop that would be carried out in Session II for their Head Start center. EPE participants returned the next week to execute the workshop they had planned for an audience of parents from their center.

Session II workshops varied in content and format, but all involved high levels of parent participation, little or no participation from the workshop leaders and placed a high priority on "real life" contributions from parents in the audience. By far the most striking EPE workshop was a skit based on the Oprah Winfrey show "Parents 'n the Hood" in which Oprah, a panel of parents, and audience members debated about what a child should be taught in response to aggression from a peer. This delightfully creative and engaging skit (conceived entirely by the parents) included a "commercial" break in which children from the Head Start classrooms were brought in to demonstrate and promote play between parents and children.

The *Conventional Parent Education* approach (CPE) involved content and format commonly found within published, professionally-designed parent training strategies. Specifically, CPE was designed to closely resemble the parent workshops typically offered by Head Start in the study's locale. Based on direct observation of workshops and extensive discussions with parents and staff during the year preceding the study, the essential elements of existing parent training strategies were identified and formed the basis for the CPE condition. Following convention, a topic area was identified by parents ("the challenges of raising a preschooler") and assigned to the professional workshop leader. For the first CPE session, the professional workshop leader was instructed to gather information from parents on 'real life' examples of common difficulties with preschool children. Parents in the conventional parent education group were also shown the "Typical Parenting Workshop" videotape. However, instead of soliciting their critique of the workshop, workshop leaders used the videotape as a catalyst to share brief stories of common preschooler difficulties. Parents were asked to record personal examples of difficulties identified on the tape (e.g., temper tantrums, fears, problems playing with other children and chores). Parents' examples were read aloud by the workshop leader who asked the group to identify how many had experienced that difficulty. The professional workshop leader led a discussion of the examples but the process of parent training was not examined (distinguishing the session from the fundamental components of the first EPE session). The parent workshop leader (her role was left relatively undefined by the experimenter) ran videotape equipment and joined minimally in the discussion of examples.

For Session II the professional workshop leader was asked to design a workshop based on her understanding of the concerns and experiences voiced by parents during the first session. She chose the topic of preschool child development in which she highlighted the emerging abilities of preschoolers in contrast to toddlers. As was customary, the professional functioned essentially as an "outside expert," engaging in instruction through the presentation of developmental information and examples. While some parents initiated comments or questions during this time of instruction, most parental input occurred during the approximately fifteen minutes structured by the presenter for questions and discussion following the lecture. The proportion of CPE workshop time allotted to instruction and discussion versus participatory, hands-on activity was comparable to that documented by Fantuzzo, Childs, Stevenson, Coolahan, Ginsburg, Gay, Debnam, and Watson (1996) in their comparison of Collaborative versus Workshop Training at a Head Start Teaching Center in this same locale. Similar to the first session, the parent workshop leader played a supportive role, running equipment and entering in to the discussion in only a peripheral manner.

Stage II: Development of "Prototypes" Videotape. In order to examine differences in the EPE vs. CPE workshops, videotapes were created containing a prototypical example of participant behaviors in each condition. The prototypes were empirically derived by the first author through a careful review of videotapes of the 14 workshops conducted during Stage I. After viewing the tapes in their entirety, an eight-minute continuous segment of each condition was preliminarily selected as prototypical of an EPE or CPE workshop. Three criteria were used to select the segments. First, the segments had to be of continuously high quality so that both audio and visual aspects could be clearly reproduced and understood by subsequent viewers. Second, the segments needed to focus on globally similar content areas. And finally, they needed to be adequately representative of the condition on two aspects of parent behavior: how often and how many parents spoke during the sessions.

In order to determine if the final criterion was met, two additional four-minute segments of each of the 14 videotaped sessions were randomly selected. (Beginning and ending sections of each session were excluded as they consisted of activities such as introductions and explanations of the measures.) The 28 segments were coded in 15-second intervals by the first author for the presence of any parent speaking and the total number of parents speaking in an interval. The EPE and CPE prototype segments were also coded so comparisons against the random samples could be made.

Coding results confirmed that the segments were suitable prototypes of the empowered and conventional conditions. Prototype means on both number of parents speaking per interval and number of intervals in which a parent spoke fell within one standard deviation of means for the respective condition as a whole.

Stage III: Assessment of Parental Perceptions of Empowerment vs. Conventional Conditions. In the final stage of the study, five groups of Head Start parents (N = 126) rated the Empowered Parent Education and Conventional Parent Education workshop conditions. Parents viewed the Prototype videotapes in randomized order, and completed the Empowered Parent Education Scale after each segment. Immediately following their ratings of both workshop conditions, a subset of participants were asked to record which condition they would attend if given the choice.

RESULTS

In order to examine whether parents' ratings on the EPES scales (Parent Involvement and Presenter Respect for Parents) differed across the two parent education strategies and by order of presentation, a three-way ANOVA was employed. The first factor was held as a between-subjects factor and corresponded to the two groups of participants randomly assigned to order of presentation of the strategies. The second factor was a within-subjects factor, which represented the empowered and conventional parent education workshops that each participant experienced, and the third factor corresponded to parents' scores on the two EPES scales (within-subjects). The purpose of these analyses was to discover significant interactions of Order of presentation or Type of workshop with the two EPES scale scores (Involvement and Respect). The repeated measures procedure is a robust data analytic strategy for this purpose, which afforded both enhanced statistical power and parsimony due to the simultaneous consideration of parents scores on the EPES scales as a repeated measure. Results of the analyses are summarized in Table 1.

Parents' EPES ratings of the empowered condition were significantly higher than ratings of the conventional one. Scores across both conditions were elevated when the conventional condition was viewed

TABLE 1. Analysis of Variance Comparing EPE and CPE on EPES Scales by Order of Presentation

Source	df	F	ω^2
	Between subjects		
Order	1	37.54**	.05
Error	124	(2.35)	
	Within subjects		
Type	1	247.01**	.42
Type x Order	1	17.51**	.03
Error	124	(2.85)	
Scale	1	3.26	
Scale x Order	1	1.66	
Error	124	(0.77)	
Type x Scale	1	8.28*	.003
Order x Type x Scale	1	19.15**	.01
Error	124	(0.58)	

Note. Values enclosed in parentheses represent mean square errors.
*p <. 005. **p < .0001.

first. Post-hoc comparisons demonstrated that the order of presentation of the conditions had differential effects on EPES subscales. The three-way Order × Condition × Dimension interaction revealed that parent involvement scores were sensitive in interaction with order and condition. Parent involvement ratings were lower for EPE when that condition was viewed first and higher for CPE when that condition was viewed first. Presenter respect scores differed as a function of order for CPE only, with CPE respect scores significantly higher when viewed first. Post-hoc comparison means for the three-way interaction are reported in Table 2.

Workshop preference scores obtained on a subset of participants (n = 52 or 41%) were overwhelmingly in favor of the empowered condition with 90% of the participants choosing this workshop, 6% selecting the conventional workshop, and 4% abstaining.

DISCUSSION

This study provides support that participants in empowering parent education strategies may be more involved and feel more respected than participants in conventional strategies. EPES ratings of the empowerment condition appear to confirm the link between empow-

TABLE 2. Three-Way ANOVA: Means and Standard Deviations of EPES Scores for Order x Workshop Type x Dimension

	EPE		CPE	
Order	PI	PR	PI	PR
A	4.25(0.96)	4.59(0.68)	1.36(1.59)	1.50(1.68)
B	4.85(0.44)	4.40(0.90)	2.63(1.66)	3.16(1.60)

Note. n = 64 (Order A), n = 62 (Order B). PI = Parent Involvement, PR = Presenter Respect. Order A: (1) EPE (2) CPE; Order B: (1) CPE (2) EPE. Data are represented in raw scores with a maximum score of five per dimension. All means are harmonic means.

erment and involvement which has been drawn in the literature (Curtis & Singh, 1996; McCann & Weinman, 1996; Rissel, Perry, Wagenaar & Wolfson, 1996). An interesting "chicken or egg" question exists in relation to these two concepts, as raised by Zimmerman and Rappaport (1988). The methods of this study are predicated on assumptions about the influence of empowerment on participation. While questions of directionality cannot be answered in a correlational, cross-sectional study such as this one, these findings are at least consistent with the view that empowering experiences create a propitious environment for participant involvement. Additionally, despite a sizable main effect for condition, qualitative observation of participants in the conventional condition spotted individuals who were more highly involved than their peers. A prime example was the parent who openly challenged the workshop leader's pronouncement that high frequencies of sibling squabbles should be considered "not normal." The presence and input of these parents who demonstrated empowerment, despite the absence of empowering conditions, also appears to support the contention that empowered individuals participate to a greater degree. Moreover, for these individuals the effects of empowerment over time may be resilient in the face of even disempowering conditions. It seems reasonable that a transactional relationship exists between empowerment and participation such that more "empowered" individuals participate at higher levels. Also, certain forms of engagement in the parent training process may have empowering effects. Participation that is meaningful for parents and which results in outcomes observable to them, as in the EPE condition, may reinforce a sense of self-efficacy and entitlement that would make it more likely for those parents to involve themselves in future opportunities.

Item analyses and scaling of the EPES lend credence to the feasibility and importance of developing assessment techniques which capture salient features of empowered participant, presenter and intervention characteristics. Thus far, parent engagement has primarily been assessed as a function of the degree of attendance in a particular setting (e.g., number of treatment sessions). Little is known about the processes that occur inside parent involvement contexts once participants have "shown up." By measuring engagement within the process, the EPES was able to distinguish two distinct participant environments, information that a simple comparison of numbers in attendance would not have revealed. A greater understanding of the relationship between specific intervention strategies and participants' engagement in those processes could mean the difference between unsuccessful and truly empowering interventions.

The importance of enhanced involvement and attributions of respect, however, lies in a hypothesized relationship between those factors and increased success in the delivery and outcomes of parent education efforts. This study did not directly test the effect of these enhanced attributions on outcome variables such as treatment completion rates or on changes in targeted training variables such as parent-child interactions. However, some evidence exists that the variables measured by this study may act as mediators for parent education outcomes. Problems of treatment delivery and outcome may occur, in part, when interventions fail to engage and promote the motivation of parents who face multiple life demands, have few supports and are assailed by unpredictability in their circumstances.

Research into the theory of achievement goals has begun to identify characteristics of adaptive motivational patterns that sustain goal directed effort over time. Several are comparable to empowerment concepts and their implementation in the EPE intervention. Ames (1992) identifies a number of features of the classroom environment which contribute to a "mastery-oriented" motivational pattern. This pattern requires that learning should be adapted to students' interests, oblige active student involvement in the form of leadership, provide for challenging but realistic choices and decision making, and foster positive, cooperative peer relationships. A mastery-orientation to learning has been associated with students' perceptions of increased competence in their own abilities and positive attitudes about school and learning. This appears to be particularly the case with at-risk students.

Frymier, Shulman, and Houser's (1996) recent study of college students lends further support to this contention in their finding of an significant association between empowering aspects of teacher communication and student motivation and learning. While a college population differs significantly from an urban, low-income, population of minority parents, the fact that empowering concepts have been effectively translated into aspects of the classroom environment and are associated with enhanced motivation is promising for parent education efforts. A connection between involvement and motivation certainly seems to be supported by the fact that parents in this investigation overwhelming picked the empowered workshop as the one they would attend if given a choice.

In addition to increasing participant involvement, increasing parents' perceptions of workshop relevance and presenter respect may be critical to designers and implementers of intervention strategies. For low-income and minority communities, interventions may be viewed as invasive, dangerous, irrelevant, or requiring the participant to become 'invisible' in order to obtain necessary resources, even in the hands of caring, ethical professionals (Ayoub & Jacewitz, 1982; Goodban, 1985). One moment in an EPE workshop powerfully illustrates the negative experiences parents have had with professional helpers. A woman who had been sharing at length about her young son's formidable conduct problems suddenly asked the group, "I want to ask you . . . do y'all think therapy really works?" Heads and shoulders turned from around the room as parents let out a spontaneous and resounding "No!" An emotionally-charged discussion of the inadequacies of "psychiatrists" ensued including the length of wait for treatment (e.g., "they called me back three months later and I said I had it all under control") and the lack of significant benefits from therapy (e.g., "you talk, they write down . . . then he said what I already told him, that I was under a lot of stress!").

Parents spoke frequently in the workshops of being made to feel angry or defensive by professionals adopting the posture of an expert, a posture that they found condescending. Especially distasteful to participants was the notion that experts conveyed the sense of "having the answer." Instead, parents repeatedly expressed their belief that "there is no one right way" to respond to parenting challenges and that professionals are most useful in helping parents know what options are available, not by saying "this is how you solve the problem."

One parent described his alternative vision for parent educators this way: "Relationships are the key. Get to know the parents, befriend them, they'll open up, relationships can grow and develop respect for each other."

Perceived relevancy in parent education may also help foster openness in parents to the degree that they will more likely derive benefit from the experience. Videotaped records of EPE workshops indicate that, compared to discussions in the conventional condition, parents were more likely to express personal material. Examples of topics unique to the empowered condition include frequent conversations about the intrusion of the local protective service agency into families' lives, frank opinions about differences in parenting styles between Black and White parents, and stories of less typical, more serious child behavior problems such as fire setting or attempted suicide.

Although the relevance of content and goals has been shown to be predictive of success in some adult educational experiences (Diekhoff & Wigginton, 1989) participants' statements in these workshops reveal the extent of irrelevance attributed to their experiences with professional helpers. These comments include describing the presenter's recommendations for child behavior management as "the Bill Cosby way," responding to workshop content and the presenter's style with "where does she get her information, does she deal with Black people?", "she needs to look at it from the 'real' side of life, you know, like a real woman," or "statistics say you're supposed to do this, that's not real life." Attempts by the CPE facilitators to elicit information from parents on public temper tantrums were consistently met with objections that this is a problem for "White people" only, since Black parents did not allow their children to "fall out."

Open, honest dialogue, then, may need to occur between parents and professionals about what and how parents are being taught; in order for professionals to design and conduct maximally effective interventions and for parents to truly benefit from them. The nature of much parent education mitigates against this sort of honesty, however. Parents may be concerned about the consequences of challenging content or process, especially in cases where parent training is a requirement to keep or have their child returned to them. Along with concerns about the threat of reprisal are the dampening effects of power differences between presenters and participants. One parent commented, "some [parents] are raised that the authority knows everything and they won't speak up and ask questions, [they think] they're not allowed to, they're intimidated." Not only this, numerous participants voiced a sincere wish not to show disrespect to professionals, and several were even concerned that their criticism might lead to the workshop presenter losing her job.

Parent education is one vital component in a comprehensive array of supports necessary for multiply-stressed communities. But not necessarily in the forms by which these techniques have been known thus far. Empowering concepts hold promise for bridging the present gap between our limited parent education strategies and the competencies and needs of poor families from diverse cultures. But the distance to be spanned is a great one. This project was a beginning attempt to empirically translate empowerment principles into assessment and intervention strategies with a low-income, urban, African American community. The hope is that increasing numbers of parent educators will begin to partner with community citizens to engineer and test new strategies built upon these principles.

REFERENCES

Ames, C. (1992). Achievement goals and the classroom motivational environment. In J. Meece & D. Schrunk (Eds.), *Student perceptions in the classroom* (pp. 327-348). Hillsdale, NJ: Erlbaum.

Ayoub, C. & Jacewitz, M. M. (1982). Families at risk of poor parenting: A model for service delivery, assessment, and intervention. *Child Abuse and Neglect, 6,* 351-358.

Barkley, R. A. (1987). *Defiant children: A clinician's manual for parent training.* New York: Guilford.

Cherniss, C. (1997). Teacher empowerment, consultation, and the creation of new programs in school. *Journal of Educational and Psychological Consultation, 8*(2), 135-152.

Clark, D. B. & Baker, B. L. (1983). Predicting outcome in parent training. *Journal of Consulting and Clinical Psychology, 51*(2), 309-311.

Curtis, J. W. & Singh, N. N. (1996). Family involvement and empowerment in mental health service provision for children with emotional and behavioral disorders. *Journal of Child and Family Studies, 5*(4), 503-517.

Diekhoff, G. M. & Wigginton, P. I. (1989). Factors of success in a volunteer adult literacy program. *Reading and Writing, 1*(2), 153-162.

Dumas, J. E. (1984). Child, adult-interactional, and socioeconomic setting events as predictors of parent training outcome. *Education and Treatment of Children, 7*(4), 351-364.

Dunst, C. J. & Trivette, C. M. (1987). Enabling and empowering families: Conceptual and intervention issues. *School Psychology Review, 16*(4), 443-456.

Fantuzzo, J., Childs, S., Stevenson, H., Coolahan, K. C., Ginsburg, M., Gay, K., Debnam, D., & Watson, C. (1996). The Head Start Teaching Center: An evaluation of an experiential, collaborative training model for Head Start teachers and parent volunteers. *Early Childhood Research Quarterly, 11,* 79-99.

Fantuzzo, J., Weiss, A., & Coolahan, K. (1998). Community-based partnership-directed research: Actualizing community strengths to treat child victims of physical abuse and neglect. In J. R. Lutzker (ed.), *Child Abuse: A handbook of theory, research, and treatment.* (pp. 213-238). New York, NY: Pergamon Press.

Forehand, R. & Kotchick, B. A. (1996). Cultural diversity: A Wake-up call for parent training. *Behavior Therapy, 27,* 187-206.

Frymier, A. B., Shulman, G. M. & Houser, M. (1996). The development of a learner empowerment measure. *Communication Education, 45*(3), 181-199.

Garbarino, J. (1995). The American war zone: What children can tell us about living with violence. *Journal of Developmental and Behavioral Pediatrics, 16*(6), 431-435.

Goodban, N. (1985). The psychological impact of being on welfare. *Social Service Review, 59,* 403-422.

Gorman, J. C. & Balter, L. (1997). Culturally sensitive parent education: A Critical review of quantitative research. *Review of Educational Research, 67*(3), 339-369.

Graziano, A. M. & Diament, D. M. (1992). Parent behavioral training: An examination of the paradigm. *Behavior Modification, 16*(1), 3-38.

Gruber, J. & Trickett, E. J. (1987). Can we empower others? The paradox of empowerment in the governing of an alternative public school. *American Journal of Community Psychology, 15,* 353-371.

Harris, Y. Gorelick, P. B., Samuels, P., & Bempong, I. (1996). Why African Americans may not be participating in clinical trials. *Journal of the National Medical Association, 88*(10), 630-634.

Harter, S. (1983). Supplementary description of Self-Perception Profile for Children: Revision of the Perceived Competence Scale for Children. Denver, CO: University of Denver.

Heflinger, C. A., Bickman, L., Northrup, D. & Sonnichsen, S. (1997). A theory-driven intervention and evaluation to explore family caregiver empowerment. *Journal of Emotional and Behavioral Disorders,* 5(3), 184-191.

Holden, G. W., Lavigne, V. V., & Cameron, A. M. (1990). Probing the continuum of effectiveness in parent training: Characteristics of parents and preschoolers. *Journal of Clinical Child Psychology, 19*(1), 2-8.

Israel, A. C., Silverman, W. K., & Solotar, L. C. (1986). An investigation of family influences on initial weight status, attrition, and treatment outcome in a childhood obesity program. *Behavior Therapy, 17,* 131-143.

Kalyanpur, M., & Rao, S. S. (1991). Empowering low-income black families of handicapped children. *American Journal of Orthopsychiatry, 61*(4), 523-532.

Kieffer, C. H. (1984). Citizen empowerment: A developmental perspective. In J. Rappaport, C. Swift & R. Hess (Eds.) *Studies in empowerment: Steps toward understanding and action* (pp. 9-36). Binghamton, NY: The Haworth Press, Inc.

Kitzman, H. J., Cole, R., Yoos, H. L. & Olds, D. (1997). Challenges experienced by home visitors: A Qualitative study of program implementation. *Journal of Community Psychology, 25*(1), 95-109.

Lieh-Mak, F., Lee, P. W. H., & Luk, S. L. (1984). Problems encountered in teaching Chinese parents to be behavior therapists. *Psychologia, 27,* 56-64.

McCann, S. & Weinman, J. (1996). Empowering the patient in the consultation: A pilot study. *Patient Education and Counseling, 27*(3), 227-234.

McMahon, R. J., Forehand, R., Griest, D. L., & Wells, K. C. (1981). Who drops out of therapy during parent behavioral training? *Behavioral Counseling Quarterly, 1,* 79-85.

Myers, H. F., Alvy, K. T., Arrington, A., Richardson, M. A., Marigna, M., Huff, R., Main, M., & Newcomb, M. D. (1992). The impact of a parent training program on inner-city African American families. *Journal of Community Psychology, 20,* 132-147.

Nickerson, K. J., Helms, J. E. & Terrell, F. (1994). Cultural mistrust, opinions about mental illness, and Black students' attitudes toward seeking psychological help from White counselors. *Journal of Counseling Psychology, 41*(3), 378-385.

Pakman, M. (1995). Therapy in contexts of poverty and ethnic dissonance: Constructivism and social constructionism as methodologies for action. *Journal of Systemic Therapies, 14*(4), 64-71.

Patterson, G. R. (1976). The aggressive child: Victim and architect of a coercive system. In L. Hamerlynck, L. Handy & E. Mash (Eds.), *Behavior modification and families, Vol. I: Theory and research.* New York: Brunner/Mazel.

Patterson, G. R. & Chamberlain, P. (1994). A functional analysis of resistance during parent training therapy. *Clinical Psychology Science & Practice, 1*(1), 53-70.

Rappaport, J. (1987). Terms of empowerment/Exemplars of prevention: Toward a theory for community psychology. *American Journal of Community Psychology, 15*(2), 121-148.

Riessman, F. (1990). Restructuring help: A human services paradigm for the 1990s. *American Journal of Community Psychology, 18*(2), 221-230.

Rissel, C. E., Perry, C. L., Wagenaar, A. C., & Wolfson, M. (1996). Empowerment, alcohol, 8th grade students and health promotion. *Journal of Alcohol and Drug Education, 41*(2), 105-119.

Wahler, R. G. (1980). The insular mother: Her problems in parent-child treatment. *Journal of Applied Behavior Analysis, 13,* 207-219.

Wallerstein, N. (1992). Powerlessness, empowerment, and health: Implications for health promotion programs. *Behavior Change, 6*(3), 197-205.

Webster-Stratton, C. (1985). Predictors of treatment outcome in parent training for conduct disordered children. *Behavior Therapy, 16,* 223-243.

Webster-Stratton, C. (1992). Individually administered videotape parent training: "Who benefits?". *Cognitive Therapy and Research, 16*(1), 31-35.

Wolfe, D. A., Sandler, J. & Kaufman, K. (1981). A competency-based parent training program for child abusers. *Journal of Consulting and Clinical Psychology, 49*(5), 633-640.

Zimmerman, M. A., Israel, B. A., Schulz, A., & Checkoway, B. (1992). Further explorations in empowerment theory: An empirical analysis of psychological empowerment. *American Journal of Community Psychology, 20,* 707-727.

Zimmerman, M. A. & Rappaport, J. (1988). Citizen participation, perceived control, and psychological empowerment. *American Journal of Community Psychology, 16*(5), 725-750.

Parental Self-Efficacy and Social Support as Predictors of Parenting Practices and Children's Socioemotional Adjustment in Mexican Immigrant Families

Charles Izzo
Laura Weiss
Timothy Shanahan
Flora Rodriguez-Brown

University of Illinois at Chicago

SUMMARY. The current study examined the hypotheses that (1) parental self-efficacy partially mediates the relationships between social

---

Address correspondence to: Charles Izzo, Department of Psychology (M/C 285), University of Illinois at Chicago, 1007 West Harrison Street, Chicago, IL, 60607-7137.

The authors express their appreciation to Dr. Kenneth Miller for help in formulating research questions and adapting measures for use with Mexican American parents. Lourdes Kaplan, Ana Nuñez, and Jackie Rupert provided invaluable assistance in translation and data collection. Many instructors and coordinators in Project FLAME worked collaboratively to provide informative data about participants and schools.

This project was supported in part by the National Institute of Mental Health Prevention Research Branch and Office on AIDS Research Training Grant T32MH19933 to Roger Weissberg, by the University of Illinois at Chicago Center for Urban Education, Research, and Development, and by the Office of Educational Research and Improvement of the U.S. Department of Education through a grant to the Mid-Atlantic Laboratory for Student Success at the Temple University Center for Research in Human Development and Education.

[Haworth co-indexing entry note]: "Parental Self-Efficacy and Social Support as Predictors of Parenting Practices and Children's Socioemotional Adjustment in Mexican Immigrant Families." Izzo, Charles et al. Co-published simultaneously in *Journal of Prevention & Intervention in the Community* (The Haworth Press, Inc.) Vol. 20, No. 1/2, 2000, pp. 197-213; and: *Diverse Families, Competent Families: Innovations in Research and Preventive Intervention Practice* (ed: Janet F. Gillespie, and Judy Primavera) The Haworth Press, Inc., 2000, pp. 197-213. Single or multiple copies of this article are available for a fee from The Haworth Document Delivery Service [1-800-342-9678, 9:00 a.m. - 5:00 p.m. (EST). E-mail address: getinfo@haworthpressinc.com].

support and both parental warmth and control, and (2) these parenting variables relate positively to children's socioemotional adjustment. First-generation, Mexican immigrant mothers were interviewed regarding social support, parental self-efficacy, parenting practices, and their child's socioemotional adjustment. Overall, results from path analyses suggest that, for Mexican immigrant families, social support relates to parenting practices partly because those with greater social support feel more efficacious as parents. Findings also showed that parenting characterized by warmth or control is associated with greater socioemotional adjustment among children. This research supports the idea that, for programs designed to influence parenting practices, simply providing social support may be less important than taking steps to enhance parental self-efficacy. *[Article copies available for a fee from The Haworth Document Delivery Service: 1-800-342-9678. E-mail address: <getinfo@haworthpressinc.com> Website: <http://www.haworthpressinc.com>]*

KEYWORDS. Self-efficacy, social support, parenting practices, child adjustment, Mexican immigrants

Mexicans constitute the largest group of immigrants to the U.S., annually (Kramer, 1994). Parents who emigrate from Mexico experience a unique range of stressors that often make it difficult for them to meet the challenge of raising families in the U.S. The migration experience frequently involves disruption of the family support network, exploitation by police and smugglers, and risk of imprisonment (Vega, Kolody, & Valle, 1987). Moreover, their later adaptation is complicated by unemployment (Kramer,1994), and having to adjust to new sets of cultural norms regarding such issues as childrearing practices, appropriate child behavior, and gender roles.

Given that hardships such as these relate to a range of negative outcomes for both parents and children (Elder, Eccles, Ardelt, & Lord, 1995; McLoyd, 1990), it would be useful to understand better what factors serve to buffer the stress that many Mexican immigrant families face. Much is known about the role of parenting practices (e.g., monitoring and controlling children's behavior to protect them from negative influences, helping children cope with crises, etc.) in mediating the link between family stress and negative child outcomes (Barber, Olsen, & Shagel, 1994; Elder et al.; MacDonald, 1992). Relatively little empirical research exists, however, on parenting among Mexican families, and even less exists for Mexican immigrants (Massey, Zambrana, & Bell, 1995). Thus, the current study assessed parenting practices within Mexican immigrant families to examine: (1) what factors predict beneficial parenting practices, and (2) what parenting practices best predict children's socioemotional adjustment. Such knowledge may inform the development and implementation of programs to promote healthy adaptation among this population by identifying key factors that need to be addressed by programs designed to facilitate optimal parenting practices.

PARENTING PRACTICES AND CHILDREN'S SOCIOEMOTIONAL ADJUSTMENT

The research literature converges on two dimensions of parenting that consistently relate to child well-being (Baumrind, 1971; Schaefer, 1959). *Parental warmth/acceptance* refers to communicating approval or expressing affection towards children, and has been found to relate positively to children's social and emotional adjustment. These behaviors reinforce children's compliance with parental expectations (MacDonald, 1992), and may help children cope with the chronic environmental stressors (Cowen & Work, 1988). *Parental control/restrictiveness* refers to guiding children and regulating their behavior, and has been widely found to influence children's social development (Baumrind; Maccoby & Martin, 1983). Theoretically, the structure and discipline parents provide helps children learn to regulate their own behavior and learn rules of social interaction (Barber et al., 1994).

Most research linking parental warmth and control to child outcomes, however, involves White or middle-income families (Baumrind, 1971), and may not generalize to Mexican immigrant families. Roosa, Tein, Groppenbacher, Michaels, and Dumka (1993) provide some support for generalizability, finding that supportive parenting in non-immigrant Mexican-American families predicted lower child depression and conduct disorder. Parental warmth and control also predict better social and emotional functioning in children from families experiencing job loss (Elder, Van Nguyen, & Caspi, 1985). Therefore, in the current study, it was expected that both parental warmth and parental control would predict better socioemotional adjustment among the families in our sample.

PREDICTORS OF PARENTING BEHAVIOR

Social support is believed to help parents cope with adversity while raising their children (Abidin, 1992; McLoyd, 1990), and has been found to relate to greater parental nurturance and control (Weinraub & Wolf, 1983). Social support may play an especially important role for immigrants, who are often separated from family and friends in their home country, and must establish new social networks (Vega et al., 1987).

Parenting practices may also be influenced by parental self-efficacy, which refers to parents' perception of their own ability to solve problems with their children, and to manage their behavior. Parental self-efficacy (Elder et al., 1995; Mash & Johnston, 1990) and similar cognitive factors (Dumka, Stoerzinger, Jackson, & Roosa, 1996; Mash & Johnston, 1983) have been found to relate to parental acceptance and warmth, and to consistent discipline practices among both European- and Mexican-American parents.

The current study proposed that social support benefits parents partly by making them feel more efficacious in their parenting role. Research by Quittner, Gueckauf, and Jackson (1990) supports this notion, suggesting that parents who experience social support perceive themselves to be more competent than do those without social support. Because perceived self-efficacy helps determine the amount of effort people will expend to meet a challenge (Bandura, 1989), it was expected that parents with greater parental self-efficacy are likely to put more effort into restricting and monitoring their children, and providing them with affection and nurturance.

Specific hypotheses were that (1) social support predicts parenting practices (warmth and control), (2) parental self-efficacy mediates the relationship between social support and parenting practices, and (3) parenting practices predict children's socioemotional adjustment. The hypotheses are consistent with other models of parenting (Abidin, 1992; Belsky, 1993; McLoyd, 1990) that relate parental cognitions (i.e., self-efficacy) and social support to parenting practices, which then relate to child outcomes. The present study is unique, however, because it proposes that social support relates to parenting practices partly because of its association with parental self-efficacy.

METHOD

Participants

Participants were 93 mothers who were first-generation immigrants from Mexico, living in low-income neighborhoods in Chicago, Illinois. All mothers were enrolled in Project FLAME, a program designed to help parents promote their children's literacy. Project FLAME recruited parents from seven public elementary schools serving mostly low-income Mexican families. On average, the student body at these schools was comprised of 89% Latinos, 41% of whom were considered to have limited English proficiency (Chicago Public Schools, 1996). In addition, the neighborhoods directly surrounding these schools, on average, had among the highest rates of violent crime in the city in the year prior to our assessment (Chicago Crime Commission, 1995). School records indicated that, on average, 96% of children in these schools received some sort of public funds for families living in poverty (e.g., school lunch subsidies, public aid).

On average, mothers in the sample were 34.1 (*range* = 18 to 52) years of age, had 7.7 (*range* = 2 to 16) years of education (all in Mexico), had resided in the U.S. for 10.3 (*range* = 1 to 28) years, and had 2.9 (*range* = 1 to 8) children at home. In 85.5% of the sample, parents or their spouses were employed. Children were 51% male and 49% female, and averaged 7.9 (SD = 2.0) years of age.

Measures

Parents completed a survey consisting of five measures assessing social support, parental self-efficacy, parental warmth, parental control, and children's socioemotional adjustment. Measures were selected that demonstrated adequate reliability and validity in past research, and that used simple language that could easily be understood by individuals with little formal education. Items assessing social support, parental self-efficacy, and parenting practices used a Likert scale ranging from 1 (*never*) to 4 (*always*), based on how often in the past month each statement was true for them. Child adjustment items used a scale ranging from 1 (*never*) to 5 (*always*). Each scale score was computed as the mean of all items in that scale, with higher scores reflecting higher levels of the construct. When existing scales were modified, items were selected based on their conceptual simplicity and their appropriateness for a Mexican American sample.

Demographic variables. In a separate interview, parents provided information on their age, years of education, number of years living in the U.S., and whether either the mother or her partner were employed. The target child's age and gender were indicated on the survey.

Parental self-efficacy. Five items (alpha = .80) measured parents' perceived abilities to manage their children's problems and to raise them effectively. Two items were drawn from a scale originally developed by Dumka et al. (1996), and research staff generated the remaining three (see Table 1).

Social support. Eight items (alpha = .79) assessed how often parents reported having social support available from friends, relatives, or other Project FLAME participants. Three items were derived from a scale by Procidano and Heller (1983), and research staff generated the remaining five (see Table 1).

Parental warmth. Seven items (alpha = .72) measured the frequency with which parents engaged in behaviors that convey approval or express warmth towards their children (e.g., "I speak to my child in a warm and friendly voice"), using the warmth/acceptance sub-scale of the Children's Report of Behavior Inventory (Schluderman & Schluderman, 1970).

Parental control. Three items (alpha = .64) measured the frequency with which parents engaged in behaviors that regulate children's behavior (e.g., "I insist that my child respect the rules I have in the house"), using the parental control sub-scale of the Children's Report of Behavior Inventory (Schluderman & Schluderman, 1970).

Children's socioemotional adjustment. Socioemotional adjustment was assessed using the competence subscale (20 items, alpha = .88) of the Parent-Child Rating Scale (P-CRS), a parent-rated version of the Teacher-Child Rating Scale (Hightower et al., 1986). It assesses four domains of children's social and academic behavior, including frustration tolerance (e.g., "Copes well with failure"), assertive social skills (e.g., "Expresses ideas willingly"), task orientation (e.g., "Functions well even with distractions"), and peer social skills (e.g., "Makes friends easily"). This scale was selected because its use of positively-valenced items made it non-threatening to parents, and because pilot testing indicated that the items were easy for parents to understand. Furthermore, past research has demonstrated the validity of the teach-

TABLE 1. Distributions of responses to parental self-efficacy and social support items.

	1 Never	2 Rarely	3 Often	4 Always
Parental Self-Efficacy Items				
When things are going badly between my child and me, I keep trying until things begin to change.	0%	9.7%	20.5%	68.8%
I know that I can help my child be successful.	0%	8.6%	28.0%	62.4%
I know what to do when my child misbehaves.	0%	14.0%	35.6%	48.4%
I feel sure of myself as a mother.	0%	7.5%	19.5%	72.0%
I can handle my child's problems.	0%	10.9%	37.6%	50.5%
	1 Never	2 Rarely	3 Often	4 Always
Social Support Items				
I have relatives or friends who help me out by watching my children when I need them to.	10.8%	36.7%	23.7%	25.8%
I can rely on my friends for emotional support.	4.3%	53.8%	16.2%	23.7%
	1 Never	2 Rarely	3 Often	4 Always
Social Support Items				
When I am feeling sad or upset, I have friends or relatives who help me feel better.	7.5%	35.5%	24.7%	30.3%
I can rely on my family for emotional support.	7.5%	31.3%	17.2%	43.0%
There are people who give me the emotional support I need.	5.4%	46.2%	20.4%	24.7%
I get emotional support from the other participants in Project FLAME.	2.2%	43.0%	24.7%	29.0%
When I have questions about raising my children, I get help from other parents in Project FLAME.	4.3%	50.5%	20.4%	22.6%
I can talk to people in Project FLAME about problems I am having at home.	2.2%	44.1%	36.6%	16.1%

Note. ns ranged from 90 to 93.

er-rated version of this sub-scale (Reynolds, Weissberg, & Kasprow, 1992).

Survey Development

Pilot testing was conducted with a group of 17 Mexican immigrant mothers who had previously been enrolled in Project FLAME. Analysis of these pilot data indicated that the items had adequate item distributions, and acceptable correlations with other survey variables. On the basis of parents' feedback, some items were eliminated and other items were modified to simplify their wording and correct awkward translations.

The appropriateness of these measures for sample participants was demonstrated by following a set of guidelines suggested by Liang and Bogat (1994) for assessing the cultural equivalence of measurement instruments. This assessment involved (1) determining the relevance of each construct for Mexican immigrant parents (*content equivalence*), (2) using independent translation and back-translation procedures (*semantic equivalence*), and (3) demonstrating that the relationships between constructs was consistent with what has previously been found in other populations (*conceptual equivalence*).

Procedure

Participants were recruited into Project FLAME by sending out letters to parents in all pre-kindergarten through third-grade classrooms in our target schools asking whether they "would like to participate in a program that would help [them] develop [their] own English literacy skills," and "help [them] improve [their] children's reading." Parents who returned the response letter to the school were formally enrolled into the program.

All parents completed the survey after having attended the program for 2 to 4 months. Parents were instructed to answer in reference to their oldest child between ages 3 and 9, or their child closest to age 9, on any question related to their child's behavior, parent-child interactions, or parental self-efficacy. Survey items were read aloud in Spanish to groups of between 10 and 40 parents, and additional Spanish-speaking research staff were always present to assist parents having difficulty with the survey. All parents provided their written consent.

RESULTS

Descriptive Statistics

Table 2 summarizes means and standard deviations for all survey variables. On average, parents reported "*often*" having social support available on most items, although item frequencies indicate that these parents have more support available from family than from friends (see Table 1). A substantial number of parents gave relatively low social support ratings, although all parents responded "*always*" or "*often*" on at least one item. Parents rated themselves relatively high on parental self-efficacy (see Table 1), parental warmth, and parental control, responding "*often*" or "*always*" on most items. Finally, children generally received favorable behavior ratings, with parents, on average, reporting that most child adjustment items described their children "*often.*"

Demographic Variation in Parent and Child Variables

The issue of whether demographic variables needed to be accounted for in the model was assessed by examining their associations with the primary variables of interest. Pearson correlation analyses (for mother's age, education, years in the U.S., and child's age) and point biserial correlation analyses (for mother's employment and child's gender) indicated that none of the six demographic variables correlated significantly with social support, parental self-efficacy, parenting practices, or child adjustment. Consequently, no demographic variables were included in any further analyses.

Correlations Among Parental and Child Variables

Pearson correlations were computed among values for social support, parental self-efficacy, parental warmth and control, and child adjustment (see Table 1). The variables correlated weakly to moderately with each other (rs = .25 to .58), and all associations were significant and positive. Notably, parental self-efficacy (rs = .36 to .67) correlated with parenting and child variables much more strongly than did social support (rs = .25 to .32).

Predictors of Parenting

Following Cohen and Cohen (1983), the issue of whether parental self-efficacy mediated the relationship between social support and parenting was assessed by determining whether the following conditions were met: (1) social support significantly predicts parenting practices, (2) social support correlates significantly with parental self-efficacy, (3) when parental self-efficacy is added as a second predictor, (a) parental self-efficacy significantly predicts parenting practices, and (b) the relationship between social support and parenting practices decreases significantly.

TABLE 2. Correlations between parent and child measured variables.

	Social Support	Self Efficacy	Parental Warmth	Parental Control	Child Adjustment
Social Support	--	.31**	.29**	.25*	.32**
Self-Efficacy		--	.56***	.44***	.40***
Parental Warmth			--	.58***	.54***
Parental Control				--	.50[a]***
Child Adjustment					--
Mean	2.73	3.51	3.60	3.66	3.82
SD	.58	.40	.37	.47	.53
n	91	92	91	92	91
Range	1.75 – 4.00	2.40 – 4.00	2.43 – 4.00	2.00 – 4.00	2.40 – 4.85

Note. ns for cortelation coefficients ranged from 90 to 92.
[a]Three cases were eliminated from this correlation because they were bivariate outliers.
*$p < .05$ **$p < .01$ ***$p < .001$

In the first set of analyses, a hierarchical regression was conducted entering social support in the first step and parental self-efficacy in the second step (see Figure 1a). Findings indicated that social support alone significantly predicted parental warmth ($B = .19, p < .01$). When parental self-efficacy was added, it significantly predicted parental warmth ($B = .59, p < .01$), and social support became non-significant. Considering that parental self-efficacy was significantly correlated with social support ($B = .22, p < .01$), all conditions have been met to indicate that parental self-efficacy mediated the relationship between social support and parental warmth.

A second hierarchical regression was conducted with parental control as the criterion variable (see Figure 1b). Again, in the first step, social support alone significantly predicted parental control ($B = .14, p < .05$). In the second step, parental self-efficacy emerged as a significant predictor of parental control ($B = .26, p < .01$), and adding it to the equation rendered social support non-significant. Thus, parental self-efficacy mediated the relationship between social support and parental control as well.

Overall, social support and parental self-efficacy together accounted for significant variance in both parental warmth ($R^2 = .46, p < .01$) and parental control ($R^2 = .16, p < .01$).

FIGURE 1a. Path diagram illustrating parental self-efficacy mediating the relationship between social support and parental warmth (n = 90).

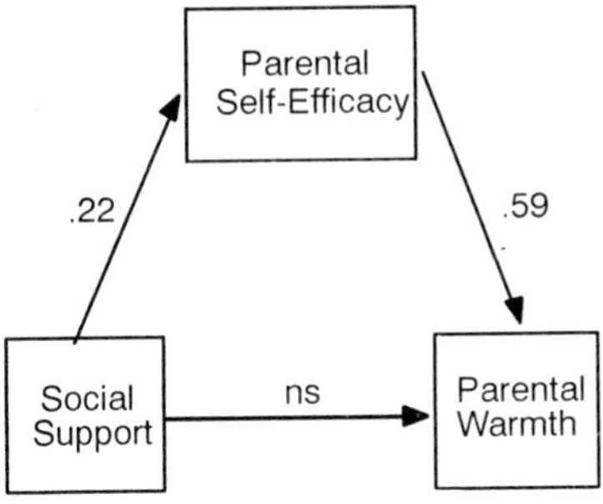

FIGURE 1b. Path diagram illustrating parental self-efficacy mediating the relationship between social support and parental control (n = 90).

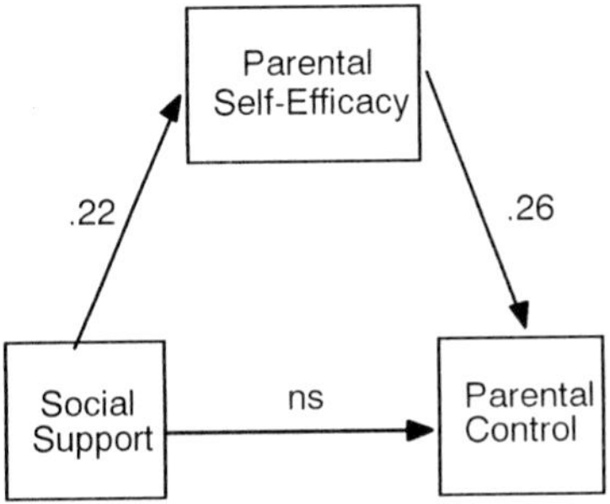

Predictors of Children's Socioemotional Adjustment

A multiple regression analysis with parental warmth and control entered simultaneously as predictors was conducted to assess their unique associations with child adjustment, and to determine how much variance they accounted for. Results indicated that, when entered together, parental warmth (B = .53, $p < .01$) and control (B = .33, p = .01) each uniquely predicted child adjustment, and, together, accounted for 34% of the variance. When entered alone in separate equations, warmth accounted for 29% of the variance in child adjustment, and control accounted for 25%.

Given the moderate correlations between child adjustment and both social support and parental self-efficacy, an exploratory analysis was conducted to examine the extent to which these variables related to children's functioning above and beyond the variance accounted for by parenting practices. A hierarchical regression was conducted predicting child adjustment, first entering social support and parental self-efficacy as independent variables in block 1, and then adding parental warmth and control in block 2 (see Figure 2).

In the first block, only parental self-efficacy significantly predicted better child adjustment (B = .53, $p < .01$). After adding the second block, both parental warmth and parental control emerged as significant predictors of child adjustment (Bs = .37 and .29, ps < .05, respectively), and both social support and parental self-efficacy were nonsignificant. The entire model explained 37% of the variance in child adjustment. Thus, both parenting variables fully mediated the relationships between child adjustment and both social support and self-efficacy, and the estimates of the variance contributions may be attributed solely to the parenting variables.

DISCUSSION

The current study sought to inform programmatic efforts to improve family well-being by promoting a better understanding of factors that relate to parenting and children's well-being, and by generalizing cur-

FIGURE 2. Path diagram illustrating the prediction of child adjustment (n = 90).

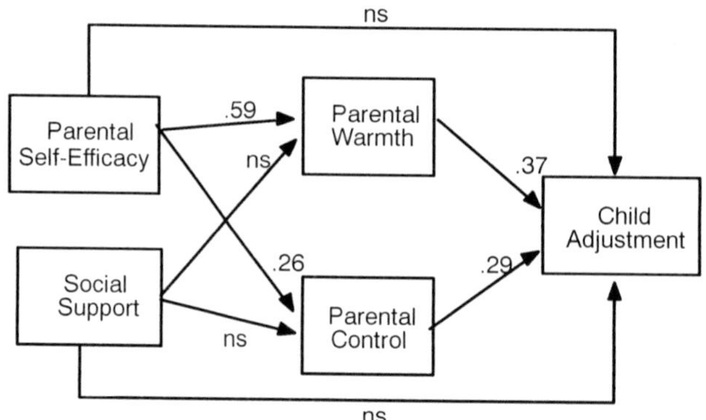

rent knowledge about parenting to families who have migrated to the United States from Mexico. Overall, the results of this study are consistent with previous research suggesting that parents who experience social support feel more efficacious about their parenting abilities (Elder et al., 1995; Quittner et al., 1990), and that both social support and parental self-efficacy predict more warm and controlling parenting (Dumka et al., 1996; Mash & Johnston, 1983; Weinraub & Wolf, 1983). The present findings are unique, however, in suggesting that social support may relate to parenting partly because it makes parents feel more efficacious. While our results do not constitute definitive causal evidence, they nevertheless suggest that programs seeking to promote effective parenting may benefit by emphasizing strategies that not only provide social support to parents, but that also strengthen parents' beliefs in their capacity to meet the challenges of child rearing. Thus, programs could plan opportunities for parents to develop supportive relationships with one another (e.g., by scheduling time for informal discussions before and after training sessions), while also explicitly incorporating activities that build their sense of competence. For example, programs might hold supportive group discussions where parents can share perspectives about child rearing, and receive positive feedback and encouragement. It may also be helpful to provide parents with a series of success experiences on progressively more challenging tasks related to parenting, followed by feedback identifying their successes, and highlighting their areas of strength. School-based programs might arrange for parents to receive feedback about the effectiveness of their efforts at parent-teacher conferences.

Our findings were also consistent with the body of research linking parental warmth and control to child adjustment (Maccoby & Martin, 1983; MacDonald, 1992), and suggest that this research generalizes to Mexican American immigrant families as well. The fact that parental warmth and control together accounted for significantly more variance in child adjustment than did either variable alone may suggest that programs serving this population should address both dimensions of parenting.

Parental self-efficacy ratings were quite high in this sample. These elevated scores probably suggest that parents who enroll in programs such as Project FLAME are likely to have greater perceived self-efficacy than parents who do not volunteer for programs such as FLAME. Additionally, parents' participation in the program may have boosted their self-efficacy beyond what might have been observed prior to their involvement.

Parents' social support ratings were also relatively high, suggesting that social isolation was not prevalent in this sample. It is likely that most parents in this study had resided in the U.S. for long enough to establish a social network, and that many probably already had family or friends here when they arrived. Interestingly, item-level analyses revealed that many parents who reported little support from family and friends indicated "often" having support available from Project FLAME participants. This finding reinforces the importance of attending to the supportive function that parent training programs can provide to their participants.

Surprisingly, social support ceased to be associated significantly with parenting once parental self-efficacy was accounted for statistically. Although it is unlikely that parental self-efficacy is the sole factor linking social support to parenting practices, the present findings may reflect a reality that this variable plays an especially important role for Mexican immigrant families. Davis' (1990) interviews with Mexican immigrants revealed that many parents had difficulty managing conflicts with children regarding adaptation to U.S. culture, and were anxious about how to protect their children from exposure to the numerous risks in their environment. To the extent that such circumstances existed among parents in our sample, confidence and self-efficacy may have been more relevant to their parenting practices than many other benefits commonly attributed to social support (Weinraub & Wolf, 1983). The lack of a unique effect for social support may also be due, partly, to a strong bias towards emotional support in the measure used in the present study. Considering the difficult economic and environmental circumstances most of these mothers face, the availability of tangible support may yield benefits to parents that could more strongly influence parenting practices.

Numerous issues limit the conclusions that can be drawn from this study. First, the findings are essentially correlational, and no causal relationships can be inferred from the data. Second, the size of the associations reported here are likely to be elevated due to the common error variance (i.e., the same person rated both predictor and outcome variables). Third, the variance was low, and the distribution negatively skewed on parental self-efficacy, parental warmth, and parental control, which may suggest that parents felt inclined to present their parenting performance favorably. Finally, because the mothers in our sample enrolled voluntarily in Project FLAME, the generalizability of our results to other Mexican immigrant families is limited. One promising direction for future research is to include assessments of parental self-efficacy into evaluations of programs that provide social support to parents, and to examine whether changes in self-efficacy account substantially for program effects on parenting. Research should also examine a wider range of factors that might influence parents' self-efficacy and child-rearing practices, including both contextual (e.g., community and family characteristics, factors related to immigration and economic well-being) and individual factors (e.g., parental depression). Finally, researchers need to incorporate parents' own perspectives, given in their own words, about what factors influence their families. Such an approach may help researchers to test the real-world validity of their findings, and to relate that information to parents' lives in meaningful ways. These steps would greatly enrich the body of knowledge about parenting in Mexican American immigrant families, and would further inform efforts to develop programs that promote family well-being.

REFERENCES

Abidin, R. R. (1992). The determinants of parenting behavior. *Journal of Child Clinical Psychology, 21*(4), 407-412.

Bandura, A. (1989). Human agency in social cognitive theory. *American Psychologist, 44*(9), 1175-1184.

Barber, B. K., Olsen, J. E., & Shagel, S. C. (1994). Associations between parental psychological and behavioral control and youth internalized and externalized behaviors. *Child Development, 65*(4), 1120-1136.

Baumrind, D. (1971). Current patterns of parental authority. *Developmental Psychology Monographs, 4,*(1, Pt. 2).

Belsky, J. (1993). Etiology of child maltreatment: A developmental-ecological analysis. *Psychological Bulletin, 114*(3), 413-434.

Chicago Crime Commission (1995). *Chicago: I-UCR Index crime by district-1995* [On-line]. Available: http://netcom.com/~chgocrcm/ucr1995.html

Chicago Public Schools (1996). *School information database* [On-line]. Available: http://acct.multi1.cps.k12.il.us/

Cohen, J., & Cohen, P. (1983). *Applied multiple regression/correlation analysis for the behavioral sciences* (2nd ed.). Hillsdale, NJ: Erlbaum.

Cowen, E. L. & Work, W. C. (1988). Resilient children, psychological wellness, and primary prevention. *American Journal of Community Psychology, 16*(4), 591-607.

Davis, M. (1990). *Mexican voices, American dreams.* New York: Henry Hold & Co.

Dumka, L. E., Stoerzinger, H. D., Jackson, K. M., & Roosa, M. W. (1996). Examination of the cross-cultural and cross-language equivalence of the Parenting Self-Agency measure. *Family Relations, 45*(2), 216-222.

Elder, G. H., Eccles, J. S., Ardelt, M., & Lord, S. (1995). Inner-city parents under economic pressure: Perspectives on the strategies of parenting. *Journal of Marriage and the Family, 57*(3), 771-784.

Elder, G. H., Van Nguyen, T., & Caspi, A. (1985). Linking family hardship to children's lives. *Child Development, 56*(2), 361-375.

Hightower, A. D., Work, W. C., Cowen, E. L., Lotyczewski, B. S., Spinell, A. P., Guare, J. C., & Rohrbeck, C. A. (1986). The teacher-child rating scale: A brief objective measure of elementary children's school problem behaviors and competencies. *School Psychology Review, 15*(3), 393-403.

Kramer, R. G. (1994). Developments in international migration to the United States. *The United States Report for the Continuous Reporting System on Migration (SOPEMI) of the Organization for Economic Cooperation and Development (OECD).*

Liang, B. & Bogat, G. A. (1994). Culture, control, and coping: New perspectives on social support. *American Journal of Community Psychology, 22*(1), 123-147.

Maccoby, E. E., & Martin, J. A. (1983). Socialization in the context of the family: Parent-child interaction. In P. H. Mussen (Ed.), *Handbook of child psychology* (4th ed., pp. 1-101). New York: John Wiley & Sons.

MacDonald, K. (1992). Warmth as a developmental construct: An evolutionary analysis. *Child Development, 63*(4), 753-773.

Mash, E. & Johnston, C. (1983). The prediction of mothers' behavior with their hyperactive children during play and task situations. *Child and Family Behavior Therapy, 5*(2), 1-14.

Mash, E. J., & Johnston, C. (1990). Determinants of parenting stress: Illustrations from families of hyperactive children and families of physically abused children. *Journal of Clinical Child Psychology, 19*(4), 313-328.

Massey, D. S., Zambrana, R. E., & Bell, S. A. (1995). Contemporary issues in Latino families: Future directions for research, policy, and practice. In R. E. Zambrana (Ed.), *Understanding Latino families* (pp. 107-129). Thousand Oaks, CA: Sage Publications.

McLoyd, V. C. (1990). The impact of economic hardship on black families and children: Psychological distress, parenting, and socioemotional development. *Child Development, 61*(2), 311-346.

Procidano, M. E. & Heller, K. (1983). Measures of perceived social support from friends and from family: Three validation studies. *American Journal of Community Psychology, 11*(1), 1-24.

Quittner, A. L., Gueckauf, R. L., & Jackson, D. N. (1990). Chronic parenting stress: Moderating vs. mediating effects of social support. *Journal of Personality and Social Psychology, 59*(6), 1266-1278.

Reynolds, A., Weissberg, R. P., & Kasprow, W. J. (1992). Prediction of early social and academic adjustment of children from the inner-city. *American Journal of Community Psychology, 20*(5), 599-624.

Roosa, M. W., Tein, J. Y., Groppenbacher, N., Michaels, M., & Dumka, L. (1993).

Mothers' parenting behavior and child mental health in families with a problem drinking parent. *Journal of Marriage and the Family, 55*(1), 107-118.

Schaefer, E. S. (1959). A circumplex model for maternal behavior. *Journal of Abnormal and Social Psychology, 59,* 226-235.

Schluderman, E. & Schluderman, S. (1970). Replicability of factors in Children's Report of Parent Behavior Inventory (CRPBI). *Journal of Psychology, 76*(2), 239-249.

Vega, W. A., Kolody, B., & Valle, J. R. (1987). Migration and mental health: An empirical test of depression risk factors among immigrant Mexican women. *International Migration Review, 21*(3), 512-531.

Weinraub, M. & Wolf, B. M. (1983). Effects of stress and social supports on mother-child interactions in single- and two-parent families. *Child Development, 54*(5), 1297-1311.

Index